T0388628

A Womanist Reading of Hebrew Bible Narratives as the Politics of Belonging from an Outsider Within

WOMANIST READINGS OF SCRIPTURE

Series Editor: Gay L. Byron

Womanist biblical scholarship is a field "coming of age." *Womanist Readings of Scripture* publishes monographs and collected essay volumes, and considers more experimental works, that demonstrate academic excellence, engage the field, and expand and enrich Womanist hermeneutical discourse about Scripture and its deployment in the academy and in contemporary ecclesiastical and social contexts.

Titles in This Series

A Womanist Reading of Hebrew Bible Narratives as the Politics of Belonging from an Outsider Within by Vanessa Lovelace
Luke, Widows, Judges, and Stereotypes by Febbie C. Dickerson

A Womanist Reading of Hebrew Bible Narratives as the Politics of Belonging from an Outsider Within

Vanessa Lovelace

LEXINGTON BOOKS/FORTRESS ACADEMIC
Lanham • Boulder • New York • London

Published by Lexington Books/Fortress Academic

Lexington Books is an imprint of The Rowman & Littlefield Publishing Group, Inc.
4501 Forbes Boulevard, Suite 200, Lanham, Maryland 20706
www.rowman.com
86-90 Paul Street, London EC2A 4NE

Copyright © 2024 by The Rowman & Littlefield Publishing Group, Inc.

All rights reserved. No part of this book may be reproduced in any form or by any electronic or mechanical means, including information storage and retrieval systems, without written permission from the publisher, except by a reviewer who may quote passages in a review.

British Library Cataloguing in Publication Information Available

Library of Congress Cataloging-in-Publication Data

Names: Lovelace, Vanessa, author.
Title: A womanist reading of Hebrew Bible narratives as the politics of belonging from an outsider within / Vanessa Lovelace.
Description: Lanham : Lexington Books/Fortress Academic, [2024] | Series: Womanist readings of scripture | Includes bibliographical references and index.
Identifiers: LCCN 2024011249 (print) | LCCN 2024011250 (ebook) | ISBN 9781978706996 (cloth) | ISBN 9781978707009 (epub)
Subjects: LCSH: Bible—Feminist criticism. | Bible—Reading. | Women—Biblical teaching.
Classification: LCC BS521.4 .L68 2024 (print) | LCC BS521.4 (ebook) | DDC 220.6082—dc23/eng/20240410
LC record available at https://lccn.loc.gov/2024011249
LC ebook record available at https://lccn.loc.gov/2024011250

♾️™ The paper used in this publication meets the minimum requirements of American National Standard for Information Sciences—Permanence of Paper for Printed Library Materials, ANSI/NISO Z39.48-1992.

For Gay Lynne Byron
(1961–2023)

Contents

Acknowledgments	ix
Introduction: Womanist Biblical Interpretation and the Politics of Belonging	xi
Abbreviations	xxxi
Chapter 1: "This Woman's Son Shall Not Inherit with My Son": The Politics of Motherhood in the Sarah-Hagar Narratives	1
Chapter 2: Outsider Within: A Vineyard, a Curse, and US Racial Politics	29
Chapter 3: Mammies, Jezebels, Prophetesses, and Royal Women: Symbolic Border Guards in the Deuteronomistic History	61
Chapter 4: Mothers in Israel, Church Mothers, and Mothers of the Nation	91
Chapter 5: Final Thoughts of an Academic Outsider Within	111
Bibliography	123
Index	143
About the Author	147

vii

Acknowledgments

This book has been many years in the making, and I am appreciative of the many people who supported me along the journey. I thank Neil Elliott (retired), Senior Acquiring Editor, Lexington Books/Fortress Academic, who submitted my manuscript proposal to the Womanist Readings of Scripture series editorial board and supported me early in the editorial process. I thank Gayla Freeman, Neil's Editorial Assistant, who became Associate Editor upon his retirement and assumed supervision of the process. I thank Mitzi Smith and Gay L. Byron, series editors. I am especially grateful for Gay, who committed to shepherding my manuscript to the end after Mitzi's departure. I thank Megan White, Acquisitions Editor, who replaced Gayla and saw the manuscript to completion despite Gay's sudden and unexpected death more than halfway through the editorial process.

I thank Claudia Camp, Erin Runions, Katara Washington Patton, Sherilyn Poole, and my Lancaster Theological Seminary colleagues, Julia O'Brien and Greg Carey, who read variations of the manuscript over the years and offered their feedback. My appreciation goes to Lancaster Theological Seminary for giving me a study leave to complete the manuscript draft. I thank Myka Kennedy Stephens and Darryl W. Stephens at Fosgail LLC for copyediting the manuscript. I thank Moravian University's Faculty Development and Research Committee for awarding me a grant to index the manuscript. I thank Barbara Fears for indexing the manuscript.

With permission from *The Journal of the Interdenominational Theological Center*, Chapter 1 is a revised and expanded version of Vanessa L. Lovelace, "'This Woman's Son Shall Not Inherit with My Son': Towards a Womanist Politics of Belonging in the Sarah-Hagar Narratives," *The Journal of the Interdenominational Theological Center* 41 (Spring 2015): 63–82.

Chapter 3 is a revised and expanded version of chapter 5 of my dissertation and Chapter 4 is a revised and expanded version of chapter 4 of my dissertation,

"Deborah and Huldah: Symbolic Border Guards in the Deuteronomistic History" (Ph.D. diss., Chicago Theological Seminary, 2012).

Words are not enough to express my love and gratitude for my spouse and partner in life, Wilfred Bentley, who has steadfastly stood beside me throughout this project and beyond. You keep me inspired. To our children, Shauna, Christopher, and Khalil.

Introduction

Womanist Biblical Interpretation and the Politics of Belonging

Theologian Karl Barth may have been known for saying that as members of society pastors needed the "Bible and the Newspaper,"[1] but for nineteenth and early twentieth century Black pastors and activists, it was the Bible and the US Constitution.[2] As enslaved and free Blacks alike argued for their right to citizenship by birth, these two documents were foundational for African Americans struggle for equal rights. Herbert Marbury demonstrates the biblical appropriation of the exodus motif in the antebellum period in his contrast of the political rhetoric of Absalom Jones and David Walker, described as "pillar of cloud politics" and "pillar of fire politics," respectively, for their different hermeneutical approaches in advocating for the full inclusion of Blacks as US citizens.[3] Clarice Martin explains that Black America's faith in the biblical witness of a God who delivered Israel from the evil of slavery in Egypt and that "was believed to be no less affronted about Black slavery . . . has always been a fundamental and bedrock tenet of African-American religious faith."[4] But, as Eddie Glaude maintained, to relegate their hopes for freedom to the spiritual realm is to miss the secular implications for such biblical appropriation. He writes, "If we only read the story of Exodus and its analogical application as examples of a community of faith awaiting an act of God, then we miss, I believe, the full significance of this mimetic act and its powerful hold on the black political imagination."[5]

Fidelity to the Constitution, likewise, was based on its promise of equal rights and full protection as citizens. Together, the Bible and the Constitution served as "primary and authoritative cultural artifacts in the history of African-American social and communal life."[6] An example are the speeches of Maria Stewart (1803–1879), abolitionist, women's rights activist, and the first Black female political writer and public speaker. In her 1831 address xii

Introduction

titled "Religion and the Pure Principles of Morality: The Sure Foundation on Which We Must Build," Stewart invoked the Bible and the Constitution to argue for the rights and liberty of Black people before a Boston audience of free Blacks:

> This is the land of freedom. The press is at liberty. Every man has a right to express his opinion. Many think, because your skins are tinged with a sable hue, that you are an inferior race of beings; but God does not consider you as such. He hath formed and fashioned you in His own glorious image, and hath bestowed upon you reason and strong powers of intellect. He hath made you to have dominion over the beasts of the field, the fowls of the air, and the fishes of the sea. He has crowned you with glory and honor; has made you but a little lower than the angels;[7] and, according to the Constitution of these United States, he has made all men free and equal.[8]

Thus, Stewart did not find any contradiction in combining sacred and secular sources in her activism on behalf of equality and justice but rather found them sufficient weapons in her battle to secure the rights that she and others believed were God-given as they faced insidious acts by Whites to disenfranchise US free Blacks. Such measures included the African colonization movement, state black laws or codes, and kidnapping of free Black people for sale into slavery. The combination of these actions made acquiring citizenship as a birthright an urgent matter for Blacks.

Despite the confidence of Stewart and others like her, such as Frederick Douglass, David Walker, and Martin Luther King, Jr., in the Bible and the US Constitution as tools to right the racial wrongs done to Africans born in America, Whites used these same texts with equal vigor to contest Blacks' right to freedom, liberty, and equality. White lawmakers used passages such as Genesis 9:20–27 and Ezra 9–10 to enact policies in support of slavery and segregation. US Supreme Court Chief Justice Roger B. Taney, in deciding Dred Scott v. Sanford, interpreted the Constitution as establishing that "no black person—enslaved or free—was a citizen of the United States" and that "black people had had no rights that whites were bound to respect."[9] Even after the passage of the Fourteenth Amendment to the Constitution making all persons born or naturalized in the United States citizens of the United States, Blacks have continued to navigate what it means to belong as a US citizen.

This is a book about belonging, more specifically the "politics of belonging," the processes used to determine who belongs as a member of a polity and who decides. Several Hebrew Bible scholars have taken different approaches to the construction of Israel's identity as nationalist, ethnic, or religious during the exilic or postexilic period based on the collection and redaction of the Hebrew Bible texts.[10] Where they tend to agree is that such

Introduction xiii

an identity was constructed in the then present, based on a past shared myth or memory of common origins from a common ancestor, and the promise of a glorious future as YHWH's chosen people bounded by covenantal fidelity. In the process, the texts also constructed borders of inclusion and exclusion in ethnic, gender, and class terms. In this book, I first read certain Hebrew Bible texts in Genesis and the Deuteronomistic Narratives (Joshua through 2 Kings) through the lens of the politics of belonging.

Next, I examine how White American pro-slavery and segregationist legislators and jurists used the same texts to defend White supremacist ideas about US-born Blacks and to place legal boundaries of exclusion around citizenship and belonging. Even without legal discrimination at their disposal, Whites enforced *de facto* social separation along racial lines. What the ancient Israelites and the White lawmakers had in common was that both groups constructed boundaries along racial/ethnic, gender, and class categories and both believed that their actions were divinely ordained.

My primary interlocutors in the book are four women whose research engages identity politics, citizenship, gender, and race. Legal scholar Kimberlé Williams Crenshaw coined the term "intersectionality" in her groundbreaking 1989 article titled "Demarginalizing the Intersection of Race and Gender," used to demonstrate how race and sex discrimination discourses fail to account for Black women's intersectional experiences of discrimination.[11] Thus, antidiscrimination discourse that excludes Black women's experiences seldom addresses their needs. Crenshaw is the first to admit that intersectionality is neither some new form of theorizing about identity nor the only way to denote the various ways that feminist and antiracist discourses tend to marginalize the multilayered discrimination borne by Black and other women of color. Sociologist Nira Yuval-Davis was among the first to offer an intersectional analytical framework for studying citizenship, identity and belonging, and the politics of belonging in theorizing nations and nationalism. Yuval-Davis argues that gender, race, and class play crucial roles in the nationalist processes that determine insiders and outsiders.

Many would consider the work of writer and poet Audre Lorde as a precursor to Crenshaw's. Lorde situated her writings from the multiplicities of her identity as a Black lesbian feminist. Lorde's paper titled "Age, Race, Class and Sex: Women Redefining Difference" (1980) delivered at the Copeland Colloquium at Amherst College (later published in *Sister Outsider*, a collection of her essential essays and speeches) explores how human differences have been misnamed and misused to divide and keep certain groups subordinate. Her remedy is to recognize, acknowledge, and redefine difference as a source of energy and vehicle for social change. Incidentally, Lorde makes an indirect reference to the Combahee River Collective (1974–1980), a

xiv *Introduction*

progressive political movement founded by Black feminist and lesbian activists in the essay.

"The Combahee River Collective Statement" composed by the group recognized that racial, sexual, heterosexual, and class oppression experienced by Black and other women of color are simultaneous and interlocking forms of discrimination.[12] This demonstrates how widely Black women have been centering their experiences of overlapping, tri-dimensional oppression in their scholarship and activism. Still others would point to the activism of nineteenth century Black women such as Sojourner Truth, Anna Julia Cooper, Frances Ellen Watkins Harper and Amanda Berry Smith, who engaged antiracist and antisexist practices simultaneously that predated these twentieth century intellectuals.

Lorde's "sister outsider" sentiment with Patricia Hill Collins's analysis of Black women in academia as "outsiders within" express for me the marginalized status of Black women in US society such that birthright citizenship does not instantaneously confer insider status. Collins's research, grounded in traditional African American culture, also examines the simultaneous and interlocking nature of race, gender, and class oppression experienced by Black women as outsiders within, which she describes as both a source of "frustration and creativity."[13] Her work is of benefit to this project for her intersectional analysis of gender, race, and the construction of US national identity.

Finally, my hermeneutical approach is womanist. The term "womanist" is a relative newcomer to the American literary landscape having first gained prominence with the 1983 publication of author, poet, and activist Alice Walker's *In Search of Our Mothers' Gardens: Womanist Prose*. There is a running narrative about the origins of the term womanist by way of introduction to most womanist scholarly works that has mostly been left unchallenged. It usually goes something like, "The term 'womanist' was coined by author and activist, Alice Walker, within her 1982 publication *In Search of Our Mothers' Gardens: Womanist Prose*."[14] This is usually accredited to her four-part poetic definition of "womanist" in the front matter of her book.

Walker begins her definition here with an adjective: "1. From womanish. (Opp. Of 'girlish,' i.e., frivolous, irresponsible, not serious)," which she expounds as originating from a Black folk expression passed from mothers to daughters.[15] Walker's use of womanish comes from her own cultural context growing up in the American South however, the term has antecedents. Womanish dates as early as the fourteenth century and meant "womanly, feminine; resembling a woman"; it was also used derogatorily of men accused of "behaving in a manner of a woman, effeminate."[16]

In Walker's definition, Black daughters were told, "'You acting womanish,' i.e., like a woman. Usually referring to outrageous, audacious, courageous or *willful* (author's emphasis) behavior."[17] Womanish girls were "Interested in

Introduction xv

grown-up doings. Acting grown up. Being grown up. Interchangeable with another black folk expression: 'You trying to be grown.' Responsible. In charge. Serious." Walker's definition demonstrates the development of the word womanish over time and within specific cultural contexts.

Although the earliest attribution of the term womanist dates to the nineteenth century and refers to a "womanizer," Walker can rightly be credited as the first person to publicly use the term in reference to the espousal of Black women's access to societal and political rights. However, she first familiarized readers with the term in a 1979 introduction to a chapter on violence and pornography titled "Coming Apart" in *Take Back the Night* edited by Laura Lederer. In the essay, Walker writes of the deleterious impact on a Black couple's marriage that the husband's taste for pornography is having on his relationship with his wife, who feels degraded by his proclivity. She reads to her husband literature by Black and White women activists, and he accuses her of being a "women's liber." Walker explains that the wife "has never considered herself a feminist—though she is, of course, a 'womanist.' A 'womanist' is a feminist, only more common."[18] Walker goes on to elaborate in an endnote that "'Womanist' encompasses 'feminist' as it is defined in Webster's, but also means instinctively pro-woman . . . It has a strong root in Black women's culture." She adds that, "An advantage of using 'womanist' is that, because it is from my own culture, I needn't preface it with the word 'Black' (an awkward necessity and a problem I have with the word 'feminist'), since Blackness is implicit in the term."[19] Although Walker does not reject the term feminist, she feels more comfortable with the accessibility of womanist as "more common."

Walker continued to develop the term womanist in her 1981 review of *Gifts of Power: The Writings of Rebecca Jackson (1795–1871), Black Visionary, Shaker Eldress* edited by Jean McMahon Humez. In an otherwise glowing review of Humez's editing skills, Walker took exception to her characterization of the relationship between Jackson and her constant companion Rebecca Perot as "lesbian" when Jackson described herself as being, "celibate" and dead to sexual desires. In searching for the words that Black women such as Jackson and Perot might use to describe their relationship, Walker imagines that they might say they "love women (sexually or not)" or refer to themselves as "whole women" or "round women" because they were concerned for all Black people, males as well as females.[20] Walker's term for such women is "womanist" because it is consistent with Black cultural values, is imbued with spirituality, and affirms a connectedness to the entire Black community and world.[21] This is not meant to detract from the quality of Humez's work but rather to signify, for Walker, the importance of Black women naming their own experience as they so choose.

xvi *Introduction*

Walker's definition of womanist culminates in her succinct four-part characterization that combines both its derivation from Black women's folk culture that labels Black girls' audacious behavior as "womanish" in "Coming Apart" and women who love other women, "sexually and/or nonsexually," as expressed in the review of *Gifts of Power*. Walker, who once described herself as sexually "curious," defined a womanist in part 2 as "a woman who loves other women, sexually and/or nonsexually . . . sometimes loves individual men, sexually and/or non-sexually."[22] Early in the development of womanist religious scholarship, there were debates whether it was suitable for Christian Black women religious scholars to appropriate the nomenclature "womanist" given its embrace of same gender-loving relationships. Some womanist religious scholars today use queer theoretical approaches in their scholarship.

Although Walker expresses that a womanist is "[a] black feminist or feminist of color," she makes clear that the terms womanist and feminist should not be conflated as she concludes that, "Womanist is to feminist as purple to lavender."[23] Speaking in familial terms, Layli Phillips explains that feminism and womanism are "cousins."[24] She adds that womanists and Black feminists are "siblings" who "favor" each other, but the terms are not interchangeable.[25] Thus, despite Walker's own words, readers should not take her comments to imply that a womanist is *simply* a Black feminist. Those who do miss the nuance (pun intended) in Walker's meaning. A Black feminist for Walker is not a racialized form of feminism but rather is like a child who resembles her kinfolk in speech and mannerisms because they come from the same stock but are not the same.

Walker continues to write that a womanist is also "traditionally universalist," a reflection of the various hues of black skin color, and "traditionally capable," as in a mother's nonchalant response to her daughter's announcement that she is taking the mother and a group of slaves on foot to Canada to freedom: "It wouldn't be the first time."[26] Although Walker's description throughout is rooted in Black women's folk culture, she emphasizes that it is not gender exclusive. Walker's characteristic of a womanist as a "round" woman introduced in the *Gifts of Power* review means that she is also concerned for the wellbeing of all Black people, regardless of gender, and therefore loves "roundness."[27] Thus, a womanist is committed to the survival and wholeness of her entire people.

Two other forms of womanist nomenclature are worth noting: Chikwenye Okonjo Ogunyemi's African womanism (1985) and Clenora Hudson-Weems's Africana womanism (1989).[28] As noted above, none of these writers coined the term womanist. Still, Layli Phillips observes that the womanist idea existed for some time waiting to be named and developed. As such, each woman created her own distinct notion of womanism independently. Their respective views of womanism demonstrate that the term is not bounded by

Introduction   xvii

geography, race, or culture. Nonetheless, womanist religious scholars consistently cite Walker's 1983 definition for their appropriation of the term. Thus, Walker's womanist terminology will be primarily engaged throughout this work when referring to womanist and womanism.

WOMANIST BIBLICAL
INTERPRETATION: AN OVERVIEW

Black women have a long history of interpreting the Bible. As Melissa Harris-Perry noted, "From slavery to the present, African American women have interpreted biblical texts in Sunday school, lectured from pulpits, and pastored unaffiliated religious bodies and informal, sometimes clandestine services."[29] Nineteenth century Black women such as Sojourner Truth, Anna Julia Cooper, Frances Ellen Watkins Harper, and Amanda Berry Smith combined biblical interpretation with their activism for racial and gender equality.[30] The genesis of academic womanist biblical interpretation can be traced to conversations among several Black women religious scholars and graduate students and their colleagues and classmates in churches and on campuses in the 1980s and 1990s. Alice Walker's writings, especially *In Search of Our Mothers' Gardens*, had an emancipating effect on them and their identity as Black women. They began to formally gather and produce scholarship using a womanist theoretical framework.[31]

In 1985 Black women members of the American Academy of Religion (AAR) and Society of Biblical Literature (SBL) organized the first session of Womanist Approaches to Religion and Society. Conversations begun at the AAR and SBL continued over the next several years at both predominately White and historically Black graduate theological schools. In 1988 Lawrence Jones, then dean of the Howard University School of Divinity (HUSD), provided the funding for Black women religious studies scholars and students to convene the first Consultation of Womanist Scholars in Religion on HUSD's campus.[32] The conversation resumed in 1989 at the AAR annual meeting with a consultation, and AAR officially recognized the womanist group in 1990.

Also in 1989, the *Journal of Feminist Studies in Religion* published "Roundtable Discussion: Christian Ethics and Theology in Womanist Perspective" to consider the "adequacy and fruitfulness of the term *womanist* as it describes black feminist theology and ethics."[33] Cheryl J. Sanders delivered the opening essay contesting the appropriation by Black women religious scholars of the secular term for doing Christian theology and ethics. The respondents, Katie G. Cannon, Emilie M. Townes, M. Shawn Copeland, bell hooks, and Cheryl Townsend Gilkes, each affirmed the value of the word xviii

Introduction

"womanist" for Black women to both embrace and critique their religious traditions from their own experience.

Just a few years later, calls were made for papers for womanist-themed biblical hermeneutics sessions at SBL annual meetings. In 1992, The African-American Theology and Biblical Hermeneutics program unit sponsored a session at the SBL annual meeting with the theme "Womanist Readings of Texts." There were only two papers presented, and both presenters were graduate students: "Rachel Wept and Miriam Sang" by Regina Smith (Jewish Theological Seminary of America) and "Some Hermeneutic Potentialities for Womanist Readers Drawn from Judges 19–21" by Koala Jones-Warsaw (Claremont Graduate School).[34] In 2006, the newly named African-American Biblical Hermeneutics unit cosponsored a session with the African Biblical Hermeneutics unit titled "African Women's and Womanist Biblical Hermeneutics: Continuities and Discontinuities." This session featured papers by South African Indian, African American, Caribbean, and Botswanan women biblical scholars. In 2008 Black women biblical scholars officially gathered at the SBL annual meeting in Boston.[35] Thus, womanist biblical scholarship made small but incremental progress in the academy.

As mentioned above, womanists frequently speak in kinship terms. One example of this is the practice of speaking of the development and growth of womanist philosophical thought in terms of "generations" rather than in "waves," which is usually associated with the development of feminist activism and thought.[36] As such, it is usually traced like a family tree with branches. However, just as biblical *toledoth* or genealogies can have duplications, omissions, and inconsistencies so also are efforts at tracing the genealogies or lines of descent or development of womanist biblical interpretation complex.[37] Attempting to classify Black women who have earned terminal degrees in biblical studies (Hebrew Bible/Old Testament and Near Eastern languages, New Testament, Early Christian origins, etc.) by generation or set of "family" members belonging to the same stage of descent is complicated by the lack of consensus around what categories should be used to group them.

Another approach is to categorize them according to the decade in which they earned their degree, which is attempted below. Still, one problem with this approach is how narrow or broad to define the category of biblical studies. Should Black women who earned degrees in Religion be counted?[38] Another issue is whether to include non-US born Black women scholars who earned their degrees from US institutions and teach in the field in the United States (as did I).[39] Finally, the decision to include as many Black women biblical scholars in the United States regardless of whether they identify themselves or their scholarship as womanist or not is a controversial one. The attempt here is not to assign to all Black women biblical scholars listed below a descriptor they themselves might not embrace. In fact, that would be counter to a central Black feminist and womanist core tenet—the power to name oneself. Rather it is meant to be as inclusive as possible so that the reader is aware of how few these women are in number and can appreciate how significant an achievement it is for these women to attain this status in a field dominated by White males.

Speaking in terms of genealogy, Clarice J. Martin and Renita J. Weems are the progenitors of what became known as womanist biblical scholarship, and the women who followed them were considered their "progeny." Martin earned a Ph.D. in New Testament from Duke University in 1985, making her the first US Black woman to be conferred a terminal degree in biblical studies. Weems, the first US Black woman to hold a doctorate in Old Testament, earned her degree from Princeton Theological Seminary in 1989. Neither woman's dissertation is explicitly womanist in its hermeneutical approach. Both scholars however were engaged in ongoing conversations with other Black women in churches and the academy about what it meant to be a womanist and wrote articles on the subject (see below).

The second generation of Black women biblical scholars includes Naomi Franklin (Hebrew Bible 1990), Wilma Ann Bailey (Hebrew Bible 1995), Edwina Wright (Hebrew Bible 1996), Mignon Jacobs (Hebrew Bible 1998) and Dora Mbuwayesango (Hebrew Bible 1998). The year 1999 was a banner one for Black women earning doctorates in biblical studies. Gay L. Byron (New Testament), Willa Johnson (Hebrew Bible), Judith Fentress-Williams (Hebrew Bible), and Ann Holmes Redding (New Testament) joined the ranks of this generation of Black women biblical scholars.

The third generation includes Cheryl Anderson (Hebrew Bible 2000), Stephanie Buckhanon Crowder (New Testament 2000), Madeline McClenney (Hebrew Bible 2001), Valerie Bridgeman (Hebrew Bible 2002), Stacy Davis (Hebrew Bible 2003), Margaret Aymer (New Testament 2004), Raquel St. Clair (New Testament 2005), Vivian Johnson (Hebrew Bible 2005), Monya Stubbs (New Testament 2005), Lauress Wilkins Lawrence (Hebrew Bible 2005), Wil Gafney (Hebrew Bible 2006), Love Sechrest (New Testament 2006), Mitzi Smith (New Testament 2006), Nyasha Junior (Hebrew Bible 2008), Amanda Mbuvi (2008), and Althea Spencer Miller (New Testament 2008).

The fourth generation includes Annie Tinsley (New Testament 2010), Terry Ann Smith (Hebrew Bible 2011), Lynne St. Clair Darden (New Testament 2011), Shanell Smith (New Testament 2012), Dorothy Akoto (Hebrew Bible 2012), Vanessa Lovelace (Hebrew Bible 2012), Lisa Marie Bowens (New Testament 2013), Jamie Waters (Hebrew Bible 2013), Janice P. De-Whyte (Hebrew Bible 2014), Jennifer Kaalund (New Testament 2015), Angela Parker (New Testament 2015), Shively Smith (New Testament 2015), Kimberly Russaw (Hebrew Bible 2016), Richetta Amen (New Testament

xx *Introduction*

2016), and Febbie Dickerson (New Testament 2017). Amen has the distinction of having earned a Ph.D. in Biblical Studies/New Testament with a complementary concentration in Womanist Hermeneutics. After a brief interval, a new generation includes Ericka Dunbar (Hebrew Bible 2020), Bridgett Green (New Testament 2021), and Kamilah Hall Sharp (Hebrew Bible 2022).[40]

Despite attempting to identify as many US Black women biblical scholars as possible, this exercise does not get us any closer to identifying womanist biblical scholars or what might be considered womanist biblical scholarship. While it is the scholar's prerogative to identify themself or their scholarship as womanist, there are external pressures that have a bearing on this decision. For one, a number of doctoral degree programs and dissertation advisors and committees discourage women and racial/ethnic minorities from drawing on their contextual situatedness as a source for doing biblical studies.[41] Therefore, some aspiring womanist biblical scholars have been informed that in order for their research to be regarded as scholarly they must use historical critical biblical methods that examine the world behind the text to the exclusion of the student's *Sitz im Leben* (setting in life). This practice is what Patricia Hill Collins refers to as the "Eurocentric masculinist knowledge validation process" that can work to suppress Black women's scholarly production.[42] Put another way, according to Collins, the processes do not necessarily have to be managed by White men; any scholar "making a knowledge claim must convince a scholarly community controlled by white men that a given claim is justified" or "credible research."[43]

Another influence is one's professional setting. Some Black women are employed at institutions (colleges, universities, seminaries) where feminist and womanist biblical hermeneutics are regarded with suspicion. Thus, academic constraints exist both for students and scholars to read the Bible as a womanist. As a result, some women wait until they are in a more secure position in their career, usually after they have earned tenure when they are less vulnerable to having their credentials withheld, before including a womanist hermeneutical approach in their scholarship.[44] Some Black Christian women and other women of color are reticent to embrace womanism due to its emphasis on spirituality rather than Christianity or its perceived conflict with Christian ethical teachings.[45] Therefore, social constraints imposed by religious institutions (or family) may also impede the production of womanist biblical scholarship. A few split the difference and self-identify using the hybridized identification of Black feminist/womanist.[46] Finally, on a practical level, many Black women were and continue to be unfamiliar with the term womanist but are familiar with Black feminist.[47]

These external pressures arguably have had a tangible impact on the production of womanist biblical scholarship in at least two ways. First, given the small number of US Black women earning terminal degrees in biblical studies over the past thirty years (we represent one percent), any move to dissuade Black women with womanist sympathies from identifying themselves or their work as womanist effectively diminished early womanist scholarly output. As such, publications that might have been under the rubric "womanist," such as revised dissertations or chapters from dissertations, either lacked a womanist approach or were tangentially associated with womanist/womanism. For example, as a Black woman biblical scholar who published a revised version of her dissertation, Renita Weems wrote about trying to be a "responsible womanist/feminist" in her acknowledgments.[48] Cheryl Anderson acknowledged her "feminist/womanist African-American female" identity as motivating her work in her introduction.[49] Kimberly Russaw describes in her acknowledgments her "feminist and womanist sensibilities" as influencing her book.[50] Gay L. Byron (2002) and Lynne St. Clair Darden (2015) engage womanist readings of ancient Christian sources but do not identify their work as "womanist." Wil Gafney mentions womanist, feminist, and African American liberationist biblical scholarship on women prophets in her introduction (2008). Jennifer Kaalund (2018) uses a postcolonial/feminist/womanist hermeneutics in her book. Only Stephanie Buckhanon Crowder (2002), Raquel St. Clair (2008), Shanell Smith (2014), and Febbie Dickerson (2019) identified their hermeneutical approach as womanist.

The second impact on scholarly womanist biblical output is opportunity.[51] An example is the scant amount of literature on womanist biblical interpretation in key feminist volumes on biblical literature. Opportunities to contribute to these volumes are mostly by invitation of the editors suggesting either familiarity with the subject and/or an acquaintance with womanist scholars professionally or personally—or both. The slow but steady growth of Black women biblical scholars since their emergence in the 1980s is evident in the publication of such volumes as the *Women's Bible Commentary* edited by Carol Newsom and Sharon Ringe. The first (1992) and expanded editions (1998) included a single entry by a Black woman (Renita Weems). By the twentieth anniversary edition (2012) edited by Newsom, Ringe, and Jacqueline Lapsley, there were several Black women included. None of these entries was explicitly womanist in their content although the editorial requirements may have limited this approach.

The groundbreaking *Feminist Companion to the Bible* series (1993–2001; 1998–2002) first edited by Athalya Brenner-Idan includes two explicitly womanist essays, although both contributors are outside the field of biblical studies.[52] To my knowledge, the New Testament and early Christianity companions edited by Amy-Jill Levine (2000 ongoing) do not include any womanist essays. *The IVP Women's Bible Commentary* (2002) edited by Catherine Clark Kroeger and Mary J. Evans includes commentaries by Anthea Butler (religious studies) and Cheryl Sanders (ethics). More recently, *Feminist*

Interpretation of the Hebrew Bible in Retrospect Vol. III (2017), the third of a three-volume set that is an overview of the progress of feminist interpretation of the Hebrew Bible includes an essay on womanist biblical interpretation by womanist theologian Karen Baker-Fletcher.[53] Thus, as important as it is to invite womanist scholars to contribute to the discipline, it is just as important to be intentional about inviting womanist *biblical* scholars to do *womanist* biblical scholarship. The Wisdom Commentary Series includes several Black feminist and womanist contributors.

DEFINITIONS OF WOMANIST BIBLICAL INTERPRETATION

There have been several articles that bring a diverse range of perspectives on defining womanist biblical interpretation. Renita Weems's article titled "Womanist Reflections on Biblical Hermeneutics" (1993) explains that an "African-American womanist perspective" on biblical hermeneutics begins with a "critique of all rationalizations for domination and exploitation both within the Bible and in scholarship," to include a critical examination of all forms of oppression and repression in the canon including sexism.[54]

Clarice Martin privileges Black Christian women's experiences as the starting point for framing womanist biblical interpretation in an essay by the same title in *Dictionary of Biblical Interpretation* (1999). According to Martin, the four tasks of womanist biblical interpreters are: 1) the recovery of women's history in the Judeo-Christian tradition; 2) the reclamation of neglected histories and stories of the presence and function of Black peoples within divergent biblical traditions; 3) to critique the persistent and still normative narrowness of vision of feminist theologians and biblical interpreters on the subject of race; and 4) the retrieval and documentary analysis of the effective history of the Bible in Western culture in general and on peoples of African descent in Black diasporic communities in particular.[55]

In *True to Our Native Land: An African American New Testament Commentary* edited by Brian Blount (2007), Raquel St. Clair's article titled "Womanist Biblical Interpretation" describes womanist biblical interpretation as resulting from the "interplay between African American women's experience and scripture."[56] St. Clair offered four tenets of what she terms a "womanist hermeneutics of wholeness" that is more christological in its perspective: 1) promotes the wholeness of African American women without prohibiting the wholeness of others; 2) is grounded in the concrete reality of African American women's lives; 3) affirms that God supports African American women in their commitment to and struggle for wholeness; and 4) asserts that Jesus' significance is his life and ministry without excluding his suffering and death.[57] Nyasha Junior's two essays on womanist biblical interpretation do not seek to define womanist interpretation but rather to lay out for the reader key features of womanist scholarship, the growth of womanist biblical interpretation by non-biblical specialists, and the future of womanist biblical scholarship.[58]

STRIDES IN WOMANIST BIBLICAL INTERPRETATION

Developments in the last decade that promise to move womanist biblical interpretation significantly beyond its formative stage include a new monograph, two edited volumes, and a new series on womanist biblical interpretation. *An Introduction to Womanist Biblical Interpretation* (2015) by Nyasha Junior is a graduate-level introductory textbook that provides the reader with key terms, historical contextual analyses of feminist and womanist biblical interpretation forerunners, and the development of contemporary womanist biblical scholarship. *I Found God in Me: A Womanist Biblical Hermeneutics Reader* (2015) edited by Mitzi Smith is a collection of classic essays on womanist religious thought, one new essay on womanist biblical interpretation and original and reprinted womanist readings of biblical texts. *Womanist Interpretations of the Bible: Expanding the Discourse* (2016) edited by Gay L. Byron and Vanessa Lovelace is a collection of original essays using innovative interpretive approaches to womanist criticism of biblical and other sacred texts. *Womanist Readings of Scripture* is a new series by Lexington Books/ Fortress Academic Press edited by Mitzi J. Smith and Gay L. Byron.[59] *Luke, Widows, Judges, and Stereotypes* by Febbie Dickerson is the first title in the series. The series description promises to "expand and enrich Womanist hermeneutical discourse about Scripture and its deployment in the academy and in contemporary ecclesiastical and social contexts." This series represents a new phase in womanist biblical hermeneutics as "coming of age" in the field of biblical interpretation to which I am pleased to contribute.

This monograph adds to this series. The first chapter explores the political project of motherhood in the politics of belonging in the Sarah-Hagar narratives. Traditional readings of the Sarah-Hagar narratives focus on God's promise and fulfillment of a son to Abram/Abraham. Feminist commentators brought the mothers in the story from the margins to the center of analysis. I examine the power dynamics between Hagar and Sarah to argue that despite the hegemonic masculine representations in the texts, Sarah still exercises a degree of power and privilege due to her ethnicity and status to exploit Hagar for her own benefit. Yet, Hagar also wields a modicum of power based on genetic and gestational motherhood. I also explore the intersection of ancient xxiv *Introduction*

laws and contemporary US population polices and race, class, and gender in the various political projects of motherhood that construct insiders and outsiders.

The second chapter reviews the history of interpretation of Genesis 9:20–27 to proffer that proslavery White Christians in the antebellum period weaponized and sexualized Genesis 9:20–27 to firmly establish the institution of slavery in America. They alleged that Noah's curse of the descendants of Canaan destined Blacks to perpetual inferiority and servitude to Whites by divine decree. This chapter shows that in order to account for the differences between Blacks and Whites, since many US Christians believed the myth that all humankind descended from one ancestor, they had to offer alternative theories for the inferiority of Blacks. These included promoting polygenesis, the theory that Blacks descended from a separate ancestor, turning to phrenology to claim that Blacks had smaller brain sizes than Whites, and defending anti-miscegenation laws out of fear that sexual relations between the races would weaken the White race and democracy.

Chapter 3 explores the embodiment of women, often mothers, as the symbolic figuration of the nation and its boundaries in the Deuteronomistic History and the United States. The two named women prophets in the Former Prophets (Joshua to 2 Kings) are juxtaposed with the royal women Jezebel and Athaliah as the limits of proper and illicit covenantal fidelity, a determinant for inclusion as a member of Israel. Deborah and Huldah are symbolic border guards along the literary boundaries. By comparison, US Black women have been saddled with the jezebel trope and its counterpart the mammy stereotype signifying sexual deviance since the antebellum period making Black women into symbolic border guards that divide the nation into "us" and "them." I argue that Jezebel and Black women, both outsiders within the nation, are depicted as dangerous *femme fatales* who use their sexuality to entice insider men to turn from God at the peril of the nation.

Chapter 4 explores nationalistic rhetoric that promotes the idea that the health and security of the nation depended largely on the status of women and their ability to produce masculine sons who would be good citizens. "Mothers in Israel, Church Mothers, and Mothers of the Nation" continues to explore the symbolic figuration of women as mothers, introduced in chapter 1, in wartime imagery, literature, and song. From Deborah a mother in Israel (Judg. 5:7) to Church Mothers in Black church traditions to contemporary US mothers of the nation, this chapter demonstrates ways that maternity functions to produce certain members of the nation, regardless of whether the woman is biologically a mother or figuratively. However, not all women can symbolically represent the polity. Non-Israelite women married to Israelite men could not qualify despite the laws on war in Deuteronomy 20:8 permitting Israelite men to take an enemy woman captured in warfare as a wife. Nor can Black women become mothers of the nation. That honor is reserved for middle-class White women. But even they are judged as good mothers or bad mothers depending on how self-sacrificing they are and how well they raise masculine sons who are healthy citizens.

The conclusion in chapter 5 offers reflections on discoveries made during the writing of this book, especially the significance of motherhood—genetic, gestational, social, mother's milk, citizenship—and the politics of belonging based on race/ethnicity, gender, and class for sons and their mothers. Additionally, it contemplates future directions of the research in this book in studies in migration and exile in the Hebrew Bible and the Black diaspora that are outside the focus of examination here. Ultimately, I boldly welcome the opportunity to write a monograph through a womanist lens as a contribution to the production of "resisting readings," biblical interpretation that goes against the grain or resists the constraints of the academy, academic institutions, religious institutions, or social institutions.[60]

NOTES

1. "Frequently Asked Questions," Center for Barth Studies at Princeton Theological Seminary, https://barth.ptsem.edu/frequently-asked-questions/.

2. The Declaration of Independence is often spoken of in tandem with the Constitution.

3. Herbert Robinson Marbury, *Pillars of Cloud and Fire: The Politics of Exodus in African American Biblical Interpretation* (New York: New York University Press, 2015).

4. Clarice Martin, "Biblical Theodicy and Black Women's Spiritual Autobiography: 'The Miry Bog, The Desolate Pit, a New Song in My Mouth,'" in *A Troubling in My Soul: Womanist Perspectives on Evil and Suffering*, ed. Emilie M. Townes (Maryknoll, NY: Orbis, 1993), 24.

5. Eddie S. Glaude, Jr., *Exodus! Religion, Race, and Nation in Early Nineteenth Century Black America* (Chicago: The University of Chicago Press, 2000), 4.

6. Martin, "Spiritual Autobiography," 26.

7. Stewart is paraphrasing Psalm 8:5.

8. Maria W. Stewart, "Meditations from the pen of Mrs. Maria W. Stewart: (Widow of the late James W. Stewart) now matron of the Freedman's hospital, and presented in 1832 to the First African Baptist church and society of Boston, Mass." (Washington, DC: Garrison & Knap, 1879), HathiTrust, https://babel.hathitrust.org/cgi/pt?id=inu.30000011406927&seq=7.

9. Martha S. Jones, *Birthright Citizens: A History of Race and Rights in Antebellum America* (Cambridge: Cambridge University Press, 2018), 131.

10. See, for example, Steven Grosby, *Biblical Ideas of Nationality: Ancient and Modern* (Winona Lake, IN: Eisenbrauns, 2002), for a national Israelite identity. For an ethnic approach to ancient Israel's identity, see E. Theodore Mullen Jr., *Narrative*

History and Ethnic Boundaries: The Deuteronomistic Historian and the Creation of Israelite National Identity (Atlanta: Scholars, 1993), takes ethnic approaches to ancient Israel's identity. See, for example, Cheryl Anderson, *Women, Ideology and Violence: Critical Theory and the Construction of Gender in the Book of the Covenant and the Deuteronomic Law* (London: T&T Clark, 2006), for a religious Israelite identity.

11. Kimberle Crenshaw, "Demarginalizing the Intersection of Race and Sex: A Black Feminist Critique of Antidiscrimination Doctrine, Feminist Theory and Antiracist Politics," *University of Chicago Legal Forum* no. 1 (1989): 139–67.

12. The Combahee River Collective, "The Combahee River Collective Statement," 1978, https://americanstudies.yale.edu/sites/default/files/files/Keyword%20Coalition _Readings.pdf.

13. Patricia Hill Collins, *Black Feminist Thought: Knowledge, Consciousness, and the Politics of Empowerment* (Boston: Unwin Hyman, 1990), 233.

14. "A Brief History of Civil Rights in the United States: The Womanist Movement," Howard University School of Law Vernon E. Jordan Law Library, https://library.law.howard.edu/civilrightshistory /womanist#:~:text=The%20term%20'womanist'%20was%20coined ,Mothers'%20Gardens%3A%20Womanist%20Prose.

15. Alice Walker, *In Search of Our Mothers' Gardens: Womanist Prose* (San Diego: Harcourt Brace Jovanovich, 1983), xi.

16. Online Etymology Dictionary, "Womanish (adj.)," https://www.etymonline .com/search?q=womanish&utm_campaign=sd&utm_medium=serp&utm_source=ds _search. "Womanism," the noun form of womanish first occurs in the nineteenth century in the *American Monthly Magazine* (1824). Womanism was defined as, "Behaviour regarded as typical or characteristic of a woman; womanishness," *Oxford English Dictionary*, 3rd ed. (Oxford: Oxford University Press, 2011). Also, Edmund Shaftesbury, *The Two Sexes: Their Functions, Purposes and Place in Nature* (Washington, DC: The Ralston Club, 1898), 13 declared that "The man who trots his nimble pace at the skirts of a domineering female is womanish. The woman who thrusts her head into the coarser stalls of the masculine duties . . . is mannish." As such, early references to womanism and womanish concerned behavior exhibited by men considered effeminate.

17. Walker, *Our Mothers' Gardens*, xi.

18. Alice Walker, "Coming Apart," in *Take Back the Night: Women on Pornography*, ed. Laura Lederer (New York: Harper Perennial, 1979), 100.

19. Walker, "Coming Apart," 100.

20. Alice Walker, "Review of Gifts of Power: The Writings of Rebecca Jackson (1795–1871), Black Visionary, Shaker Eldress," *The Black Scholar* 12, no. 5 (September/October 1981): 67.

21. Walker, 67.

22. Walker, *Our Mothers' Gardens*, xi.

23. Walker, xi.

24. Layli Phillips, ed., *The Womanist Reader* (New York: Routledge, 2006), xxxiii.

25. Phillips, xxxiv.

26. Walker, *Our Mothers' Gardens*, xxxiv.

27. Walker, xxxiv.

28. See Phillips, *The Womanist Reader*, for a comprehensive overview of Ogunyemi and Hudson-Weems's work.

29. Melissa Harris-Perry, *Sister Citizen: Shame, Stereotypes, and Black Women in America* (New Haven: Yale University Press, 2011), 232.

30. For a brief survey of the use of scripture in the activism of the nineteenth century forerunners to contemporary womanist biblical interpreters, see, for example, Nyasha Junior, *An Introduction to Womanist Biblical Interpretation* (Louisville: Westminster John Knox, 2015).

31. For an introduction of womanist theology, see, for example, the two-volume classic, James H. Cone and Gayraud S. Wilmore, eds., *Black Theology: A Documentary History*, Volume One: 1996–1979 and Volume Two: 1980–1992 (Maryknoll, NY: Orbis, 1993).

32. Delores Carpenter, "Theological and Spiritual Empowerment of Black Women in Ministry," in *The Quest for Liberation and Reconciliation: Essays in Honor of J. Deotis Roberts*, ed. Michael Battle (Louisville: Westminster John Knox, 2005), 153–64; Howard University School of Divinity celebrated the 30th anniversary of the gathering, "Continuing the Womanist Consultation" on March 29–30, 2019. Cheryl J. Sanders, Gay L. Byron, Judith Fentress Williams, and Renita J. Weems were among the panelists.

33. "Editors' Introduction," *Journal of Feminist Studies in Religion* 5, no. 2 (1989): 4.

34. The respondents were Danna Nolan Fewell, then Perkins School of Theology, Southern Methodist University and M. Shawn Copeland, Yale Divinity School. A revised version of Koala Jones-Warsaw's SBL paper was published as "Toward a Womanist Hermeneutic: A Reading of Judges 19–21," in *A Feminist Companion to Judges*, The Feminist Companion to the Bible 4, ed. Athalya Brenner (Sheffield: Sheffield Academic, 1993), 172–86.

35. Stephanie Buckhanon Crowder, *When Momma Speaks: The Bible and Motherhood from a Womanist Perspective* (Louisville: Westminster John Knox, 2016), xii. The Womanist Group first appears in the SBL Program Book in 2009 at the annual meeting in New Orleans. Note: Since the completion of this manuscript, SBL added a Womanist Interpretation Section with Renita Weems and Mitzi Smith as the program unit chairs.

36. One approach is to trace the trajectory of womanist biblical interpretation from the recovery of women and Black people in the Bible, the centering of the Black church and historical critical methods as the frame of analysis, to the analysis of race, gender, class, sexuality, and masculinity using various methodological approaches and religious perspectives, to include queer theory, postcolonial theory, social-sciences, trauma theory and Coptic, Hindu, and other sacred texts.

37. Mitzi Smith acknowledges the same challenges in *I Found God in Me: A Womanist Biblical Hermeneutics Reader* (Eugene, OR: Cascade, 2015), 4 n14.

xxviii   *Introduction*

38. Cheryl Kirk-Duggan is often included as a womanist biblical scholar. Kirk-Duggan earned her Ph.D. from Baylor University in Religion (Theology and Ethics) in 1992.

39. Womanist biblical interpreters from the Global South include South African Madipoane Masenya and South African Indian Sarojini Nadar.

40. This list is based on the author's research of Black women scholars who earned a terminal degree in Hebrew Bible/Old Testament or Near Eastern languages, New Testament, or Early Christian origins in the United States and does not claim to be comprehensive.

41. Frank Yamada, Executive Director of the Association of Theological Schools, who is of Japanese ancestry, shared his doctoral experiences with Forum for Theological Exploration doctoral fellows in Chicago in 2008. Yamada discussed how his dissertation committee dissuaded him from writing from his contextual situatedness as a Japanese American. He was advised that he could pursue such work after he completed his dissertation. See also Smith, *I Found God in Me*, for similar observations.

42. Collins, *Black Feminist Thought*, 203.

43. Collins, 204.

44. See also Smith, *I Found God in Me*. In contrast, for a perspective of Black women religious scholars who felt pressure to identify as "womanist" on the academic job market and by publishers, see Monica Coleman, "Roundtable Discussion: Must I Be a Womanist?" in *Journal of Feminist Studies in Religion* 22, no.1 (2006): 85–134; Junior, *An Introduction to Womanist Biblical Interpretation*.

45. See, for example, Cheryl J. Sanders, "Christian Ethics and Theology in Womanist Perspectives," *Journal of Feminist Studies in Religion* 5, no. 2 (Fall 1989): 83–91.

46. See, for example, Wil Gafney, "A Black Feminist Approach to Biblical Studies," *Encounter* 67, no. 4 (August 2006): 391–403; and Wil Gafney, "Translation Matters: A Fem/Womanist Exploration of Translation Theory and Practice for Proclamation in Worship," https://www.sbl-site.org/assets/pdfs/Gafney.pdf.

47. In a 1985 survey, no Black women seminarians identified as womanist. The same survey conducted in 1990 found two-thirds of respondents so identified. Carpenter, "Theological and Spiritual Empowerment," 153–64.

48. Renita Weems, *Battered Love: Marriage, Sex, and Violence in the Hebrew Prophets* (Minneapolis: Fortress, 1995), xiv.

49. Cheryl Anderson, *Women, Ideology and Violence: Critical Theory and the Construction of Gender in the Book of the Covenant and the Deuteronomic Law* (London: T&T Clark, 2006), 19.

50. Kimberly D. Russaw, *Daughters in the Hebrew Bible* (Lanham, MD: Lexington Books/Fortress Academic, 2018), viii.

51. It should not go without mention the adverse impact on the production of womanist biblical scholarship of tenure denial or inability to acquire tenure-track positions in the first place, and even deaths of Black women biblical scholars.

52. Jones-Warsaw, "Toward a Womanist Hermeneutics," 172–86; Cheryl Kirk-Duggan, "Divine Puppeteer: Yahweh of Exodus," in *A Feminist Companion to Exodus to Deuteronomy*, Second Series, ed. Athalya Brenner (Sheffield: Sheffield Academic, 2000), 75–102.

Introduction xxix

53. Tina Pippin also published an article in this volume on ideological criticism as a feminist/womanist methodological approach, "Biblical Women as Ideological Constructs toward Justice," in *Feminist Interpretation of the Hebrew Bible in Retrospective, vol. III*, ed. Susanne Scholz (Sheffield: Sheffield Phoenix, 2017), 261–77.

54. Renita Weems, "Womanist Reflections on Biblical Hermeneutics," in *Black Theology: A Documentary History Volume Two: 1980–1992*, ed. James H. Cone and Gayraud S. Wilmore (Maryknoll, NY: Orbis, 1993), 219.

55. Clarice J. Martin, "Womanist Biblical Interpretation," in *Dictionary of Biblical Interpretation*, ed. John H. Hayes (Nashville: Abingdon, 1999), 655.

56. Raquel St. Clair, "Womanist Biblical Interpretation," in *True to Our Native Land: An African American New Testament Commentary*, ed. Brian K. Blount and Clarice J. Martin (Minneapolis: Fortress, 2007), 57.

57. St. Clair, 59–60.

58. Nyasha Junior, "Womanist Biblical Interpretation," in *Engaging the Bible in a Gendered World: An Introduction to Feminist Biblical Interpretation in Honor of Katharine Doob Sakenfeld*, ed. Linda Day and Carolyn Pressler (Louisville: Westminster John Knox, 2006), 37–46; Nyasha Junior, "Womanist Interpretation," in *The Oxford Encyclopedia of Biblical Interpretation* (Oxford University Press, 2013), https://www.oxfordreference.com/view/10.1093/acref:obso/9780199832262 .001.0001/acref-9780199832262-e-89.

59. Mitzi Smith resigned as co-editor of the series in 2022.

60. Bible and Culture Collective, "Feminist and Womanist Criticism," in *The Postmodern Bible* (New Haven, CT: Yale University Press, 1995), 244–45.

Abbreviations

AAR	American Academy of Religion
AT	Author's Translation
ATLA	American Theological Library Association
BDB	*Brown-Driver-Briggs Hebrew and English Lexicon*
DH	Deuteronomistic History
DTR	Deuteronomistic historian, Deuteronomist
DtrH	Deuteronomistic history
DtrN	Deuteronomistic nomist
DtrP	Prophetic Deuteronomist
ESV	English Standard Version
HALOT	*Hebrew and Aramaic Lexicon of the Old Testament*
HUSD	Howard University School of Divinity
IVP	InterVarsity Press
JBL	*Journal of Biblical Literature*
JPS	*The New Jewish Publication Society Translation of the Hebrew Bible*
JSOT	*Journal for the Study of the Old Testament*
JSOT sup	*Journal for the Study of the Old Testament: Supplement Series*
KJV	King James Version
LXX	Septuagint
MENA	people of Middle Eastern and North African origins
MT	Masoretic Text
NIV	New International Version
NRSV	New Revised Standard Version
RSV	Revised Standard Version
SBL	Society of Biblical Literature

Chapter 1

"This Woman's Son Shall Not Inherit with My Son"

The Politics of Motherhood in the Sarah-Hagar Narratives

The relationship between the biblical women Sarah and Hagar has captured the attention of Black women for more than a century. The appeal for me grew out of my interest in the work of Black women religious scholars who focused their attention on the biblical figure Hagar because her experience of God resonated with their own experiences as Black women. For example, Delores S. Williams found in Hagar a prototype for African American women's quest for "survival/quality-of-life";[1] Wilma Ann Bailey (1994) asked whether Anabaptist feminists might adopt Hagar as a role model that reflects the lived experience of women from multiple racial, ethnic, and socioeconomic classes; and Diana L. Hayes (1995) proclaimed in her manifesto to Black Christian women:

> We are the daughters of Maria Stewart, of Ida B. Wells Barnett, of Harriet Tubman, of Sojourner Truth, of Mary McLeod Bethune, of Rebecca Jackson, of Zora Neale Hurston, and of Hagar, the rejected and cast-out slave, mother of Ishmael, concubine of Abraham and threat to Sarah, his barren wife.[2]

These scholars are heirs to an older tradition of biblical Hagar's appropriation by Africans enslaved in America, who empathized with the plight of the exploited, abused, and abandoned Egyptian slave woman exiled with her son. She became their spiritual mother and they "Hagar's children." However, the interest extends beyond Black women.

U.S. News and World Report contributor Julia Klein published an article titled, "Why Scholars Just Can't Stop Talking About Sarah and Hagar" (2008). The article addressed such issues as female rivalry, surrogate motherhood,

2   *Chapter 1*

inheritance customs, and the Israeli-Palestinian conflict. Although one might conclude from those cited in the article that it is mostly female scholars who cannot stop talking about the two women, many readers of all genders are fascinated by Sarah and Hagar's story. Examples are the commentary on Sarah and Hagar by Sarah Towne Smith Martyn in *Women of the Bible* (1868), James Arthur MacKnight's novel *Hagar: A Tale of Mormon Life* (1889), and Cothburn O'Neal's fictional retelling of Sarah and Hagar's story in *Hagar* (1958).[3]

That interest is due in part, as biblical scholar Naomi Steinberg, who was interviewed by Klein suggested, to the issues of belonging raised in the stories: "What does it mean to be a member of society—who's in and who's out?"[4] I agree with Klein and Steinberg that the story of Sarah and Hagar located in the so-called Abraham cycle or saga consisting of Genesis 12–25 contains narratives about belonging, identity construction, and boundary maintenance.[5] However, more importantly, I contend that the stories of Sarah and Hagar are about the *politics of belonging*.

In this chapter I enter the ongoing conversations about Sarah and Hagar to explore the politics of belonging, the political projects engaged to construct the boundaries that include and exclude members of the nation of Israel, and the intersection of gender and sexuality in the process. While on one level the Sarah-Hagar narratives are about who belongs as a member of biblical Israel, on another level, it is about the political processes that determine who is a member and who has the power to decide. I contend that it is Sarah, despite her limitations as a woman in a patriarchal society, who uses the political project of motherhood to enforce the boundaries delineating insiders and outsiders. Thus, in the politics of belonging, the contested terrain of motherhood in Genesis 12–25 demonstrates that narratives of national identity construction are often written on the bodies of women as their symbolic boundaries of difference.

THE POLITICS OF BELONGING

Without debating whether or not ancient Israel should be understood as a nation in the modern sense of the term, I am reading Genesis 12–25 as national narratives helping to give shape to biblical Israel as a nation through Benedict Anderson's concept of "nation" as an "imagined community."[6] According to Benedict Anderson, nations are "imagined" because "the members of even the smallest nation will never know most of their fellow-members, meet them, or even hear of them, yet in the minds of each lives the image of their communion."[7] Therefore, they live into a common future with a shared identity divided into "us" and "them."

When talking about the politics of belonging, it is important to make the distinction implied above between "belonging" and the "politics of belonging." Nira Yuval-Davis describes the former as an emotional attachment, such as the warm sentiments one gets about feeling "at home." The latter comprises the political projects that construct belonging to a specific polity, which she explains are themselves "being constructed in these projects (i.e., whether or not, according to specific politics of belonging, Jews can be considered to be German, or abortion advocates can be considered Catholic)."[8] Yuval-Davis adds that the politics of belonging is always situated and multilayered, which, according to her, "serves to contextualize them both locally and globally, and affect different members of these collectivities and communities differently."[9] John Crowley describes the politics of belonging as "the dirty work of boundary maintenance"[10] because it involves the drawing and redrawing of boundaries—physical and symbolic that separate people into "us" and "them." As such, the politics of belonging refers to the mechanisms or political processes that socially construct people into groups of insiders and outsiders, the meting out of benefits to those who belong and withholding the same from those who do not, and who has the power to decide.

As Yuval-Davis explains, "Belonging is where the sociology of emotions interfaces with the sociology of power, where identification and participation collude."[11] But she adds that within hegemonic constructions, belonging becomes "naturalized" and "invisible" so long as the individual feels safe; it is only when that stability is threatened that "narratives of belonging become politicized" and emotions of fear and hate are evoked "to build higher walls around the boundaries and borders of the national collectivity and to mobilize the people toward exclusionary politics."[12] Significantly, the boundaries of the politics of belonging that separate people into us and them are always symbolic and often contested.

Such emotional attachments to belonging and their relationship to boundary construction and the politics of belonging are what Sara Ahmed refers to as the "cultural politics of emotion."[13] According to Ahmed, emotions such as fear and hatred can move individuals to create borders. Emotions explain how individuals are affected by others or moved by others. Emotions can also move individuals to defend the established borders once they feel that they have been transgressed.

The politics of belonging consist of multiple political projects of belonging, each with its own requirements for inclusion as a member of the polity. Yuval-Davis's favorite example of a political project of belonging is the infamous British "Cricket Test." The boundaries of belonging were established along the lines of sports team loyalty: "if people watched a cricket match between Britain and a team from the country from which they or their family had originated and cheered for that latter team, this meant that

4   *Chapter 1*

those people did not really 'belong' to the British collectivity, even if they had formal British citizenship, and had been born and reared in it."[14] Other examples of organizing principles of belonging identified by Yuval-Davis are shared biological origins (or at least the myth of common descent), a common culture, religion and/or language, and loyalty and solidarity based on common values.[15]

Yet, Floya Anthias, Yuval-Davis, and other feminist theorists of nation and nationalism point out that although nationalist projects are nearly exclusively thought to be the interests of men and reflect male aspirations, women are not only affected by nationalist projects and processes, but also affect them. Anthias and Yuval-Davis identified at least five ways women affect and are affected by nationalism: as biological reproducers of members of the nation; as central participants in the ideological reproduction of the boundaries of the group; as transmitters of the nation's culture; as symbolic signifiers of national difference; and as participants in national, economic, political, and military struggles.[16] Thus, they emphasize not only that gender and sexuality play crucial roles in nationalist projects but also acknowledge that there are differences in the way women from separate social categories and racial/ethnic groups are constructed by nationalist projects.

READING SARAH AND HAGAR—AGAIN

The biblical story of Abraham is the story a man whom God chose to become the progenitor of the people of Israel.[17] According to the story, the deity YHWH called a man named Abram from Ur of Chaldea in Mesopotamia to leave his homeland, his inheritance, and his father's household for the land of Canaan with the promise to make of him a great nation (Gen. 12). Abram obeys YHWH's command and leaves for Canaan, where he settles with his wife, Sarai. The narrator shares with the reader that she is barren (Gen. 11:30). Of course, this statement builds suspense regarding the fulfillment of the promise.

YHWH later makes a covenant with Abram consisting of a threefold promise: that he would be the father of a multitude of nations; he would have abundant offspring; and he would possess all the land of Canaan (Gen. 17:2–8, 15–16). YHWH also proceeds to change their names from Abram to Abraham, the "father of a multitude of nations" and Sarai to Sarah, who would be "the mother of kings," as a sign to future generations that they would continue to flourish. YHWH's words harken back to the earlier statement that Sarai is barren. Specifically, YHWH declares that Sarah would give birth to a son, who would be Abraham's heir of the covenant, and whose descendants would become the nation of Israel (vv. 17–19) despite her present condition.

Israel's history is told mostly in narratives about the nation's origins and identity shared by the groups that were its intended audience. In the context of the exile, these narratives of the past gave comfort and hope for the future to the deportees since despite their current condition, YHWH would restore their land, their fecundity, and their perpetuity because YHWH promised it to Abraham their ancestor. Given that national narratives "always implicitly or explicitly refer to the future of the nation, national narratives are often more than historical accounts of the collective past."[18] Up to now in our story, that future was still undetermined: Would Abraham have a male heir? Who belongs as a member of Abraham's family? And who decides?

A selective survey of commentaries on Genesis 12–25 reflects historical-critical readings of the text by mostly male biblical scholars that are concerned with the world behind the text and focus primarily on the theme of the fulfillment of the promise that YHWH made to the patriarch Abraham.[19] These readings were concerned with Sarah and Hagar either to the extent that Sarah's barrenness and Hagar's birth of Ishmael represented a delay of or threat to the promise,[20] how their stories represent a conflict narrative, specifically a "conflict between women,"[21] "the struggle between the two women,"[22] or Abraham and Sarah's lack of faith in God by turning to Hagar.[23] There is the work, however, of feminist biblical scholars who were less interested in the patriarch Abraham and the promise-fulfillment motif than in the recovery of the presence of women in the narrative and the reconstruction of their world. For example, Naomi Steinberg (1993) explores certain social customs operating behind the text to explain why Sarah's son prevailed over Hagar's son as Abraham's lineal descendant. She writes that, "Through kinship studies the legal situation becomes clear: the son borne by the primary wife is automatically entitled as his father's heir."[24]

Phyllis Trible's groundbreaking book *Texts of Terror* is a feminist literary-rhetorical critical reading of the Sarah-Hagar narratives. Trible's examination of gender, ethnicity, and class in her analysis paved the way for others to follow. Trible's investigation demonstrates how the plot moves in the two narrative cycles in Genesis 16 and 20 to reveal how the ethnic and class disparities between the two women result in Hagar's bondage, expulsion, and homelessness. Trible concludes that, "Her story depicts oppression in three familiar forms: nationality, class and sex."[25]

Following Trible are such works as Sharon Pace Jeansonne's (1990) treatment of Sarai/Sarah and Hagar that attends to the power dynamic issues of wealth, status, and foreignness between the two women and Katharine Doob Sakenfeld's reading, that also recognizes the ethnic and economic divide between Sarah and Hagar. Sakenfeld explains, "The two women were divided from one another both by ethnicity (one a Hebrew, the other an Egyptian), and by economic class (Sarah as the one with relative economic power, Hagar

6   *Chapter 1*

dependent upon her as slave who had to our knowledge no personal economic resources)."[26]

Although feminist and other women biblical scholars were continuing to exegete the texts using historical critical methods, as well as newer methodological approaches, such as queer theory, postcolonial theory, and social-science criticism, some were just beginning to name their social location as part of their analysis. Many Black women religious scholars entering the field in the late 1980s were direct in acknowledging that they were reading the biblical texts from theirs and the experiences of other Black women. Some of these scholars preferred to self-identify as "womanist" instead of "feminist."

Delores Williams's reading of Hagar was the first womanist interpretation of this narrative cycle. Using a constructive theological approach, Williams read Hagar's story through the lens of African American women's historic experiences of slavery and surrogacy—involuntary and voluntary during the antebellum and postbellum periods. Williams named this female-centered tradition of African American biblical appropriation "survival/quality-of-life tradition of African-American biblical appropriation"[27] because God was neither concerned with nor involved with Hagar's liberation, but rather God provides her with the resources to survive and have a quality of life.

The same year that Williams's book was published womanist biblical scholar Renita Weems published *Just a Sister Away: A Womanist Vision of Women's Relationships in the Bible*, which included a chapter on Sarah and Hagar. Weems combined social-historical criticism and literary criticism with African American oral tradition to interpret their stories from the perspective of African American women's experiences. She describes Sarah and Hagar's encounters as reflecting "ethnic prejudice exacerbated by economic and sexual exploitation."[28]

More recently Wil Gafney has analyzed the texts on Sarah and Hagar using an approach she refers to as *womanist midrash*, a combination of rabbinic midrash, literary and contextual approaches, and Black women's feminism to reimagine the stories of often overlooked and unnamed female characters in the Hebrew Bible. Although Gafney acknowledges that Sarah and Hagar share gender peril despite being separated by economic status, social privilege, and national origins, her sympathies are also with Hagar. She reads Hagar's story "through the prism of the wholesale enslavement of black peoples in the Americas and elsewhere."[29]

Not all Black women biblical scholars who focus on Hagar in their scholarship identify their approach as either Black feminist or womanist. For example, Nyasha Junior's *Reimagining Hagar: Blackness and Bible* (2019) is a reception history approach that explores the link between the biblical Hagar as an enslaved Egyptian and the Black Hagar tradition of African American women religious scholars. She focuses on the development over time of Aunt Hagar traditions that are the production of Black communities independent of biblical Hagar rather than reading Hagar from Junior's own social location as an African American woman.

In this chapter I read the stories of Sarah and Hagar through a womanist hermeneutic, although a little differently. Unlike Williams and others, I do not read Sarah and Hagar's relationship through modern American racial categories that regard the differences between Hagar and Sarah as the tensions between enslaved African women and their White mistresses. Instead, I contend that the differences between Hagar and Sarah are ethnicity and class or legal status. The ancient world would have viewed the Egyptian Hagar and the Mesopotamian Sarah as belonging to different ethnic groups, not different racial categories.[30] Where ethnicity refers to the common cultural traits (language, geographic locale or place of origin, religion, food habits, etc.) that distinguish one group of people from another (but are transmissible and subject to change), race is a modern (nineteenth century) cultural invention about human differences that assigns special worth and status to some groups and lower status to others based on skin color and phenotype. Class refers to a group of people categorized by shared economic condition.[31]

Renita Weems concedes as much by recognizing the ethnic differences between the two women but still adds, "The story of the Egyptian slave and her Hebrew mistress is hauntingly reminiscent of the disturbing accounts of black slave women and white mistresses during slavery."[32] This does not negate the reality that "[Hagar speaks to] generation after generation of black women because her story is their story of suffering at the hands of white women."[33] Amanda Mbuvi adds that although the biblical story cannot be equated with American racial politics, it "provides a much-needed occasion to reflect upon the manifold injustices of slavery and the complex legacy it has produced. Moreover, one cannot see beyond black slaves and white mistresses without seeing them first."[34]

In fairness to Williams, nineteenth and early twentieth century US White and Black women writers such as Harriet Beecher Stowe, Susan Warner, and Eloise Bibb wrote from their social and racial locations of antebellum and postbellum domestic relations to racialize biblical Sarah and Hagar as White and Black, respectively; Sarah as the White mistress and Hagar as the Black slave and domestic.[35] In the twenty-first century some White feminist scholars reading from their own social location also identify Sarah as White or at least see themselves as White women in the position of Sarah. For example, Elizabeth Durant explains that as a White, middle-class lesbian she immediately responds by "identifying myself with Sarai."[36] Jayme Reaves has written how she is challenged by womanist religious scholars such as Delores Williams to, "recognize that, because of my position as a white woman, I

8 *Chapter 1*

have wittingly or unwittingly been in the role of Sarah more often than I have been in the role of Hagar."[37]

While acknowledging that modern racial categories would have been alien to Hebrew Bible authors, ancient peoples were aware of differences in skin color. Thus, in contemporary US society, Sarah would be regarded just like Hagar as a "woman of color" having originated from Ur of Chaldea in Mesopotamia, so I call Sarah "sister" as well.[38] Another difference that I bring is the social scientific approach of theory of nation and gender. In addition to examining the Sarah-Hagar narratives through the politics of belonging, I explore issues of fertility, surrogacy, and reproduction in the ancient world and contemporary US population policies as they relate to Black women. Despite our diverse approaches, I along with Weems and Williams arrive at the conclusion that despite being a woman in a patriarchal society, Sarah still uses her privilege and status to subjugate and exploit Hagar. Therefore, I build on the womanist tradition of reading Sarah and Hagar through the simultaneously overlapping experiences of oppression and discrimination based on race/ethnicity, class, and sexual identities.

COMPETING POLITICAL PROJECTS OF BELONGING

An analysis of the Sarah-Hagar narratives in Genesis returns us to the point mentioned above that YHWH promised to bless Abram with descendants too numerous to count, but we know that his wife Sarai is barren. When Abram complained that he had no offspring and concluded that the heir of his house would be his steward Eliezer, YHWH rejected this plan and promised Abram that he would have a child who would come from his own body (Gen. 15:24). One chapter later Abram indeed gets a biological heir when Sarai's Egyptian handmaid bears him a son after they had been in the land of Canaan ten years (Gen. 16:3).

The attention in many commentaries on Genesis 16 is on the promise and its fulfillment. Thus, the focus is on the birth of Ishmael, leaving the reader with the impression that being born Abram's son to the slave woman Hagar was sufficient criterion for Ishmael to be accepted as a member of Abram's family and the heir YHWH promised to Abram. This would suggest that the biological or genealogical dimension was the organizing principle of belonging in this passage. However, a closer look suggests a different emphasis. Given the importance of women's reproduction in national and ethnic discourses as the biological producers of members of the nation, the child's mother is usually of significance, as in being born to the "right" mother.[39] However, God's promise to Abram that he would have a son of his own issue in Genesis 15 leaves the mother's identity open ended. In fact, the birth of Ishmael at the end of chapter 16 is treated matter-of-factly suggesting that the mother's status and ethnicity were of no concern to the Yahwist writer believed to have been active during the preexilic period.

Along with biology being used to construct national or ethnic boundaries, the more elastic autochthonous or indigenous dimension of the politics of belonging is introduced. Yuval-Davis explains that a common feature of autochthonous exclusionary politics is to establish one's right to belong territorially based on where one's ancestors are buried.[40] The Yahwist source, which among other criteria is interested in legitimizing Abraham and his descendants as the true possessors of the land of Canaan as promised by YHWH (e.g., Gen. 12:7; 13:15; 26:3, 28:4) is supported in Genesis 16 by the mention of the length of Abram's stay in Canaan, establishing his residency in the land (Gen. 16:3) and Ishmael as indigenous to the land.

Konrad Schmid observes that the older Genesis material does not regard the ancestors as foreigners in Canaan but rather, "through them, Israel was settled in the land."[41] According to Schmid, the canonical form of Genesis regards Israel as "just as indigenous to its land as its neighbors."[42] From the perspective of the exile, the ancestral tradition of Abraham as indigenous to the land could belong to elite Judahites who remained in the land. Laying claim to descent from Abraham gave them the right to remain in the land.[43]

Yvonne Sherwood points out the awkwardness of a group identity that lays claim to the land through an autochthonous political project given that,

> The Abrahamic family is emphatically not *autochthonous* (emphasis original), or aborigine or indigenous. Their claim on the land is not validated by nature or by human agreement. Abraham comes from Babylon/Iraq and is called to Canaan by God . . . The relation to the land is never naturalized. It depends on human agreement as well as divine promise.[44]

Thus, Sherwood notes that Abraham negotiated for land to bury Sarah in upon her death (Genesis 23) because he is not native to the land.[45] Nonetheless, the Chronicler's construction of Israel's identity is one with autochthonous origins. In its lists of genealogies that trace their descent from Adam to the postexilic community, Israel naturally belongs to the land. "In other words, the Israelites emerge 'from the soil,' as it were, with the land thus belonging to them because of their status as its first inhabitants."[46] As such, it rejects the conquest narrative of the Israelites' entry in the land.

Despite claims to the land through Abraham, it soon becomes evident that neither the autochthonic politics of belonging nor the political project of biological descent secures Ishmael's status as an insider born in Canaan, despite being the firstborn of Abraham's loins and apparent patrilineal heir to the

10   Chapter 1

promise. Instead, one chapter later a different political project of belonging prevails, leading to his eventual expulsion from Abraham's household.

Scholars attribute Genesis 17 to the Priestly school, a group of religious leaders in postexilic Judah/Yehud. God (Elohim) makes a covenant with Abraham in Genesis 17 declaring that there would be a sign of the covenant. This is a new wrinkle in the promise. The sign was the circumcision of the flesh of the foreskin of every male, including Abram, now Abraham, in his household and every generation thereafter on the eighth day of birth (Gen. 17:10). Circumcision indicated participation in the covenant and any of Abraham's male descendants who did not undergo this symbolic act should be "cut off" from the people of Israel (Gen. 17:14).[47] The fact that the cutting was to be applied to the male genitalia was a reminder to the male recipients that both they and any future progeny could be excised from the covenant community. Thus, Ilona Rashkow writes that the penis "serves as a physical reminder both of inclusion *in* the community and exclusion *from* it (italics original). Circumcision, taken over from other cultures and reinterpreted, defines males and males only as the full members of the covenant community."[48]

The Priestly redaction of the Abrahamic covenant in Genesis 17 reconceptualizes Israel primarily in terms of the Abrahamic covenant of circumcision.[49] This results in a shift from a political project of autochthony to a political project that is theologically determinative of the rite of male circumcision. Yuval-Davis describes this political process as a political project of belonging based on the construction of culture and tradition as a religious identity. Thus, a secular rite such as circumcision can become differentiated and delineated from the secular realm by designating it as sanctified by the deity.[50] While some scholars argue that male infant genital circumcision is a uniquely Israelite rite, others demonstrate that circumcision was widely practiced among other ancient societies.[51] For example, material remains show that some ancient Egyptian males underwent circumcision as part of initiation rites at puberty, although it seems that this was limited to higher class or Priestly classes.[52] Jack Sasson maintains that male circumcision was "reserved for either a period of prenuptial ceremonies or, more likely, for initiation into the state of manhood."[53] The rite did not appear to have religious significance in ancient Egypt, thus demonstrating its malleability.

The announcement a few verses later by God that Isaac, the son yet unborn to his wife, Sarah and not Ishmael will be Abraham's patrilineal heir (Gen. 17:19) does not immediately result in Ishmael's displacement. As Amanda Mbuvi observes, "Having revealed that Ishmael is not 'the one,' [the narrative] does not immediately lose interest in him and focus on Isaac. Instead, [the narrative] recounts Ishmael's circumcision before embarking on the story of Isaac's birth. Ishmael stands alongside Abraham as his son

(17:23–26)."[54] Abraham only reluctantly accepts the deity's plan to replace Ishmael with Isaac pleading with God, "O that Ishmael might live in your sight!" (Gen. 17:18). There is no mention of the place of Abraham's secondary wife Hagar in this covenantal community.

The competing political projects of belonging presented in Genesis 16 and 17 establish boundaries, but the degrees to which people are included or excluded as members of what became known as the nation of Israel varies from less to more exclusionary. Each son lays claim to belonging through their relationship to Abraham. The political project with the autochthonous dimension is more flexible requiring only having been born a descendant of Abraham in the land of Canaan. The political project with the cultural dimension is more exclusionary requiring the circumcision of male descendants of Abraham and Sarah for membership. The fact that two seemingly contradictory narratives survive simultaneously in the same canon might seem confusing. However, drawing on the work of Homi Bhabha, Yuval-Davis observes that on the one hand, national narratives "seek to construct national boundaries of the 'us' against the outside 'them' and on the other hand, they include discourses which provide space for cultural and other forms of difference within the nation."[55]

POLITICAL PROJECTS OF MOTHERHOOD

If circumcision represents fruitfulness and fullness, then barrenness represents infertility and emptiness. In the ancient world, fertility was understood in agricultural terms. A female's womb was akin to a field and the male fertilized it with his "seed." Thus, if a woman was unable to conceive, the belief was that her field was unproductive. Wil Gafney observed that "nowhere in the Bible is a man accused of having 'bad' seed" despite the knowledge in the ancient world that other factors besides poor ground conditions caused crop failure.[56] However, since infertility is gendered, Marianne Kartzow writes that even contemporarily, "Women tend worldwide to bear the major burden of infertility; they are blamed for the reproductive failing, they experience personal anxiety, frustration, grief, fear and social stigma."[57]

In the world of the Hebrew Bible, if infertility is gendered feminine, fertility is gendered male. For example, in speaking of the Priestly school's preoccupation with procreation and genealogy, Howard Eilberg-Schwartz explains, "Impressing a symbol of fertility on the male organ of reproduction establishes a connection between procreation and masculinity and creates a community of men who are linked to one another through a similar mark on their male members."[58] Sandra Jacobs continues the horticultural imagery by describing the view of infant circumcision in antiquity as analogous to immature fruit trees being trimmed and readied to produce fruit.[59]

Sarah's barrenness may bring her shame, but there are other ways to achieve motherhood. After determining that YHWH is the source of her infertility, she uses the legal means at her disposal to take matters into her own hands. She gives her slave woman to her husband as a secondary wife to bear her a child (Gen. 16:2). The Hebrew verbal root *banah* ("to build") most often interpreted in English as "to obtain children" (KJV and NRSV) or "have a son" is used figuratively to mean to "perpetuate and establish a family" (BDB s.v.). Thus, Sarah resorts to surrogacy to be "built up." Sarah does not act out of benevolence towards Abram. The Hebrew is clear that she gives Hagar to Abram so that *she* may "be built up." Sarah would increase in honor or esteem in the eyes of other women through motherhood. In a patriarchal world where a woman's barrenness was considered a "misfortune of overwhelming proportions,"[60] many women would welcome the opportunity to achieve motherhood even if their social status and wealth held this possibility beyond their reach. Sarah's social status as a wealthy freewoman not only accorded her the privilege of owning a slave girl but also the power to use her body for Sarah's benefit. And Sarah had the law in her favor.

Ancient family legal codes granted Sarah the prerogative as a barren wife to use her slave as a surrogate to attain motherhood.[61] But the state of motherhood is not a single category. Explains Marianne Kartzow, "Motherhood, traditionally connected to pregnancy, birth giving, and breast feeding, is renegotiated and divided into three stages or qualities"[62] in the discourse on surrogacy: the genetic mother whose eggs were fertilized to produce the child; the gestational or biological mother who carries and delivers the baby; the juridical or social mother who legally has the right to raise the child as her own.[63] The dynamics of surrogacy in Genesis 16 and 21 demonstrate that the categories of motherhood are not fixed but are subject to change.

Up to this point, Hagar does not speak, so we can infer that this is done without her consent. Even if she had consented, the unequal power dynamics between Hagar and Sarah and Abraham subjected Hagar to their will. She is a foreigner, an outsider, and a slave. Even her name Hagar (*ha-gar*), which sounds similar to the Hebrew word for "foreigner" (*ger*) with the Hebrew definite article *ha*, appears more like an epithet than a personal name.[64] The one with the "bio-genetic reproductive capital" is pressed into service to bear a child for the couple who "lack such capital but had juridical and economical reproductive capital."[65]

The power dynamics being what they were, Hagar had no control over her reproductive capital. As Sarah's female slave, Hagar's sexuality and reproductive capacity were her mistress's possessions to "exploit or dispose of . . . like any other beneficial aspect of property."[66] Thus, if Hagar were harmed or

"This Woman's Son Shall Not Inherit with My Son"

sexually violated by someone other than Sarah, it was a violation of Sarah's property rights, not Hagar's, and compensation would be due Sarah. While most surrogacy arrangements today require consent, the use of female slaves as biogenetic mothers for barren mistresses was an acceptable practice in the Hebrew Bible (Gen. 30:3, 9–12). According to Tikva Frymer-Kensky, "Using another person's body as a surrogate for one's own is part of the fabric of slavery" in ancient societies.[67] Ancient family and property legal codes aside, what Hagar experienced is a form of rape.

Too many of us are familiar with stories of relatives who were domestic workers who were raped or sexually harassed by male employers or their sons with the tacit or explicit approval of the wife or mother on one hand, or denial on the other hand. In a collection of oral-history narratives of Black female domestic workers and their White employers in the first half century of the U.S segregated South, Susan Tucker wrote about the experiences of Black women domestics serving in White homes. She observed that while Black women domestics were vulnerable to sexual advances, such risks largely went unnoticed by White women. Tucker observed, "What I came to see was that white women, indeed, usually denied ever hearing of sexual exploitation of black domestics."[68]

Likewise, an early twentieth century quasi-autobiography by a Black nursemaid recalls that not only were some White women aware that their husbands were having sexual relations with Black women domestics in their employ but knew of "more than one colored woman who was openly importuned by white women to become the mistresses of their white husbands, on the ground that they, the white wives, were afraid that, if their husbands did not associate with colored women, they would certainly do so with outside white women."[69] White women employers under such circumstances might not have intended to "build up" a family but children certainly resulted from unions between White male employers and Black female employees. Whether or not the White wives approved of such arrangements, visibly pregnant Black female servants under the circumstances surely engendered tension in the home.

In speaking of Sarah and Hagar, Katharine Sakenfeld acknowledges the possibility noting, "The difference in power between the two women that begins with the mistress-slave relationship continues as Hagar becomes the secondary wife,"[70] albeit it in unexpected ways. When Hagar realizes that she has conceived, Sarah becomes slight (*qalal*) in Hagar's eyes (Gen. 16:4). Sarai recognizes her new status in Hagar's eyes (Gen. 16:5), bringing to awareness that "female slaves' reproductive capital could destabilize the fixed hierarchy between slave and free," if only momentarily.[71]

Despite the unintended consequences, by building a family Sarah succeeds where YHWH and Abram have thus far been slow to do—perpetuate

14 *Chapter 1*

and establish a family for Abram. In this regard, she is following the legal custom in Deuteronomy 25:5–6, which declares that if one of two brothers living under the same household should die, the wife of the deceased becomes the wife of her brother-in-law in order to bear a son to perpetuate her dead husband's name. If he refuses, she may appeal to the elders, charging her brother-in-law with refusing to "build up his brother's house" (Deut. 25:9). The Hebrew verb *banah*, "to build" used in Genesis 16:2 is the same in Deuteronomy 25:9. In the words of Joseph Blenkinsopp, "What was fundamentally important was paternity and inheritance, the extension of the man's 'house' into the future."[72] Thus, although she is not a widow, Sarah takes it upon herself to be built up by building her husband's house.[73]

The law may have been intended to protect the economic interests of the husband, but Sarah knows enough to understand that in the event Abram died and left her without a male heir she could call her own, she would be in a precarious economic situation with no one to care for her. Therefore, although Hagar was the genetic and biological mother to Ishmael (Gen. 16:15), it was in Sarah's personal interests that she be Ishmael's socio-legal mother. By providing Abram with a legal heir and legatee, Sarah both retains her status and secures her economic future through motherhood. However, her actions up to this point do nothing to jeopardize Ishmael's status as a member of Abram's family. Things take a turn in Genesis 21.

Commentators often refer to Genesis 21 as the account of Isaac's birth and the fulfillment of YHWH's promise of descendants to Abraham through the birth of a son of his seed—never mind that he already had a son of his loins. However, picking up where Gen. 17:16–19 left off, this narrative is just as much about Isaac's birth to Sarah. As mentioned above, Abraham was content to have Ishmael as his only son and lineal heir. However, God told him that Sarah would conceive and give birth to a son who would be his heir. According to Steinberg above, the reason that Sarah must give birth to a son is because only Abraham's son by his primary wife could be his patrilineal heir. As such, Ishmael's status as the son of a secondary wife, despite his primogeniture and circumcision—a sign marking him as a covenantal member—prevented him from being Abraham's lineal heir. Yet, in a more recent work Steinberg contends that Ishmael would have maintained his status as the patrilineal heir despite his mother's status if Isaac had not been born.[74] Sarah's shift from a socio-legal mother to a genetic/biological mother is of importance.

The narrator reports that YHWH remembered Sarah and fulfilled the earlier promise to give her a son. Abraham named him Isaac as God had instructed him in chapter 17. Sarah's exuberance is evident as she proclaims, "'God has brought laughter for me; everyone who hears will laugh with me.' And she said, 'Who would ever have said to Abraham that Sarah would nurse children" (Gen. 21:6–7 NRSV).[75] Until now, motherhood has been spoken of in terms of conception and birth. However, this verse introduces the element of breastfeeding for the first time in reference to either Sarah or Hagar. While acknowledging the genetic, biological, and judicial/social categories of motherhood, another type of motherhood is breastfeeding. Thus, a woman may not belong to either of the other three categories, but nursing an infant is another maternal function.[76]

Cynthia Chapman's analysis of maternal kinship in the Hebrew Bible demonstrates that in the ancient world breastmilk was understood as more than just a source of nutrition. She finds that "the act of breastfeeding was first and foremost an act understood to inculcate in the child culturally defined personal boundaries and to transmit maternal traits from mother or wet nurse to child."[77] Likewise, Sharon Jacob and Jennifer Kaalund's work on wet nurses in the contexts of African American slavery and the British colonization of India illustrates the often inconsistent, contradictory views of the milk flowing from the breasts of Black and brown women to nourish the master's children. While appropriating the surplus milk of the wet nurses for their own children, the masters nonetheless feared that the milk produced by these women might contaminate the suckling's character.[78]

This raises the question why the narrator not only reports that ninety-year-old Sarah nursed Isaac but also "stretches credulity" by insisting that she nursed him until he was weaned, usually around the age of three.[79] It was not only common but expected that a woman of Sarah's social and economic status (and age?) would hire a wet nurse to breastfeed her newborn (e.g., Exod. 2:9), especially given Hagar's presence in the household. In fact, the reader has probably taken for granted that Hagar nursed Ishmael for Sarah back in Genesis 16. Why wouldn't she be expected to do the same in Genesis 21? What difference did it make who nursed the two boys? For the two competing narratives on identity and origin, it mattered.

Amanda Mbuvi offers the first clue when she notes that, "The ambiguity as to whether or not Hagar nursed Isaac parallels the ambiguity as to whether or not Sarah went through with her plan to claim Ismael as her own son. These arrangements create a certain fluidity in the relationships between the mothers and the sons . . . Both women potentially stand in a mothering role toward both children."[80] Thus, there should not have been an issue with the four living together in the same household. However, things are not that simple.

As has already been established, motherhood was not new to Sarah. Legally, she was the socio-juridical mother of Ishmael and motherhood elevated her status in the eyes of the community if not in the eyes of her slave girl. But God decreed that Sarah would give birth to Isaac and he would be Abraham's heir to the promise (Gen. 17:19). Therefore, giving birth to Isaac in fulfillment of this promise should have ended this episode. Instead, we

16 *Chapter 1*

have the notice that Sarah nursed Isaac instead of Hagar. Thus, there must be a more significant reason, which Cynthia Chapman helps explain. According to Chapman, it was believed in the ancient world that a woman transferred her ethnicity or status (royal or priestly) to her suckling through her breast milk.[81] More specifically, breast milk confers ethnic insider status on a child, as evidenced in the foundational birth narratives of male heroes in the Hebrew Bible (see, for example, Exod. 2:7). The ambiguity raised by Mbuvi surrounding who nursed Isaac is not by accident.

Commentators such as Gerhard von Rad maintain that Genesis 21:1–7 reflects the handiwork of the Priestly source, especially in verses 2a–5, where it refers back to Genesis 17.[82] Verses 1–8, on the other hand, are regarded as belonging to an independent source. Chapman agrees, noting however the significance of the addition of verse 7, which has not been carried over from Genesis 17. According to Chapman, the division between verses 7 and 8 is important because "when Genesis 21:1–5 was brought together with Gen 21:8–21, a redactor noted and sought to clarify the ambiguity concerning who had nursed Isaac."[83] Given that the verb for "to wean" in verse 8 is passive, one might be left with the impression that Hagar was a wet nurse to Isaac. As such, the redactor disabuses the reader of any such notion by inserting verse 7. This still does not explain why it mattered which woman nursed Isaac.

Chapman proffers that it mattered whether Sarah nursed Isaac because it was important that she be recognized as having bestowed Isaac with the appropriate insider ethnic and royal status. Chapman goes to lengths to establish Sarah's credentials as belonging to "Terahite stock," the same patrilineage of Abraham (Gen. 11:29; 12:5; cf. 20:12; 12:19) and royal status (Gen. 17:15–16).[84] Neither of these points is disputed. However, they are not what is important. Chapman is right that the redactor is concerned about which woman's breastmilk nourishes Isaac, but the reason is simpler than Sarah's ethnic or royal status. If, as it has been argued, that breastmilk does more than nourish the suckling but also transfers the nursing woman's cultural traits and defines ethnic boundaries, then the older tradition with Hagar nursing both Isaac and Ishmael is problematic. Not only would Hagar's breastmilk imbue both boys with the cultural traits of the Egyptian slave woman but also forge them in kinship bonds that could result in lifelong ties.[85] Sarah's elevation in status as a genetic-biological and socio-judicial mother would all be for naught. Thus, the redactor removes the ambiguity and relieves the reader of any doubt that Sarah, who enjoys insider status, has passed her traits to Isaac.

The narrator reports that Isaac grew and was weaned, which occasioned Abraham to hold a great feast (Gen. 21:8). The narrator reports that Sarah observed Ishmael "Isaacing" (*metsacheq*) and her emotions turned from the joy of motherhood to disgust and hatred. The English translations for *metsacheq* are usually "playing with" (NRSV) or "mocking" (KJV and NIV). The word is from the same Hebrew root *tsachaq* for "to laugh," as in Sarah's laughter in Genesis 21:6 and Isaac's name ("he laughs"). However, I translate *metsacheq* as "Isaacing" because in my opinion, Sarah saw Ishmael behaving in some way that mirrored Isaac. Although the text is silent regarding what Sarah saw, Tammi Schneider notes that "the feast and what it symbolizes cause Sarah to consider the relationship between Ishmael and Isaac in a new light because of Isaac's new situation."[86]

The shift between the celebration and Sarah's mood change is abrupt. Sarah becomes enraged and orders Abraham to get rid of Hagar and Ishmael, proclaiming, "Cast out this slave woman and her son; for the son of this slave woman shall not inherit with my son Isaac" (Gen. 21:10 NRSV), suggesting an economic motive for the outburst. Gender, ethnicity, class, and the cultural politics of emotions intersect here to "other" Hagar and Ishmael and transform them from outsiders within to outsiders without. Hagar, who is not mentioned in the first eight verses is twice referred to by Sarah as an *'amah*, a Hebrew term for "female slave," emphasizing her lower social status.[87] Likewise, she is twice referred to as "slave woman" by the deity, reinforcing her lowly position. Only the narrator refers to her by name. Ishmael, on the other hand, is never mentioned by name but rather as the "son of Hagar the Egyptian" (Gen. 21:9), "son of this slave woman (v. 10), "son of the slave woman" (v. 13), Abraham's son (v. 11), "the boy" (v. 12), or "the child" (v. 14). The deity refers to him as *na'ar* ("boy" or "lad"), a non-familial Hebrew term that further distances Ishmael from being an insider of Abraham's household.

Sarah's emotional outburst precipitates the expulsion of Hagar and Ishmael from Abraham's household and establishes them as outsiders. She attributes the source of her angst to Ishmael's proximity to Isaac. As Yvonne Sherwood observes, a surrogate is someone who stands in the place of another and as long as Hagar and Ishmael remain close by, they threaten Sarah's security through Isaac.[88] So concerned is Sarah that she is willing to use force to remove Ishmael and Hagar from her presence. The verb *garash* translated as "to cast" in verse 10 is used only three times in the Hebrew Bible (Gen. 21:10; Exod. 11:1; Prov. 22:10). In each context it means to forcibly remove or drive out.

What is it about Isaac's weaning that instigates Sarah's reaction? Amanda Mbuvi proffers, "The weaning of Isaac may provide the opportune time for the expulsion of Hagar and Ishmael because Hagar was the one doing the nursing"[89] as several scholars believe that Genesis 21:8 is independent of 21:7. Whether Sarah nursed Isaac is ambiguous. The significance of Isaac's weaning, therefore according to Naomi Steinberg, is that it signaled that he had reached the stage to be regarded as a member of Abraham's family.[90] Thus, Sarah had to wait until Hagar's services to Isaac were no longer needed before she could expel Hagar and Ishmael from Abraham's household.[91]

In the political project of motherhood, the redactor responsible for the final form of Genesis 21 has demonstrated that neither biology, birth order, place of origin, nor theologically determinative male genital circumcision combined make one an insider in Israel. The requisite for belonging is a biological and socio-judicial relationship to motherhood through the wealthy Sarah, which gives Isaac the right credentials. Once the patrilineal line of descent has been safely secured by Isaac, "Sarah works to secure a firm and future position for herself in Abraham's household through the birth of her son [for] . . . a woman's power comes through her son."[92] Steinberg rightfully notes that "Sarah becomes the agent of change by which Isaac replaces Ishmael as primary heir to Abraham."[93] Sarah's actions delineated the boundaries between the insider Israelites, represented by Sarah and Abraham, and the outsider Ishmaelites, Egyptians, and the descendants of Abraham's sons born to his third wife Keturah (Gen. 25:1).[94]

Some feminist scholars defend Sarah, arguing that Abraham is ultimately responsible for expelling Hagar and Ishmael. In her article on the abjection or rejection of Hagar as part of Israel's becoming, Cheryl Exum writes:

> There is confusion within the self, seen in the conflict between Sarah and Abraham, both of whom represent Israel. Abraham is ultimately responsible for the abjection, since only he, and not Sarah, has the authority to send Hagar and Ishmael away. In each version, however, the narrator makes the patriarch Abraham look better by having Sarah bear the brunt of the blame.[95]

It is true that Abraham appears to be the more sympathetic character in both versions. However, while the Priestly version of the Sarah/Hagar narrative identifies Hagar the slave woman as belonging to Abraham, in Genesis 16:6 Abraham makes clear that Hagar is Sarah's slave woman to do with as she pleases. Of course, more than one person is complicit in Hagar and Ishmael's expulsion. A central concern of the patriarchal narratives is who belongs as a member of Israel and who does not, who is included among God's "chosen people" and who is not. It is God who establishes the boundaries by determining which boy would be given which benefits and God who completes the abjection of Hagar and Ishmael in the binding of Isaac when God commands Abraham in Genesis 22:2 to "Take your son, your *only son* Isaac, whom you love" (emphasis author's) (NRSV), amounting to an erasure of Ishmael, if only for the moment.[96] By expelling Ishmael, according to Exum, Abraham is rejecting a part of himself, but such abjection is required in boundary construction.

Still, once the boundaries are established, they need enforcement and constant maintenance. Up to now, with Hagar and Ishmael's presence, the boundaries remained fluid. Thus Sarah, using the political project of motherhood, steps forward to do the "dirty work" of boundary maintenance in Genesis 21. Sarah has been described pejoratively as "calculating."[97] However, I would counter that as a woman in a patriarchal society, Sarah used whatever means for securing her future were at her disposal. Giving her the benefit of the doubt, Tammi Schneider points out that although God makes clear to Abraham in Genesis 17:21 that the covenant would be with Isaac, the son borne by Sarah, "This is information that Abraham has, based on his conversation with the Deity, though there is no clue in the text that Sarah knows this."[98] On the other hand, Sarah may understand God's plan better than Abraham does. From forced surrogacy to forced removal instigated by an emotional outburst, Sarah has wielded the apparatuses of different political projects of motherhood to protect her and her son. In doing so, she shows more astuteness and courage than Abraham to carry out God's plans by enforcing the boundaries.

The Yahwist writers accepted the ancient cultural practices of its time for sustaining the hegemonic national family narrative that made the male heir born to Sarah and Abraham through a surrogate acceptable. However, the Priestly school rejected this narrative and regarded only Sarah as the legitimate mother of Israel through her lineage and marriage to Abraham. The different narratives woven together in the Abraham-Sarah-Hagar cycle in their final form appear cohesive to many readers. Yet, competing narratives of political projects of motherhood are detectible because they simultaneously meet the needs of different constituent groups within the collectivity.

The two women and their sons were constructed as insiders and outsiders according to different political projects of belonging. Hagar the Egyptian slave woman and her son are constructed as outsiders within what would become the nation of Israel in the Hebrew Bible narratives. They live within Abraham's household and Ishmael is Abraham's firstborn son, but both Hagar and Ishmael are considered outsiders due to Hagar's ethnicity and social status.[99] Sarah, in contrast, is constructed as an insider within the collectivity as the legitimate mother of the heir of the covenant due to having the right ethnicity and pedigree. Yet, only Hagar functions as a symbolic signifier of national difference. Still, as Esther Fuchs noted, as an Israelite *woman*, Sarah too is an outsider within the nation. In the gendering of the nation, while Sarah has the proper credentials, in representing the nation as a sexual and maternal subject, her body is "constructed as defective or damaged sexually and reproductively" and dependent on "supplementary assistance"[100] first from a surrogate and secondarily from the deity.

THE EMOTION OF ANGER AS A WOMANIST
POLITICAL PROJECT OF BELONGING

Sarah and Hagar are divided among ethnic and class lines. And while it was mentioned above that the biblical texts should not be read through modern racial constructs, readers are nonetheless led down that path beginning with the Hebrew Bible's depiction of Egyptians as sexually deviant (e.g., Lev. 18; Ezek. 23:20). Thus, Hagar as an Egyptian becomes othered in the final form of the Hebrew Bible canon by being guilty by association of sexual immorality. Julianna Claassens notes that in a rabbinic interpretation of Genesis 16 Hagar's ethnicity is associated with fecundity and hypersexuality.[101] As the tradition goes, Abraham impregnated Hagar after their first sexual encounter. This feeds into the modern myth that Black women are hyper-fertile "baby-making machines" since as an Egyptian Hagar is regarded as African or US Black in US nineteenth and twentieth-century literature.

The truth is, according to government studies on reproduction and infertility, US Black women are nearly twice as likely as White women to experience impaired fecundity and the infertility rates among Black women are rising.[102] The reasons for the racial disparity in infertility are unknown although they are likely related to the racial inequalities in healthcare in the United States. For Black women who turn to assisted reproductive technology such as *in vitro* fertilization or artificial insemination to conceive, even accounting for socioeconomic status and risk factors, they had lower rates of live births than White women.[103]

Some women who are involuntarily childless hire a gestational surrogate to carry a fetus for the genetic mother. The enslaved Egyptian woman Hagar is often touted as the archetype for surrogacy despite the involuntary nature of her gestational motherhood. For example, the former website The Hagar Center, which provided assisted reproduction and adoption services, advertised that "Surrogacy is not new: it goes back to the Old Testament and Hagar, who carried a child—Ishmael—for Abraham and Sarah" to promote its services.[104] An article discussing the legal and psychological issues concerning gestational surrogacy cited Genesis 16:1–15 in its opening, maintaining that "This story is often referred to as the first known case of surrogacy, although this custom was apparently prevalent in ancient Mesopotamia as far back as 1900 B.C.E."[105] As Marianne Bjelland Kartow remarked, "Surrogacy is legitimated by creating an illusion of an unproblematic continuum from 'biblical days' to our present time."[106]

Yet, there are inequalities in individual experiences of surrogacy and motherhood based on race, class, and gender locations. For one, US Black gestational surrogates are mostly gestators for White women. However, in custody battles where the gestational mother's class, marital status, and race are considered, courts consistently rule in favor of the genetic couple, giving preference instead to "configurations of the family that fit the nuclear family model of white, middle- to upper-middle-class heterosexual couples."[107] Given that US Black women are three times more likely to die in childbirth than Hispanic or White women and experience an infant mortality rate that is twice the rate of White women, Black women's participation in the commercial gestational surrogate industry is at great risk to them and the infants.

The different political projects of belonging in the Sarah and Hagar narrative demonstrate the challenges of the various organizing principles of belonging, especially the political project of motherhood. There are ethnic, class, and cultural differences between Sarah and Hagar, differences that affect modern US women from different racial/ethnic, socioeconomic backgrounds in disparate ways. The significant disparities faced by Black women across their reproductive lives, regardless of income, documented by a group of obstetricians-gynecologists led them to conclude that the outcomes were not only "statistically significant, but morally significant and fundamentally unjust."[108] This prompted them to claim a space within the medical field for what they coined "evidence-based outrage" in response to the statistics and to challenge obstetricians-gynecologists to pursue racial equity in their research to improve health for US Black women. Their outrage is the manifestation of what I refer to as the emotion of anger as a womanist political project of belonging. By embracing the #BlackLivesMatter to express the urgency and frustration with the persistent inequities for African Americans, the obstetricians-gynecologists demonstrated that anger or outrage is an appropriate emotional response.

I originally chose the emotion of righteous indignation as a justified reactive emotion of anger in response to the simultaneously occurring, overlapping forms of discrimination experienced by US Black and other women of color. However, Sara Ahmed cautions that feminists (and womanists) should not make their emotion of anger into a sign of truth, as if their anger is always right. "When anger becomes righteous it can be oppressive; to assume anger makes us right can be a wrong."[109]

Yet, as Audre Lorde maintains, not only do Black women maintain a "well-stocked arsenal" of anger for use against oppression, but also require anger for their survival.[110] Some Black women might be discomfited by displaying their anger or outrage at their personal or collective oppressions for fear of being stereotyped as an "angry Black woman." As Melissa Harris-Perry observed, rather than being acknowledged as a legitimate reaction to unequal circumstances, Black women's anger is seen as pathological and irrational.[111] According to Lorde, Black women's anger also produces guilt and defensiveness in White women. However, she opines, "The angers between

22   *Chapter 1*

women will not kill us if we can articulate with at least as much intensity as when we defend ourselves against the manner of saying . . . But anger expressed and translated into action in the service of our vision and our future is a liberating and strengthening act of clarification."[112] The emotion of anger can be used to create distance between the rational "us" and the "irrational" them, therefore the maintenance of such boundaries demands stifling Black women's rage because it can lead to Black women's empowerment. But to interpret Lorde another way, for Black women to stifle their anger is to invite certain death and so we rage on.

NOTES

1. Delores Williams, *Sisters in the Wilderness: The Challenge of Womanist God-talk* (Maryknoll, NY: Orbis, 1993), 8.

2. Diana Hayes, *Hagar's Daughters: Womanist Ways of Being in the World* (New York: Paulist, 1995), 3.

3. See also, Vanessa Lovelace, "Intersections of Ethnicity, Gender, Sexuality, and Nation" in *The Hebrew Bible: Feminist and Intersectional Perspectives*, ed. Gale A. Yee (Minneapolis: Fortress, 2018), 75–107.

4. Julie Klein, "Why Scholars Just Can't Stop Talking About Sarah and Hagar," *U.S. News and World Report*, January 25, 2008, https://www.usnews.com/news/religion/articles/2008/01/25/why-scholars-just-cant-stop-talking-about-sarah-and-hagar.

5. See Tikva Frymer-Kensky, *Reading the Women of the Bible* (New York: Schocken, 2002), who refers to this cycle as the Abraham-Sarah Cycle.

6. The term "nation" is commonly defined as a collectivity with a shared myth of common descent, history, and land. A major debate on nation is the antiquity or modernity of nations. Theorists in support of the former are called "primordialists" and the latter are called "modernists." This debate extends to the study of ancient Israel. Scholars are at odds whether ancient Israel is continuous with the modern nation, for example, Adrian Hastings, *The Construction of Nationhood: Ethnicity, Religion and Nationalism* (Cambridge: Cambridge University Press, 1997); Steven Grosby, *Biblical Ideas of Nationality: Ancient and Modern* (Winona Lake, IN: Eisenbrauns 2002); Aviel Roshwald, *The Endurance of Nationalism: Ancient Roots and Modern Dilemmas* (Cambridge: Cambridge University Press, 2007); or whether nation is anachronistic to ancient Israel, for example, Elie Kedourie, *Nationalism* (London: Hutchinson University Library, 1960); Ernest Gellner, *Nations and Nationalism* (Ithaca, NY: Cornell University Press, 1983); Eric Hobsbawm, *Nations and Nationalism Since 1780* (Cambridge: Cambridge University Press, 1992).

7. Benedict Anderson, *Imagined Communities* (London: Verso, 1983), 6–7.

8. Nira Yuval-Davis, *The Politics of Belonging: Intersectional Contestations* (London: Sage, 2011), 10.

9. Yuval-Davis, vii.

10. John Crowley, "The Politics of Belonging: Some Theoretical Considerations," in *The Politics of Belonging: Migrants and Minorities in Contemporary Europe*, ed. Andrew Geddess and Adrian Favell (Brookfield, VT: Ashgate, 1999), 30.

11. Nira Yuval-Davis, "Borders, Boundaries, and the Politics of Belonging" in *Ethnicity, Nationalism, and Minority Rights*, ed. Stephen May, Tariq Modood, and Judith Squires (Cambridge: Cambridge University Press, 2009), 216.

12. Yuval-Davis, 216.

13. Sara Ahmed, *The Cultural Politics of Emotions*, 2nd ed. (Edinburgh: Edinburgh University Press), 2014.

14. Yuval-Davis, *The Politics of Belonging*, 22.

15. Yuval-Davis, 20–21.

16. Floya Anthias and Nira Yuval-Davis, eds., *Racialized Boundaries: Race, Nation, Gender, Colour and Class and the Anti-Racist Struggle* (London: Routledge, 1992); See also, Nira Yuval-Davis, *Gender & Nation* (London: Sage, 1997).

17. The limited focus of this essay does not allow for an examination of the competing traditions of Israel's origins in the ancestor narratives in Genesis and the Moses story in Exodus. For a detailed treatment see, Konrad Schmid, *Genesis and the Moses Story: Israel's Dual Origins in the Hebrew Bible*, trans. James D. Nogalski (Winona Lake, IN: Eisenbrauns, 2010).

18. Elizabeth Malone, Nathan E. Hultman, Kate L. Anderson, Viviane Romeiro, citing Sheafer, Shenhav, and Goldstein in "Stories about ourselves: How national narratives influence the diffusion of large-scale energy technologies," *Energy Research & Social Science* 31 (2017): 2.

19. Other investigations have focused on the origins of the tribal Ishmaelites in Genesis 16 and the ancient Mediterranean legal codes behind the women's actions in the text.

20. Infertility is not the only threat to the promise. In Genesis 12 the "endangered ancestress" motif figures in the taking of Sarai as a wife by Pharaoh.

21. Claus Westermann, *Genesis 12–36*, trans. John J. Scullion S.J. (Minneapolis: Fortress, 1995), 235.

22. John Van Seters, *Abraham in History* (New Haven: Yale University Press, 1975), 192–96.

23. See also, Walter Brueggemann, *Genesis. Interpretation: A Bible Commentary for Teaching and Preaching* (Atlanta: John Knox, 1982); Gerhard von Rad, *Genesis: A Commentary*, Old Testament Library, trans. John H. Marks (Philadelphia: Westminster, 1972).

24. Naomi Steinberg, *Kinship and Marriage in Genesis: A Household Economics Perspective* (Minneapolis: Augsburg, 1993), 78–79.

25. Phyllis Trible, *Texts of Terror: Literary Feminist Readings in Biblical Narratives* (Philadelphia: Fortress, 1984), 27.

26. Katharine Doob Sakenfeld, *Just Wives? Stories of Power and Survival in the Old Testament* (Louisville, Westminster John Knox, 2003), 15.

27. Delores Williams, *Sisters in the Wilderness: The Challenge of Womanist God-talk* (Maryknoll, NY: Orbis, 1993), 6.

28. Renita Weems, *Just a Sister Away: A Womanist Vision of Women's Relationships in the Bible* (San Diego: Lura Media, 1988), 2.

29. Wil Gafney, *Womanist Midrash: A Reintroduction to the Women of the Torah and the Throne* (Louisville: Westminster John Knox, 2017), 44.

30. See, for example, Gay L. Byron, *Symbolic Blackness and Ethnic Difference in Early Christianity* (New York: Routledge, 2002) and Edwin Yamauchi, *Africa and the Bible* (Grand Rapids, MI: Baker Academic, 2004).

31. Audrey Smedley and Brian Smedley, "Race as Biology is Fiction, Racism as A Social Problem is Real: Anthropological and Historical Perspectives on the Social Construction of Race," *American Psychologist* 60, no. 1 (January 2005): 16–26. See also, Patricia Hill Collins, "It's All in the Family: Intersections of Gender, Race, and Nation," *Hypatia* 13, no. 3 (1998): 62–82.

32. Weems, *Just a Sister Away*, 7.

33. Williams, *Sisters in the Wilderness*, 15.

34. Amanda Beckenstein Mbuvi, *Belonging in Genesis: Biblical Israel and the Politics of Identity Formation* (Waco, TX: Baylor University Press, 2016), 124.

35. See, for example, Marion Ann Taylor and Heather E. Weir, eds., *Let Her Speak for Herself: Nineteenth Century Women Writing on Women in Genesis* (Boston: Boston University Press, 2006); Eloise Bibb, "Poems," American Verse Project, 1895, http://name.umdl.umich.edu/BAD9461.0001.001. For a different perspective on the racialization of Sarah and Hagar, see Nyasha Junior, *Reimagining Hagar: Blackness and Bible* (Oxford: Oxford University Press, 2019).

36. Elizabeth Durant, "It's Complicated: Power and Complicity in the Stories of Hagar and Sarah," *Conversations with the Biblical World* 35 (2015): 86.

37. Jayme Reaves, "Sarah as Victim and Perpetrator: Whiteness, Power, and Memory in the Matriarchal Narrative," *Review & Expositor* 115, no. 4 (2018): 484.

38. This is a play on the titles of both Weems's and Williams's books and the adoption of fictive kinship to include Sarah as a "Black" woman or "sister."

39. Patricia Hill Collins, "Producing Mothers of the Nation: Race, Class and Contemporary US Population Policies," in *Women, Citizenship and Difference*, ed. Nira Yuval-Davis and Pnina Werbner (London: Zed, 1999), 118–29; Nira Yuval-Davis "Nationalist Projects and Gender Relations" *Nar. Umjet* 40, no. 1 (2003).

40. Yuval-Davis, *The Politics of Belonging*, 100.

41. Schmid, *Genesis and the Moses Story*, 84.

42. Schmid, 112.

43. Mark Brett, ed., *Ethnicity and the Bible* (Boston: Brill, 2014).

44. Yvonne Sherwood, "Hagar and Ishmael: The Reception of Expulsion," *Interpretation: A Journal of Bible and Theology* 68, no. 3 (2014): 289–90.

45. Sherwood, "Hagar and Ishmael," 290.

46. Julie Kelso, *O Mother, Where Art Thou? An Irigarayan Reading of the Book of Chronicles* (London: Equinox, 2007), 8.

47. This is a play on the phrase translated in English as "to make a covenant." In Hebrew to make a covenant is literally to "cut a covenant" from the verb "to cut" (Heb. *karat*) and the noun "covenant" (Heb. *berit* or *brit*; Gen. 15:18).

"This Woman's Son Shall Not Inherit with My Son"　　25

48. Ilona N. Rashkow, *Taboo or Not Taboo: Sexuality and Family in the Hebrew Bible* (Minneapolis: Fortress, 2000), 75.

49. Schmid, *Genesis and the Moses Story*, 245.

50. Yuval-Davis, *The Politics of Belonging*, 92.

51. See, for example, Jack Sasson, "Circumcision in the Ancient Near East," *Journal of Biblical Literature* 85, no. 4 (1966): 473–76; John Goldingay, "The Significance of Circumcision," *Journal for the Study of the Old Testament* 25, no. 88 (June 2000): 3–18; Sandra Jacobs, *The Body as Property: Physical Disfigurement in Biblical Law* (New York: Bloomsbury T&T Clark, 2014).

52. Jacobs, *The Body as Property*, 30–31.

53. Sasson, "Circumcision in the Ancient Near East," 474.

54. Mbuvi, *Belonging in Genesis*, 140.

55. Yuval-Davis, *The Politics of Belonging*, 97.

56. Gafney, *Womanist Midrash*, 30–31.

57. Marianne Bjelland Kartzow, "Reproductive Capital and Slave Surrogacy: Thinking about/with/beyond Hagar," in *Bodies, Borders, Believers: Ancient Texts and Present Conversations*, ed. Marianne Bjelland Kartzow, Anne Hege Grung, and Anna Rebecca Solevag (Cambridge: Lutterworth, 2016), 400.

58. Howard Eilberg-Schwartz, "People of the Body: The Problem of the Body for the People of the Book," *Journal of the History of Sexuality* 2, no. 1 (1991): 24.

59. Jacobs, *The Body as Property*, 33.

60. Westermann, *Genesis 12–36*, 235.

61. A document on marriage and divorce customs from the ancient Near Eastern city Nuzi closely corresponds to Genesis 16. The document, translated here by E. A. Speiser, records that a certain Shennima married a woman named Gilimninu (*Harvard Semitic Studies* 5 no. 67). We are told that if "Gilimninu bears children, Shennima shall not take another wife. But if Gilimninu fails to bear children, Gilimninu shall get for Shennima a woman from the Lullu country (i.e., a slave girl) as concubine. In that case, Gilimninu herself shall have authority over the offspring," E. A. Speiser, "Genesis," *Anchor Bible Dictionary* (New York: Doubleday, 1962), 120.

62. Kartzow, "Reproductive Capital and Slave Surrogacy," 401.

63. A child can technically have three mothers based on these scenarios.

64. Tikva Frymer-Kensky, *In the Wake of the Goddesses: Women, Culture, and the Biblical Transformation of Pagan Myth* (New York: The Free Press, 2002); Gafney, *Womanist Midrash*, 2017.

65. Kartzow, "Reproductive Capital and Slave Surrogacy," 401–02.

66. Raymond Westbrook, "The Female Slave," in *Gender and Law in the Hebrew Bible and Ancient Near East*, ed. Victor H. Matthews, Bernard Levinson, and Tikva Frymer-Kensky (New York: T&T Clark, 2004), 215.

67. Frymer-Kensky, *In the Wake of the Goddesses*, 227.

68. Susan Tucker, *Telling Memories Among Southern Women* (Baton Rouge: Louisiana State University Press, 1988), 19. As an example, white segregationist Senator Strom Thurmond (R-SC) had sexual relations with Carrie Butler, a Black teenager employed as a maid by his parents in 1925. The liaison resulted in Thurmond fathering a child with Butler. Essie Mae Washington-Williams, *Dear Senator: A Memoir by*

26   *Chapter 1*

the Daughter of Strom Thurmond (New York: HarperCollins, 2005). See also Anne Moody, *Coming of Age in Mississippi* (New York: Dell, 1968); and Grace Halsell, *Soul Sister* (New York: Fawcett Gold Medal, 1969).

69. "'We Are Literally Slaves': An Early Twentieth-Century Black Nanny Sets the Record Straight," *History Matters*, 1912, http://historymatters.gmu.edu/d/80/.

70. Sakenfeld, *Just Wives?*, 12.

71. Kartzow, "Reproductive Capital and Slave Surrogacy," 398.

72. Joseph Blenkinsopp, "The Family in First Temple Israel," in *Families in Ancient Israel*, ed. Leo G. Purdue, Joseph Blenkinsopp, John J. Collins, and Carol Meyers (Louisville, KY: Westminster John Knox, 1997), 63.

73. On biblical widowhood, Paula Hiebert makes the distinction between the modern concept of the widow as a woman whose husband has died and her obligations to him are terminated, and the biblical notion of a woman whose husband has died, and she has no father-in-law or sons to care for her. Paula Hiebert, "Whence Shall Help Come to Me: The Biblical Widow," in *Gender and Difference in Ancient Israel*, ed. Peggy Lynne Day (Minneapolis: Augsburg Fortress, 1989), 125–41.

74. Naomi Steinberg, in *The World of the Child in the Hebrew Bible* (Sheffield: Sheffield Phoenix Press, 2013), 84–85, examines the effects of being a child in a polygamous household in the Hebrew Bible. Here she argues that when Ishmael was Abraham's only son he was entitled to the rights and privileges of the firstborn son. However, Isaac's birth reconfigures the household from a monogamous to a polygamous one. Steinberg is defining "monogamous household" here as Abraham, Sarah, and Ishmael (Gen. 16:16). The household shifts to a polygamous one after the birth of Isaac, where two mothers now reside: Sarah, Isaac's mother and Hagar, Ishmael's mother (Gen. 21:2).

75. Isaac's name, which is Hebrew for "he laughs" (*yitzchaq*) is from the same root צ-ח-ק as the noun *tzechoq* for "laughter" and the verb *tzachaq* for "laugh" in verse 6.

76. Kartzow, "Reproductive Capital and Slave Surrogacy," 398.

77. Cynthia Chapman, *The House of the Mother: The Social Roles of Maternal Kin in Biblical Hebrew Narrative and Poetry* (New Haven, CT: Yale University Press, 2016), 126.

78. Sharon Jacob and Jennifer Kaalund, "Flowing from Breast to Breast: An Examination of Dis/placed Motherhood in African American and Indian Wet Nurses," in *Womanist Interpretations of the Bible: Expanding the Discourse*, ed. Gay L. Byron and Vanessa Lovelace (Atlanta: SBL Press, 2016), 209–38.

79. Chapman, *The House of the Mother*, 138.

80. Mbuvi, *Belonging in Genesis*, 132.

81. Chapman, *The House of the Mother*, 152.

82. Von Rad, *Genesis*, 231.

83. Chapman, *The House of the Mother*, 140.

84. Chapman, 139.

85. Chapman, 133.

86. Tammi Schneider, *Sarah: Mother of Nations* (New York: Continuum, 2004), 93.

87. Hagar's status goes from a *shifchah* in Genesis 16:3 to an *'amah* in Genesis 21:10, 12. *Shifchah* is usually translated "handmaid" and *'amah* is translated "female

slave." Biblical scholars do not agree on whether the status of one is higher than the other.

88. Sherwood, "Hagar and Ishmael," 292.

89. Mbuvi, *Belonging in Genesis*, 131.

90. Steinberg, *The World of the Child*, 38–39, 83.

91. Chapman, *The House of the Mother*, 140.

92. Steinberg, *Kinship and Marriage in Genesis*, 78.

93. Steinberg, *The World of the Child in the Hebrew Bible*, 85.

94. Keturah is called Abraham's wife *(ishshah)* in Genesis 25, and his concubine *(pilegesh)* in 1 Chronicles 1:32–33. Some scholars believe that the *pilegesh* was a non-Israelite woman.

95. J. Cheryl Exum, "Hagar en Procès: The Abject in Search of Subjectivity," in *From the Margins I: Women of the Hebrew Bible and Their Afterlives*, ed. P. S. Hawkins and L. C. Stahlberg (Sheffield: Sheffield Academic, 2009), 5–6.

96. Ishmael is not mentioned again until 1 Chronicles in the genealogy (1 Chron. 1:28, 31).

97. Von Rad, *Genesis*, 227.

98. Schneider, *Sarah: Mother of Nations*, 95.

99. Ishmael's abjection is not complete. For one, he joins Isaac in burying Abraham (Gen. 25:9) and Isaac's son, Esau, marries Ishmael's daughter, Mahalath (Gen. 28:9).

100. Esther Fuchs, "Intermarriage, Gender, and Nation in the Hebrew Bible," in *The Passionate Torah: Sex and Judaism*, ed. Danya Ruttenberg (New York: New York University Press, 2009), 74, 77.

101. Juliana Claassens, "Just Emotions: Reading the Sarah and Hagar Narrative (Genesis 16, 21) through the Lens of Human Dignity," in *Verbum et Ecclesia* 32, no. 2 (2013).

102. See, for example, Ashley Wiltshire, et al., "Infertility Knowledge and Treatment Beliefs among African American Women in an Urban Community," in *Contraception and Reproductive Medicine* 4, no. 16 (2019), https://doi.org/10.1186/s40834-019-0097-x.

103. Wilshire, et al., "Infertility Knowledge."

104. Attorney Mark Eckman, immigration, adoption, gestational surrogacy, and traditional surrogacy law specialist, maintained the now defunct website The Hagar Center archived at http://web.archive.org/web/20220526050653/https://hagarcenter.org/.

105. Susan C. Klock and Steven R. Lindheim, "Gestational Surrogacy: Medical, Psychosocial, and Legal Considerations," *Fertility and Sterility* 113, no. 5 (2020): 889.

106. Marianne Bjelland Kartzow, "Navigating the Womb: Surrogacy, Slavery, Fertility—And Biblical Discourses," *Journal of Early Christian History* 2, no. 4 (2012): 47.

107. Deborah Grayson, "Mediating Intimacy: Black Surrogate Mothers and the Law," *Critical Inquiry* 24, no. 2 (Winter, 1998): 106.

108. Kacey Eichelberger, et al., "Black Lives Matter: Claiming a Space for Evidence-Based Outrage in Obstetrics and Gynecology," *American Journal of Public Health* 106, no. 10 (2016).

28 *Chapter 1*

109. Sara Ahmed, "Feminist Killjoys (And Other Willful Subjects)," *S&F Online* (Summer 2010): 4.

110. Audre Lorde, *Sister Outsider: Essays & Speeches by Audre Lorde*, new foreword by Cheryl Clarke (Berkeley: Crossing, 2007), 127.

111. Melissa Harris-Perry, *Sister Citizen: Shame, Stereotypes, and Black Women in America* (New Haven: Yale University Press, 2011), 95.

112. Lorde, *Sister Outsider*, 131, 127.

Chapter 2

Outsider Within

A Vineyard, a Curse, and US Racial Politics

One of the most popular stories of the Bible is the tale of Noah and his family (Gen. 6:11–9:17). Many a nursery room in homes and churches is decorated with an ark carrying pairs of male and female animals floating atop a sea of water with a rainbow above them. Fascination with the biblical tale of a deity who becomes disillusioned with the wickedness and corruption of human beings and sends an epic flood to destroy them—save a righteous man named Noah, his family, and a select few animals—has fueled the imaginations of readers for centuries. The myriad artistic and literary representations of the biblical story of a watery deluge, commonly referred to as Noah's flood—including Renaissance artist Michelangelo's "The Flood" (1508–12), American artist Edward Hicks's "Noah's Ark" (1846), *Noye's Fludde* (*Noah's Flood*), a medieval one-act play later set to music by Benjamin Britten (1913–1976),[1] and Darren Aronofsky's film *Noah* (2014)—attest to this story's staying power, despite the fact that it is neither the only nor the oldest recorded diluvial myth.[2] Still, the biblical tale remains the most recognized and, arguably, the most popular of all deluge stories in the western hemisphere.

Notwithstanding the animal-stuffed ark and rainbow decor in nurseries and illustrated children's Bibles, these adorable images belie darker themes of diluvial mayhem, death, destruction, and alienation that follows postdiluvian. Genesis 9, on one hand, is about defining who belongs as a member of the nation of Israel and the boundaries between insiders and outsiders. On the other hand, for many African American readers, the story of Noah and his sons is a "text of terror"[3] that conjures images of blackness as a curse, racial inferiority, slavery, and segregation. The story of Noah's curse of his grandson Canaan, interchangeably referred to as Noah's Curse, the misnomer Curse of Ham, and the Curse of Canaan has been used in US racial politics

30   *Chapter 2*

to rationalize the enslavement of Blacks and the separation of Blacks from Whites in public and private spaces.

While the curse of blackness has been used to justify the enslavement of Blacks, the reality is that the doctrine of Black inferiority was developed after the institution of slavery to legalize racial prejudice against Blacks. As Leon Higginbotham puts it, "Although the law came to enforce the precept [of Black inferiority], it did not create it."[4] Thus, as Stephen Steinberg explained, "In these various forms of racial domination and exploitation, the nation, under the guise of a racist mythology, had established a precedent for not only tolerating extremes of inequality but also imparting them with political and moral legitimacy as well."[5] As a result, whiteness both culturally and legally conferred rights and privileges on one segment of society and excluded non-Whites from the same benefits. This would serve to make Blacks outsiders within their birthplace, to deny them birthright citizenship, and later relegate them to second-class citizenship despite being granted "equal protections under the law" by the Fourteenth Amendment.

By citizenship, at its most fundamental, I am referring to formal membership in a nation-state.[6] The French Enlightenment thinker Jean-Jacques Rousseau (1712–78) is recognized for conceptualizing the democratic (political) nation as representative of actively engaged citizenry. Rousseau equated citizenship with the "mutual interdependence of fellow citizens . . . of 'general will'" and not "given to the 'tyranny' of his fellow citizens."[7] Citizenship today has been understood both as a reciprocal relationship of "rule and being ruled" and a "form of legal status, with specific rights and responsibilities."[8] Yet, when the framers of the United States Constitution grappled with the issue of slavery, they were in effect defining the identity and values of its membership. According to Natalie Masuoka and Jane Junn, "By creating limits on who could be a member, citizenship laws also promoted the idea of virtuousness and exclusivity."[9] As Winthrop Jordan explained, along the binary moral paradigm of race, "White and black connoted purity and filthiness, virginity and sin, virtue and baseness, beauty and ugliness, beneficence and evil, God and the devil."[10] The result was the creation of a national identity "premised on the ascription of moral, social, symbolic, and intellectual characteristics to real or manufactured phenotypical features which justify and give normality to the institutional and societal dominance of one population over other populations."[11]

These beliefs aided by the story of Noah and his sons in the antebellum period would serve to secure in the minds of generations of White Christian Americans (as well as some Black Christian Americans) the inherent inferiority of Blacks to Whites despite the story also depicting the equality of all human beings as descended from the same ancestor. According to Thomas Peterson, "No story was more symbolically persuasive in resolving certain

Outsider Within 31

tensions between White Southerners' racial values and their most fundamental religious beliefs than was the myth of Ham."[12]

In this chapter I explore how the politics of belonging has been influenced by the racialization and sexualization of Noah's Curse in Genesis 9:20–27 throughout its history of interpretation in America to promote the political project of White superiority. I argue that in the United States, proslavery Americans weaponized Noah's curse to enforce a racial hierarchy of belonging and citizenship that granted full citizenship to Whites and excluded Blacks from membership and belonging based on race. I demonstrate that the political project of White superiority adopted the ascriptive social location of blackness as an organizing principle of society. It was intended to keep Blacks in a subordinate position to Whites by dehumanizing Black humanity, morality, intellect, and sexuality and codified such inferiority as divinely decreed.

THE INTERSECTION OF GENDER, SEXUALITY, AND NOAH'S CURSE

A quick survey of scholarship on Noah's curse demonstrates that it is not a story that has greatly interested feminist and womanist biblical critics despite the issues of gender and sexuality raised in the text. This is perhaps on account of the near absence of women in the narrative, except as nameless wives.[13] The fact that women are mentioned at all is in reference to their relationship to Noah: "your wife . . . your sons' wives" (Gen. 6:18, 7:6, 13, 8:16, 18) and their unmentioned role in repopulating the earth with their husbands. Yet feminist readings of the flood narrative in Genesis 6–9 barely reference women in the text, if at all. Ilona Rashkow's psychoanalytic treatment of Genesis 9:18–27 makes no remarks on the women but rather addresses the possibility that Noah initiated an act of father-son incest.[14] Tikva Frymer-Kensky discusses Genesis 9:25–27 and the curse of Canaan to explain the disdain the biblical writers held for the Canaanites.[15] Wil Gafney does not include Noah's wife or his daughters-in-law in her womanist midrash on women in Genesis.[16] An exception is Julie Ringold Spitzer's brief commentary on Mrs. Noah in *The Women's Torah Commentary*.[17]

A surprising omission is Susan Niditch's commentary (1998, 2012) on women in the book of Genesis between Genesis 6:1–4 and 12–50 in the *Women's Bible Commentary*.[18] Skipping over the flood story, the only mention of women is the reference to the absence of women in the genealogical lists in Genesis 1–11, except Genesis 4:19. Thus, anyone interested in women's roles in the Hebrew Bible could be excused from addressing a narrative that only mentions Noah's wife and daughters-in-law in passing reference, giving readers with such interest little to work with.

32   *Chapter 2*

On one hand, arguably women as a group should not be disregarded for their supposed irrelevance to the flood narrative. The tale of Noah and his family functions much like other national narratives. In the process of building a national identity, storytelling, in this case stories about family, is but one means of establishing the boundaries between insiders and outsiders of the polity.[19] For the community responsible for collecting and editing this story, women's reproductive roles are essential to the national discourses that contribute to boundary construction. A polity needs members, and as Nira Yuval-Davis explains, women are "biological 'producers' of children/people," and therefore also the "'bearers of the collective' within these boundaries."[20] However, as demonstrated in chapter 1, womanist interests in whose reproductive roles matter for determining who is included as a member must be investigated. Nonetheless, Noah's instruction to bring the male and its mate of every kind on the ark, to include Noah's sons and their wives (Gen. 7:2; cf. 6:19, 7:3:), and the later blessing to "be fruitful and multiply" (Gen. 9:1, 7; cf. 8:17; cf. 1:28) would be of significance to a displaced *golah* (exile) community that faced existential threats from assimilation and intermarriage.[21] The promised fecundity is divine assurance to the readers that the returning community would have an equally secure future.

On the other hand, the genealogies in Genesis 5 and 11 attributed to the Priestly school, which form an inclusion around the flood story, genders procreation as male.[22] The men do the begetting in these genealogical lists, with the formulaic male "PN *yalad* ('begot')" followed by the name of his firstborn son; and then he begot other sons and daughters and died (e.g., Gen. 5:6). In her analysis of genealogies and gender in the Priestly writings, Elizabeth Goldstein quotes Nicole Ruane as stating, "The genealogies portray men as having procreative power for themselves. Women are not members of the procreative line [although] they of course give birth."[23] Thus, even when women's role in reproduction is implied, in nationalist discourses such as the Priestly genealogical records in the book of Genesis, it is often men who "sire" nations.[24]

Yet, genaeology and reproduction are not the interests of the Yahwist in Genesis 9. The use of the verb *yalad* ("to beget") in Genesis 5 denotes having fathered a son ("became the father of") in contrast to Genesis 9:18, where the mention that Ham was the father of Canaan omits any verbs of procreation. For another, where God's command to the humans to be fruitful (*parah*), multiply (*ravah*), and fill (*mala'*) the earth in the Priestly version of creation (Gen. 1:28; cf. 9:1, 7) uses procreative language, the verb in Genesis 9:18 that means to repopulate the earth (*nafatz*) literally means to "disperse" or "be scattered"). Thus, rather than emphasizing the Israelite lineage as descended from Adam in P, the Yahwist's focus is on establishing the relationships between the sons of Noah and their ancestors who represent the nations descended from them. From the broad view of all nations to the narrowly defined relationship between Israel and Canaan, Genesis 9:20–27 has become a convenient text throughout history for defining a racial group as sexually deviant and thus deserving of enslavement by divine consent.

A TALE OF DRUNKENNESS AND NAKEDNESS

Genesis 9:18–27 introduces a new episode in the story of Noah and his sons. Beginning with the report that Shem, Ham, and Japheth would be scattered to all the earth, effectively explaining the origins of other nations, there is an editorial report in Genesis 9:18b: "Ham was the father of Canaan." Martin Kessler and Karel Deurloo raised the question asked by many readers when they arrive at this place in the narrative: "Why is it said of Ham, in parentheses, that he is the father of Canaan?"[25] Traditionally, scholars have argued that the statement serves as an ethnological notice reflecting an earlier tradition concerning Shem, Japheth, and Canaan to introduce the geopolitical realities between the Israelites and the Canaanites.[26] Such scholars regard the appearance of Ham as the work of a redactor. For example, John Skinner asserted that the circumstantial clause "Ham, the father of Canaan" was a gloss in Genesis 9:18b and 22 by an editor who attempted to smooth the transition from verse 18, which includes Ham as a son of Noah, to verses 24–25, which identify Canaan as the youngest brother of Shem and Japheth.[27]

Gerhard von Rad agreed that the original story was oriented toward Canaan and the Palestinian context but argued that Ham was inserted to bring him into harmony with the ecumenical scheme of nations in chapter 10 by maintaining, "A redactor attempted to remove the inconsistency by making Ham, and not Canaan, appear in the story. He did this by inserting in v. 18 and v. 22 the words *ḥām hū' 'abī* ('Ham, the father of') before the name of 'Canaan.'"[28] The general consensus is that a redactor fused together two traditions about Ham and Canaan.[29] Nonetheless, most would agree with the observation by Thomas Brodie that the first appearance of Canaan in verse 18 is "jolting."[30] Rather than smooth over the inconsistencies, such effort instead created more confusion for modern readers. At a minimum, one can fathom that in dramatic structure and plot, the reference to Canaan serves to introduce tension or suspense in the story, alerting the reader to be prepared for a development concerning Canaan later in the narrative that will be of some consequence. Genesis 9:18–19 conclude the flood episode and provide the bridge to the postdiluvian world. What follows is a story about Noah that includes an abstruse incident between Noah and Ham resulting in interpretations infused with sexual overtones about Noah, Ham, and peoples of African descent.

34   *Chapter 2*

Beginning in Genesis 9:20, Noah is portrayed as a "man of the ground," having planted a vineyard. The association of Noah with the earth links him with the first human (Adam), who is formed from the "dust of the ground" (Gen. 2:7) and his son Cain who is a "worker of the ground" (Gen. 4:2 AT), like his father before him (Gen. 2:15; cf. 2:5). Noah's vocation in viticulture—the first to do so—suggests that he is the first man of culture after the flood (cf. Gen. 4:17–22). However, Noah's earthiness is not the only characteristic that he shares with his two predecessors. Each one of them is also characterized by a planting that leads to scandal: "the tree of knowledge, Cain's produce, Noah's vine each set the stage for the fall that is to occur."[31]

The narrator wastes no words getting to Noah's indiscretion in verse 21: he drank, he was drunk, he lay uncovered. Noah, who imbibed too freely of the fruit of the vine, is left lying drunk and uncovered in his tent. Once more, the writer reaches back to Genesis 3 by associating the taking and eating of fruit with nakedness. Noah's nakedness and drunkenness, in and of themselves, are of no moral consequence to the ancient reader. As noted by Walter Brueggemann, "Verse 21 cannot be interpreted as a negative comment on drinking, alcohol, or drunkenness . . . The drunkenness of Noah is only presented as a context for what follows."[32] More specifically, the drunkenness is the context for the nakedness, which is a pretext for Noah cursing Canaan. What happens next in this passage is an unfortunate sequence of reactions—Ronald Gowan refers to them as a series of "non sequiturs that have left every scholar baffled," becoming the genesis of a long history of interpretation of Genesis 9:20–25 that eventually found its way into American racial discourse.[33]

Having established that Noah's drunkenness from planting the vineyard is the situation and not the problem, the problem is soon revealed. The narrator reports that "Ham, the father of Canaan, saw the nakedness of his father" (Gen. 9:22 NRSV). Thomas Brodie, who also recognized the allusions to the planting of the tree in the garden of Eden with the report of the planting of the postdiluvian vineyard, locates the problem in both situations with intruders into the text. Brodie contends, "The trouble starts therefore (both in Eden and here) not with the nakedness but with an intrusive visitor—the serpent (in chap. 3) and now Ham."[34] Readers who maintain that Ham invaded his father's privacy assume that Ham had no business being in his father's tent unannounced. However, John Skinner argues that the earlier tradition represents Noah's sons as minors living in their father's tent.[35] Although the later version presents Shem, Ham, and Jephthah as married adults (Gen. 7:13), they nevertheless could have all lived together under one tent, as was customary in ancient times, with curtains to divide the tent into separate dwelling spaces. Therefore, despite some speculations about the reasons why Ham would have entered his father's tent, he could very well have belonged there.

Outsider Within   35

Still, what has intrigued interpreters for centuries is the seeing of his father naked in the tent.

The Hebrew noun עֵרוָה translated "nakedness" in Genesis is a feminine noun that usually means *pudenda*, the external male or female genital parts. This should be understood in contrast to the US context, where a woman is also considered naked if her breasts, especially her nipples, are bare. On one level, Ham seeing his father's nakedness should be understood as having literally seen Noah's genitalia. Two other references to male private parts using the same noun are in Exodus 20:26 and 28:42. They belong to the Covenant Code and refer to proper cultic conduct before the altar.[36] In each instance the concern is that the altar steps should not be exposed to male genitalia, whether by the worshiper in the former or the priest in the latter. Of course, the prohibition in Exodus 20:26 could also have been intended to prevent exposing the genitalia of the one ascending the altar steps to the view of the those below.

Except for Genesis 2:25, being seen naked often brought shame to not only the one whose genitalia has been exposed but also his or her family members. Even the Latin root for the noun *pudenda* derives from the verb "to make or be ashamed," especially in reference to women's genitalia.[37] An example is Michal, Saul's daughter's rebuke (twice) of her husband David's shameful display of his genitalia before the lowest members of society, like some commoner. Apparently, his leaping and dancing in celebration of returning the ark to Israel exposed his private parts to the public (2 Sam. 6:20). Thus, at the very least, Ham's seeing his father's עֵרוָה should be taken euphemistically as having seen his genitals. Still, although Exodus 28:42 uses the verb כסה ("to cover") with עֵרוָה straightforwardly to mean covering the priests' genitalia with undergarments, Exodus 20:26 uses עֵרוָה with גלה ("to uncover"), which is also an idiom for sexual intercourse.

The Holiness Code (Lev. 17–26) includes a list of sexual offenses to avoid, including uncovering the father's nakedness, which is also the mother's nakedness: "You shall not uncover the nakedness of your father, which is the nakedness of your mother; she is your mother, you shall not uncover her nakedness" (Lev. 18:7–8; cf. 1 Sam. 20:30).[38] On its face, it is understood that it is taboo for a son to engage in sexual relations with his mother, leading some scholars to suggest that Ham engaged in an incestuous relationship with his mother.[39] Scholars of this opinion argue that Genesis 9:22 should be read intertextually with Genesis 19:30–38 to interpret the violation as parent-child incest.[40] What this interpretation fails to recognize is that Ham did not "uncover" his father's nakedness but rather the Hebrew verb stem used indicates that Noah uncovered or exposed himself. Johannes Botterweck is also unconvinced contending, "Whether Lev. 20 can be used to interpret the

36   *Chapter 2*

story in Gen. 9:22–23, suggesting that Ham had sexual intercourse with his father's wives, is highly dubious."[41]

Nonetheless, taken together some scholars suggest that the idioms in Leviticus 18 and 20 leave open the possibility that Ham committed a sexual offense, despite the text's ambiguity. For example, Devora Steinmetz maintains, "It seems clear to me that the text suggests a sexual violation by Ham of his father . . . clearly the 'seeing of nakedness' implies a sexual violation, as it does throughout the biblical text in both legal and narrative passages."[42] Some scholars have gone so far as to use Leviticus 18:7a to argue that Ham engaged in homosexual relations with Noah. As an example, Anthony Phillips, insists that the text's ordinary meaning should be taken as prohibiting sexual relations with either parent. As such, "we should perhaps understand this incident as more than an immodest looking at his drunken and naked father but rather as his actual seduction while unconscious."[43] Randall Bailey, who maintains that Ham's sin was voyeurism, nonetheless agrees that the exilic editor has intentionally planted the sexual innuendo in the reader's mind based on Noah's response.[44]

While the debate continues regarding whether Ham committed a sexual offense in seeing his father's nakedness, the seeing is not really the issue—it is the telling. Ham reacts to the spectacle by reporting to his brothers outside what he has observed inside. Turning for a moment to the Mediterranean model of honor and shame, honor and shame are reciprocal moral values conferred on individuals by their social group that are deemed acceptable or offensive, respectively, that play out in the public sphere.[45] What specifically Ham recounted to his brothers is left unsaid. As Bailey points out, there is no modifier to support the verb "to tell." Accordingly, he notes that, "It [Gen. 9:22] states neither 'He told them what he saw,' nor 'He told them what he did.'"[46] However, in a world where what happened in the tent should have remained Noah's business, Ham took it public. By doing so, he brought shame to his father. Noah, who has been regarded by some as a paragon of righteousness, is dishonored by Ham.

The writer's contempt for Ham is barely concealed, as evidenced by the contrast between the actions of Ham and his brothers. More than a few commentators have noted the brevity with which the narrator recounts Ham's seeing and telling. By comparison, each of Shem and Japheth's actions is reported with the deliberateness with which they are taken. The two take a garment, lay it upon their shoulders, walk backwards, and cover their father's naked body (Gen. 9:23a). The second clause makes plain the writer's evaluation of the brothers: "their faces were turned away, and they did not see their father's nakedness" (v. 23b). The fact that they took careful consideration of their father's condition and that their actions are the reverse of Ham's—they do not see, they cover their father's nakedness, they remain silent—makes plain that the writer regards Shem and Japheth as more honorable than Ham. At the least, the writer suggests that Ham is guilty of violating the commandment to honor one's parents (Exod. 20:12; cf. Deut. 5:16).

Once the wine's effects wear off and Noah awakes from his drunken stupor, the narrator reports that Noah "knew what his youngest son had done to him" (Gen. 9:24). As mentioned above, the debate over just what it is that Noah knew was done to him is left open to the reader's imagination. Complicating the text's ambiguity is what Noah does in response. In the history of interpretation, his actions will reverberate for centuries with implications for the intersection of religion, anti-blackness, and Black sexuality in the development of the American racial hierarchy.

THE CURSE OF CANAAN

Noah retaliates by cursing Canaan, Ham's son, and blessing Shem and Japheth (vv. 26–27). Noah's curse, recorded in poetic structure, consigns Canaan to be a slave to his brothers. He is condemned not only to slavery but also to be the "lowest of the slaves" (v. 25), literally "slave of the slaves" in the MT. This is the first time in the Bible that a human has pronounced a curse on someone.[47] Scholars are quick to point out at least a couple of interpretive issues raised by verses 24 and 25. Not least among them, as noted by F. W. Bassett, is the nature of the offense that led Noah to curse Canaan. However, ascertaining the identity of the offender is a real conundrum.[48] Addressing the latter first, the adjective "youngest" before son, as in Noah knew what he had done to him, is confusing. As shown above, the genealogical notices list Ham as the middle, not the youngest son (Gen. 5:32, 6:10, 7:13; cf. 9:28). Once again raising the argument that "Ham, father of Canaan" should be regarded as a gloss and that the original genealogical list should read Shem, Japheth, and Canaan. This would be a solution to the problem of who Noah meant by "his youngest son" (Gen. 9:24) and, therefore, why Canaan and not Ham was cursed. However, the text as we have received it identifies Ham as the offender.

In regards to the issue raised by Bassett as to the nature of the offense, the text remains silent not only on this, but also on how Noah knew what the offender had done to him that caused his reaction.[49] Such an omission has led interpreters to insist that Ham (or whoever) was not just guilty of being a peeping Tom, but of having left some physical evidence on Noah. Hermann Gunkel, following the older tradition regarding Canaan, insisted that "v 24 presupposes that Canaan 'did' something to him (not just said something about him)."[50] Therefore, he and others concluded that Canaan/Ham must

38   *Chapter 2*

also have committed an act so heinous to justify Noah's curse of Canaan that the text has suppressed the details.

Some scholars who support the interpretation that the offense was maternal incest in violation of Leviticus 18 argue that Canaan was the offspring of this illicit affair.[51] A few remarks in rabbinic midrashic, talmudic, and later medieval texts reviewed in more detail below supposed that the infraction was either that Ham castrated Noah or sexually abused him. Therefore, since Ham deprived Noah of a fourth son by castrating him, Noah retaliated by cursing Canaan, Ham's fourth son to serve his brothers.[52]

Despite the narrative's silence regarding Noah's motive for cursing Canaan, Thomas Mann sums up the effect by stating that "it is at least implied that the political subjection of a particular people within its own land is a result of a curse pronounced on its founding father as punishment for moral turpitude."[53] According to Randall Bailey, without the sexual prohibitions of the Holiness Code in Leviticus 18 and 20, as noted above, the reader would conclude that Ham was guilty of voyeurism. Still, he contends that the text's "ambiguity leads the reader to resolve that something sexual has transpired, and, regardless of the act, it was enough to justify a curse of slavery upon at least one of the descendants of Ham."[54] The narrative concludes with Noah's death notice (Gen. 9:29).

As we can see, Noah's story on its own is confined to a story about shame, dishonor, and future geopolitical conflicts. Yet, when interpreted through the intertextual perspective of the law codes the narrative takes on a darker, more dangerous interpretation. Several scholars have noted that the biblical legal codes serve an identity construction role rather than a juridical one. For example, Cheryl Anderson offers, "In the context of biblical laws, their ability to define appropriate behavior for an Israelite . . . is the way that these various identities are developed."[55] A consequence is that the Canaanites, who were originally insiders, become outsiders by the group that has been elevated due to the curse. As Jennifer Knust explains, "The curse as now presented was designed to heap blame on the Canaanites, who were to be subjugated, and to anticipate Israel's elevation to the status of blessed, an elevation that, in later books at least, would come at the Canaanites' expense."[56]

The outcome is that Ham's (unidentified) shameful act becomes sexualized as deviant and links Canaanite enslavement to sexual aberration, thus serving to differentiate the Israelites from their neighbors. Henrik Barth's groundbreaking research on ethnicity and boundaries demonstrates that despite their commonalities like shared origins or geographical territory, ethnic groups distinguish "us" versus "them" by establishing and maintaining boundaries around such differences as culture and behavior.[57] For the Canaanites, later redactors included additions that disparaged their culture and sexual behavior to justify their enslavement and elimination by the Israelites.

Once the sexual deviance of the Canaanites was firmly established, later readers were open to racial theories that coupled Ham's shame to the curse of blackness, which in turn racialized Ham and his descendants as Black. As such, Noah's curse of Canaan would eventually be regarded as a prophecy fulfilled concerning the condition of African-descended people as Ham's descendants condemned to be the "slaves of the slaves" to White Americans. How then did we get from a family story about filial dishonor to Black "hereditary slavery [having] been scripted as a biblical curse"?[58] The politics of belonging and the intersection of Noah's curse and racial boundary maintenance offer some answers.

BLACKNESS, SLAVERY, AND THE HEBREW BIBLE

The question of when blackness became associated with slavery accompanied by whether the Bible is responsible has been hotly debated since the late twentieth century. Three factors contribute to why the Bible came to be identified with the origin for associating blackness with slavery: they are geography, etymology, and proximity. The putative ancestors of Ham—Kush, Egypt, Put, and Canaan (Gen. 10:6ff; 1 Chron. 1:8)—and their geographical designations helped to fuel ideas that Ham was Black. Kush or Meroe has long been regarded as located in Africa south of Egypt. Put is believed to be in northeast Africa in modern-day Libya, and Canaan is northeast of Egypt in what is referred to as the southern Levant (also Transjordan). Taken together, Ham's lineage would cover parts of Africa, the Arabian Peninsula, and the Levant.

Many scholars point out that the groups listed here should not be regarded as representative of modern racial or ethnic groups or as accurately aligned to modern (or ancient) territorial designations.[59] Yet, there are still a number of scholars, ancient and modern, who claim with certainty the ability to locate the geographical designations of the peoples and nations identified as the putative ancestors of Kush, Egypt, and Put in ancient literature including the Bible, patristic texts, and medieval literature. However, there is no consensus around this matter.[60] For example, few scholars today agree that Kush identified in Genesis 10:6 is the ancestor of the Kassites through Nimrod in Genesis 10:11 who built a kingdom in Babylonia. Yet, despite the geographical and ethnic diversity of the areas supposedly inhabited by Ham's descendants and the difficulties with harmonizing the biblical genealogy in Genesis 10 with territories, these lands are widely regarded as representative of Black Africa in certain traditions and interpretations.[61] The phrase "sons of Ham" and "children of Ham" found in Jewish, Christian, and Islamic literature also

40   *Chapter 2*

frequently refers to Cushites, Ethiopians, and Nubians as Black Africans, which brings us to etymology as another contributing factor.

When it comes to the terms "Kush/Kushites" and "Ethiopia/Ethiopians," a number of scholars have noted the inconsistencies and inaccuracies in translations from the Hebrew to the early Greek and Latin.[62] For example, the terms Ethiopia and Ethiopian are the Greek and Latin translations from the Hebrew for Kush and Kushite. The Greek term *aithiops* (*aitho-* "burnt" + *ops-* "face") translated "Ethiopian" refers to African peoples, perhaps in comparison to the lighter-skinned Greeks.[63] Ancient sources regarded Africa as the furthermost edge of the earth. The Africans' darker-skin color was explained as due to Africa's proximity to the sun. The name "Kush" in the Hebrew Bible is largely regarded as a loan word from the Egyptians for the land adjacent to Egypt to the south, which the Egyptians also referred to as Nubia.[64] According to its order of appearance in Genesis 10:6, it is also the personal name for Ham's first-born son. Numerous researchers and onomastic lists have suggested a range of meanings for the term Kush from "darkness" and "blackness" to "dust" or "dirt." Yet, the meaning of the term Kush in Egyptian is indeterminate. Therefore, David Goldenberg suggests that these renderings are dependent on Greek translations of Ethiopia for Kush and not from Egyptian etymology. As such, Kush and the Kushites of the Hebrew Bible are not necessarily the same as Ethiopia and the Ethiopians of the New Testament.

Rodney Sadler notes the discontinuity between how the Hebrew Bible's authors knew the people they called Kushites and the reception by their Greek-speaking descendants of Kushites "not by their place of origin or ethnicity (Cush), but by an essentialist assessment of their phenotypical presentation, 'burnt face.'"[65] Where the etymological and geographical link between Kush and Ethiopia and black skin color is made by Greek observers can be understood, the same conclusion cannot be credibly made for Ham. Yet, Hebrew lexicons and Bible dictionaries list the name Ham both as the personal name of Noah's second son and as an adjective for "black," "brown," or "hot."[66] Still, BDB and HALOT do not offer an etymology for the name. David Neiman suggests that it derives from the Egyptian term *Khemi* for "Black Land" for Egypt.[67]

M. G. Kyle regards this etymology as "very attractive, but phonetically very improbable, to say the least."[68] By contrast, Kyle suggests that the etymology can be traced to the Egyptian god Min, who was also known by the name Khem, which he maintained was an exact Egyptian equivalent to Ham, Noah's second son. Kyle lets his racial bias show by further adding the sentiment, "That Ham the son of Noah should be deified in the Egyp [sic] pantheon is not surprising. The sensuality of this god Min or Khem also accords well with the reputation for licentiousness borne by Ham the son of Noah."[69] Goldenberg challenges all such etymologies for Ham as well. Instead, he suggests that its root is from Epigraphic Arabic for "to feel bad, ill," "to stink," "to go bad (of food),"[70] although he concedes that this origin of Ham's name also isn't definitive. Despite the lack of any conclusive evidence for the etymology of Ham as black or hot, Goldenberg notes the centuries-long identification of Ham with African lands.

A third factor, similar to geographical location for the linkage of blackness and slavery, is proximity. As previously mentioned, early contact with sub-Saharan Africa and its inhabitants exposed Greek and later Romans to a people who were markedly different from them in dress and appearance, whom they viewed as having "burnt" or black skin because they lived so close to the sun. Later, the expansion of Arab traders into East Africa, which turned into wars and conquests, expanded the growing numbers of non-Blacks having contact with Africans. Slavery was an accepted practice in the ancient world. Although a member of one's own ethnic or national group could be enslaved by another member, such as debt slavery (Exod. 21; Lev. 5), the tendency to enslave foreign peoples was greater. The likelihood of the enslavement of a foreigner, especially one who looked markedly different than oneself and spoke a different language was even greater. The increased contact between Black Africans and non-Blacks resulted in a marked expansion of the enslavement of Black Africans in antiquity. Yet, the increase in Black slaves in foreign lands did not mean that most slaves were Black but rather that their features made them more readily identifiable as a foreign slave. David Goldenberg remarks,

> The physiognomy of the black African is more readily distinguishable from the Greek, Roman, and Arab than, say, the physiognomy of the Syrian or the Persian. For this reason, and since most foreigners were slaves, the Black would more commonly be identified as a slave.[71]

Through increased contact between sub-Saharan Africans and Greeks and Romans, frequent incursions into the land by Arabs to acquire slave labor, and the foreign status of slaves who were more frequently becoming Black Africans, proximity became another influencing factor. Thus, geography, etymology, and proximity each contributed to the ideology associating blackness with slavery. However, the biblical text does not racialize Ham and his descendants as Black or as having Black skin. So how then did blackness and slavery come to be linked as divinely sanctioned on account of Noah's curse of Canaan?

42   *Chapter 2*

THE BLAME GAME

Ever since Winthrop Jordan's 1968 publication *White Over Black: American Attitudes toward the Negro, 1550–1812* was received with critical acclaim, it became popular to champion the assertion that midrashic, talmudic, and other rabbinic texts contributed to anti-Black sentiment which linked blackness and slavery. Although not the first, Jordan's was the most widely read on race relations in the United States.[72] A subject of analysis in Jordan's book is the progression of attitudes from antiquity to modernity after first encounters by non-Africans with Black Africans. He reported mindsets ranging from bemused by the novelty of black skin to inquiring about the origin of black skin color and the superiority of whiteness to blackness to outright anti-Black hostility. Of particular interest for some readers was his treatment of Jewish interpretations of Genesis 9:18–27 from antiquity and medieval times. For example, Jordan wrote,

> Talmudic and Midrashic sources contained such suggestions as "Ham was smitten in his skin," that Noah told Ham "your seed will be ugly and dark-skinned" and that Ham was "father of Canaan who brought curses into the world."[73]

For some reason the argument that such passages as those shown above were the source of anti-Black prejudice grew in influence. Over the last half century, several historians, religious scholars, and non-scholars alike have cited Jordan's book in support of such claims. For example, Hebrew Bible scholar Gene Rice citing Jordan in 1972 wrote, "The earliest evidence of a racist interpretation of Gen. 9:18–27 is found in Bereshit Rabbah."[74] Rice was referring to the early fifth century collection of rabbinic commentary on the book of Genesis located in Midrash Rabbah. Bereshit Rabbah 36:7 includes commentary on Genesis 9:25 that attempts to explain the age-old question why Canaan and not Ham is cursed. For example, one rabbi suggests that Noah cursed Ham's fourth son to be ugly and dark because Ham prevented Noah from begetting a fourth son (see above). However, further rabbinic back and forth adds that Ham came forth from the ark "black skinned" and that his descendants will be "ugly and dark-skinned" because Ham copulated in the ark (36:8).[75]

Midrash Tanchuma 12–15 (ca. 800–850 CE), expands on Genesis Rabbah 36: 3–8 in its interpretation of Genesis 9:18–27. Midrash Tanchuma Noach 12:9 notes that Ham was afflicted with dark skin for engaging in sexual relations on the ark. However, Stacy Davis observes, "Although the reading may not be the most enlightened explanation for the presence of melanin, it does not make a clear connection between blackness and perpetual servitude."[76] The same can be said for Bereshit Rabbah.

Some of these explanations attribute the origin of black skin color to sexual misconduct and even go so far as to maintain that Blacks are inherently sexually deviant because they descend from Ham. However, experts on the Talmud and Midrash point out that these texts comprise vast compilations of interpretations that developed over several centuries and contain a variety of genres, including history, fables, legends, theology, and ethics. The rabbinic deliberations on Genesis 9:24–27 represent fewer than eight texts in relation to the entirety of the collection.

Still, in the 1990s several Black religious scholars repeated the assertion that midrashic, talmudic, and medieval Jewish texts were the origins of anti-Black racism. For example, Charles B. Copher attributed to rabbinic sources the so-called "Old Hamite View," which based on Genesis 9:24–27, purportedly establishes that "Ham and/or Canaan, more often Ham, was turned black as a result of Noah's curse, and his descendants were doomed to bear the same color."[77] Cain Hope Felder, a colleague of Rice's, argued that Midrashim were responsible for providing the theological justification or *sacralization* of Genesis 9:18–27 in order to serve an ethnic group's agenda. He contended, "[W]e have much evidence of such sacralization in the Midrashim."[78] As late as 2008, Edward Wimberly repeated Copher's claim that rabbinic literature is to blame for the so-called curse of Ham and anti-Black bias. Wimberly noted, "In fact, Copher wrote that it is difficult to talk about the black presence in the Bible because the dominant perspectives for doing so come not from the biblical texts themselves but from rabbinic interpretations of some biblical texts."[79] They argue that American anti-Black biases can be traced to rabbinic literature.

Many scholars who make this claim also contend that Christian writers in antiquity were free of anti-Black bias until they discovered and borrowed Jewish interpretations of Genesis 9:18–27 in the medieval era. For example, Charles Copher wrote that Jewish and Christian interpreters adopted the Old Hamite View from midrashic and talmudic writings.[80] Similarly, Gene Rice maintained that a negative view of Blacks was not advanced in the ancient world, as it was "largely free of color prejudice."[81] However, there were Christian writings in antiquity that came to similar conclusions about black-skinned people based on Genesis 9:18–27 independent of the influence of Jewish writings. Origen (ca. 185–254) was just one among the church fathers to proffer that Ham's descendants were dark-skinned on account of Ham having dishonored his father.

The *Book of the Cave of Treasures* (sixth century CE), an anti-Semitic Syriac Christian work which expounds biblical stories, claims that Canaan was cursed because he revived the sin of Cain by making musical instruments and reintroduced dancing, singing, and lascivious behavior. The curse upon Canaan, to be a servant of servants, extended to his posterity, "that is

44 Chapter 2

to say, to the Egyptians, and the Cushites, and the MÛsâyê (Mysians), [and the Indians, and all the Ethiopians, whose skins are black]."[82] Thus although the author of *Cave of Treasures* does not explicity associate the curse with blackness, he does directly link slavery with sin. In contrast, Muslim stories passed down as early as the late sixth century implicitly associate slavery and blackness with Noah's curse. Through the combination of Muslim dark-skin etiologies and Noah's curse of slavery, Muslim stories of the biblical Noah were transformed into an independent dual-curse tradition with Ham as the one cursed by Noah.[83] Ham is twice cursed in Muslim traditions with enslavement and blackness.

Scholars point to the expansion of the Muslim world into sub-Saharan Africa, an increase in the African slave trade resulting from that expansion, and the growing association of blackness with hereditary servitude as contributing to the development of such narratives.[84] As the African slave trade grew in the Muslim world, various versions of the story of Noah's curse of Ham arose. According to Bernard Lewis, the theory of the descendants of Ham who were enslaved changed to suit the context: "The slaves of the Arabs were not Canaanites but blacks—so the curse was transferred to them, and blackness added to servitude as part of the hereditary burden"[85] while the non-Black descendants of Ham were excluded from the curse.

Versions of Noah's curse continued to be shared in the Muslim world, but the theory of Noah's curse did not gain significantly in Christianity until the fifteenth century when Europeans began to import slaves from Africa to British colonies.[86] With the exportation of Africans to the British colony in Virginia, pro-slavery Christians adopted the theory that Ham, whom they regarded as the ancestor of Black Africans, was the one who Noah cursed and thus justified slavery.

As documented above, Jewish, Muslim, and Christian writers interpreted Ham's transgressions and aftermaths from their own seats in life. Over time Noah's curse of Canaan was supplanted by Ham being the one cursed. On one hand, the theory of the Curse of Ham could not have taken on the racial overtones it acquired without the later biblical addition of the genealogical table of Ham's descendants in Genesis 10. It is from there that Ham became known as the progenitor of black-skinned people. On the other hand, racial constructions of black-skinned people as sexually perverted, licentious, bestial, and subject to hereditary slavery—thus unfit for citizenship—did not need a biblical curse for validation. Black people were already scripted culturally different than Europeans (and Muslims). As Kathryn Manzo explains, "the understanding of Africans as culturally inferior to Europeans meant that they could not be considered members of nations that defined themselves in cultural terms."[87] Therefore, while some believed that the change in environment by being removed from Africa improved the Africans' cultural status, "God's curse, on the other hand, was devoid of an expiration date; Ham's descendants were doomed to permanent exclusion."[88] Nonetheless, the exclusion of Blacks as belonging as members of the nation was supported on several fronts, but the theory of the Curse of Ham in the antebellum period provided the theological underpinning for the racial hierarchy that placed Whites at the top and Blacks at the bottom.

NOAH'S CURSE AND NINETEENTH CENTURY RACIAL POLITICS OF BELONGING

When the theory of the Curse of Ham became deeply rooted in American pro-slavery rhetoric is debated. The earliest use of the curse in America in the defense of African enslavement was in the seventeenth century. However, according to Edwin Yamauchi, scholars such as Elizabeth Fox-Genovese, Eugene D. Genovese, and B. Wood maintained that the theory of the Curse of Ham was not widely appropriated in America until the antebellum period leading up to the civil war.[89] Ronald Hendel describes the brewing theological dilemma in the mid-nineteenth century over how to interpret the legitimacy of slavery based on the book of Genesis. According to Hendel, in antebellum America, Genesis became a theological cudgel used by both liberal Christians and fundamentalist Christians to defend their positions on slavery.[90] In fact, Hendel states that there were three positions on the legitimacy of slavery based on the Bible: "the Bible supports slavery, the Bible opposes slavery, and slavery is wrong no matter what the Bible says."[91] Stephen Haynes contends that the crisis was developing even earlier. He wrote,

> By the 1830s—when the American anti-slavery movement became organized, vocal, and aggressive—the scriptural defense of slavery had evolved into the 'most elaborate and systematic statement of proslavery theory, Noah's curse had become a stock weapon in the arsenal of slavery's apologists, and references to Genesis 9 appeared prominently in their publications.[92]

According to John Patrick Daly, by the antebellum period the dissemination of publications using racist arguments in defense of slavery were pervasive. He writes, "Racist religious ideologies based on scripture, such as the so-called 'curse of ham' in Genesis 9, were used to justify enslavement of Africans before slavery was instituted in America. No society in history, however, produced nearly the volume of religious proslavery writings that appeared in the antebellum South."[93]

Fueling the popularity of anti-Black, proslavery religious literature was the growing strength of the abolitionist movement. They were also publishing an

46 Chapter 2

abundance of pamphlets, books, and speeches denouncing slavery. The invention of the cotton gin in 1793 increased the need for slave labor in the South to support their major source of economic productivity. The anti-slavery movement threatened to diminish such economic gains. White southerners would use whatever resources were within their reach, including combining race, science, and religion to protect their economic interests.

While some commentators have argued that intellectual elites eschewed linking Ham with blackness and slavery, there were historians and scientists who ascribed racial slavery to Ham and his descendants. Of course, supporters of the theory of Ham both secular and religious had to contend with how to account for racial diversity among the peoples of the earth if Noah and his sons were of the same race and the fact that not all of Ham's descendants were enslaved. Both were committed to using race to consign Blacks to servitude to Whites on the basis that their innate blackness made them morally, intellectually, and sexually inferior.

Many literalist readers of the Bible adhere to "monogenesis" or the theory that all humanity descended from a common ancestor Adam, who in their minds is White.[94] Therefore, they are left to contend with the challenge that if Noah and his sons were White then how did Ham become Black. One theory was that black skin color was the result of Africans having adapted to their environment after migrating geographically south close to the sun.[95] Another theory, although unsubstantiated by the Bible, was that although all humans descended from a common ancestor, Ham's skin color was changed black by a divine act.[96] However, an old theory with an American twist in the 1830s by proslavery advocates was "polygenesis" or "pre-Adamism."[97]

Polygenesis is the theory that the different races did not have a common ancestor but rather that each race had a separate and distinct ancestor contrary to the account in Genesis of a single human ancestor. Proslavery advocates adopted the racial theories of polygenists to argue that the lowly condition of Blacks as slaves was supported by science. Richard Colfax published the pamphlet *Evidence Against the Views of the Abolitionists* (1833) in defense of the view that Blacks could never belong as members of the nation because Blacks were by nature culturally and intellectually inferior to Whites. In his opinion, "*His want of capability to receive a complicated education renders it improper and impolitic, that he should be allowed the privileges of citizenship in an enlightened country!*" (italics in original).[98] Colfax based his claims in part on the science of phrenology, which purported that the allegedly small brain size of Blacks correlated with their lesser intelligence.

American naturalist and physician Josiah Clark Nott was a foremost defender of this theory in the antebellum period. He was well known for his controversial publication *Types of Mankind* (1854) coauthored with George Robins Gliddon. The book included exaggerated sketches of the facial features of Blacks to defend their position that Blacks were more apelike than human. Nott believed that Blacks possessed fixed behavioral traits, intellect, and a moral disposition that predisposed them to biological and cultural inferiority to Whites. He argued vociferously that, "under no conditions should we assume that the physical effects of the environment upon the human form could 'change a White man into a Negro.'"[99] *Types of Man* was well received by proslavery advocates; it sold out its first print and was reprinted for another nine editions. Although Nott maintained that his theories were based on science not theology, he nonetheless accepted the widely held Christian belief that the White race originated from Noah's sons.[100]

Men like Nott did not find slavery and racism antithetical to the democratic and egalitarian principles upon which the nation was founded. In the preface to Josiah Priest's tract *Slavery, as It Relates to the Negro, or African Race*, the publisher wrote in defense of Southern rights and institutions that the "peculiar institution" was in harmony with "the genius of republicanism, and the spirit of true Christianity" as it was in the "best interests of the inferior or African race in particular, in securing to him that protection and support which his native imbecility of intellect disqualifies him from accruing for himself."[101] Whether or not those who argued from anthropological, ethnological, or natural positions saw themselves as intellectual elites, the theologically determinative justification for slavery appears to have been the most widely accepted.

It should be said that many abolitionists, including Black clergyman Alexander Crummel, protested the misinterpretation of Noah's curse to justify slavery. In his 1853 pamphlet essay titled "The Negro Not Under a Curse," Crummel points to the plain reading of the text to insist, "Canaan was the person subjected to this curse. Neither directly nor indirectly is Ham, the father, denounced by Noah; and therefore we have the authority of the word of God, for the affirmation that the curse was *not* pronounced upon Ham" (emphasis original).[102] Concerning the argument that Blacks were under the prophetic judgment of a curse as the children of Ham, Crummell contended:

> The facts of the case warrant the most positive denial of the assertion that the Negro race are the descendants of Canaan. *In fact, of all of the sons of Ham, Canaan was the only one who never entered Africa* (emphasis original). Of this there is abundant evidence, sacred and profane.[103]

Crummell's point was that regardless of whether Noah's malediction was intended for Ham or Canaan, the argument made by proslavery proponents for the enslavement of Blacks based on Genesis 9:25, even some of the most learned divines of his time, was a deliberate misinterpretation for self-interests.

48   Chapter 2

Yet, Josiah Priest's tract perhaps did more to advance proslavery apologetics in the antebellum period using the Curse of Ham, than any other effort.[104] Priest offers a fanciful tale of the origin of the Africans' black skin complexion and racial slavery. According to Priest, first Adam and then Noah, his wife, and son Shem had red skin complexions, but God turned Japheth's skin white and Ham's skin black in their mother's womb. He claimed, as others before him, that the name Ham was Egyptian for "black." Priest's belief that Ham was the progenitor of the African race was not an outlier. Nor was his position that Noah cursed Ham by divine judicial decree for Ham's display of filial disrespect for his father.[105] On this count, Stephen Haynes agrees that Southern antebellum readings of Genesis 9:20–27 "understood the transgression as a violation of familial loyalty [that] marked Ham and his African descendants as utterly devoid of honor and thus fit for slavery."[106] However, Priest's interpretation beyond the honor-bound southern interpretation had far reaching implications.

A CURSE, RACE, GENDER, AND SEXUALITY

Abolitionist arguments against the denigration of Black humanity to justify slavery did not prevent the likes of Josiah Priest to go so far as to sexualize Ham's transgression in Genesis 9:22, 24 in their defense. Priest repeats the sexual innuendo of earlier biblical interpreters that Ham was guilty not just of seeing his father's nakedness and violating his honor by failing to cover him but also of engaging in sexual relations with his father's wife. Priest commented, "On account of *this* passage, it has been believed that the crime of Ham did not consist alone of seeing his father in an improper manner, but rather of his own mother, the wife of Noah, and of violating her."[107] Priest wrote that this was in keeping with the whole character, nature, and constitution of Ham and the Black race, which he described as sensual, devilish, lewd, promiscuous, and indifferent to the "regulations of virtuous principles."[108] Therefore, he maintained, "For these things, as foreseen, they were adjudged judicially, together with Ham, as an inferior race of men, and could never be elevated on account of their natures.[109] Priest's sexually provocative account of Ham's curse was widely shared in a short period of time and was reprinted eight times in a five-year period.[110]

Following from his belief that Blacks were sexually degenerate, Priest and likeminded White supremacists viewed sex between the races with disgust, an act which they saw as a transgression against the laws of nature and God. Polygenist Josiah Nott referred to the offspring of White and Black unions as "hybrids" with a shorter life span, more prone to disease, and less capable of hard work.[111] For some, race mixing was akin to bestiality and would thus

Outsider Within

49

diminish the White race. His peer, Richard Colfax challenged his readers to examine the "detestable and disgusting scheme of amalgamation in all its bearings, let us analize [sic] the *principle* which dictated it, the *persons* who proposed it, and above all let us consider who are to be benefitted by this revolting attempt to destroy our nationality" (italics in original).[112] Each one appealed to Noah's curse for justification against interracial sexual relations. The intersection of race, gender, and sexuality is on display in dividing "us" and "them" based on a biblical mandate.

David Croly coined the term *miscegenation*—from the Latin *miscere*, "to mix" and *Genus*, race—or "the blending of the various races of men" in an 1864 pamphlet titled *Miscegenation: The Theory of the Blending of the Races, Applied to the American White Man and the Negro*. The pamphlet, circulated anonymously, purported to support race mixing by claiming that it was essential for the progress of humanity. It included such claims as, "Providence has kindly placed on the American soil for his own wise purposes four millions of colored people . . . By mingling with them we become powerful, prosperous, and progressive."[113]

By contrast, White supremacists believed that the superiority of the White race would be weakened by mixing with the Black race. They took on the issue of miscegenation to discredit the anti-slavery movement by arguing that abolitionists wanted to "marry negresses to your sons" and "give your daughters to negroes."[114] When President Abraham Lincoln ran for re-election on the campaign platform that he would not end the war until the south rejoined the north and abolished slavery, supporters of his opponent, George McClellan, published a racist political cartoon exploiting "White Americans' fears about interracial sex. The political caricature depicted a fictional 'Miscegenation Ball at the Headquarters of the Lincoln Central Campaign Club'"[115] that featured White men frolicking with Black women. The message was: if Lincoln were re-elected racial mixing was ensured. It turns out that the miscegenation pamphlet by Croly was a hoax intended to inflame anti-abolitionist sentiments and influence the election. Although his election interference failed, he succeeded in keeping interracial relationships objectionable.[116]

In White supremacists' and segregationists' minds, the best way to prevent this was to keep the races separate. From school boards to state legislatures, racially discriminatory statutes were enacted across the country prohibiting interracial dating and marriage. The same scientific and biblical arguments that made slavery constitutional were deployed to segregate schools and ban miscegenation by law. For example, Keith Sealing cites a state legislator, arguing against miscegenation in the context of the monogeny/polygeny debate, who stated, "[I] do know from Holy Writ that the negro race, whether they belong to the same race as we do or to a higher order of animals, are under the ban of heaven—a curse that was pronounced upon them by

50   *Chapter 2*

Almighty God still remains upon them."[117] For White supremacists, their belief that Black racial inferiority posed a threat to democracy if Blacks were given equal rights forced them to resist all efforts at full inclusion of Blacks as full citizens of the United States by birthright or naturalization. The political project of White superiority was securely in place.

CONCLUSION

The political project of White superiority constructed citizenship and belonging along a racial caste system that marked Whites as the "'default category' of Americanness"[118] and Blacks as the racially inferior other. Although Whites used several processes to construct boundaries excluding Blacks as members of the nation, the theory of the Curse of Ham proved effective in advancing slavery and discrimination against Blacks. Hebrew Bible authors did not link blackness and perpetual slavery. Rabbinic, Islamic, and Christian writings connected blackness and sexuality. But the biblical writers did not imagine that Noah's curse would be used by nineteenth century White slaveholders and segregationists to divide the world into "us" and "them." They linked blackness, perpetual servitude, and sexuality. Blackness, slavery, and sexuality intersected to construct and maintain the boundaries of separation in the United States.

The racist biblical justifications for the enslavement of Blacks were not new to the American nationalist project. However, the growing influence of the abolitionist movement in the antebellum period engendered a proliferation of proslavery sermons, tracts, and books by clergy espousing the Curse of Ham to denigrate Black sexuality and humanity. As Kelly Brown Douglas stated, "Such dehumanization [has] made it easier to enslave Black people and to treat them merely as property and labor commodities rather than as human beings."[119] Nineteenth century Americans may have accepted the then commonly held belief that the biblical account of human descent from a common ancestor and Noah's curse on the descendants of Ham, "the original negro" sanctioned the enslavement of Blacks.[120] But it was the judicial system, deeply imbued with the doctrine of Black inferiority, that emboldened proslavery apologists and segregationists, as the opinion of Supreme Court Chief Justice Roger Taney in *Scott v. Sanford* (1857) demonstrated.

Taney's opinion was that Blacks descended from enslaved Africans were not American citizens with standing to sue in federal court. Taney was predisposed to deny Black citizenship based on his belief that Blacks were of a human order inferior to Whites, beliefs that he appeared to share with fellow segregationists in the superiority of Whites to Blacks and other non-Whites based in biblical teachings. Thus, the two documents most valuable to

Blacks—the Bible and the Constitution—were used to deny them citizenship based on race. Yet, the pursuit of freedom and citizenship was never far from the American Blacks' minds. As Martha Jones explains, for Blacks, particularly free Blacks, "Birthright citizenship was a fully formed idea by the early 1850s" not to be denied them without a struggle.[121] She quotes Frederick Douglass's address to the 1853 Colored National Convention in Rochester, New York, advocating for Black citizenship: "By birth, we are American citizens; by the principles of the Declaration of Independence, we are American citizens."[122] As such, for Blacks, Taney's question whether the negro, whose ancestors were kidnapped and bought and sold as chattel could become full US citizens under the Constitution with all rights pursuant, the answer was a resounding yes—because the Bible told them so.

NOTES

1. *Noye's Fludde* is one among the *Chester Miracle Plays*, a collection of 25 short dramas based on biblical stories written by Sir Henry Francis (ca. 1375) of England, Carl Gerbrandt, *Sacred Music Drama: The Guide*, 2nd ed. (Bloomington, IL: AuthorHouse, 2006), 90–91.

2. That distinction goes to the Sumerian myth about a pious hero named Ziusudra in the third millennium BCE, who is warned by a deity of the impending flood, builds an ark for survival, taking his family, animals, and seeds aboard with him. This story, referred to by modern scholars as the Eridu Genesis, named for Eridu, the first city raised by the Mesopotamian gods and where Ziusudra hailed from, inspired the later Babylonian flood myths in the Epic of Atrahasis and the Epic of Gilgamesh. For an analysis of Ham and Noah in Darren Aronofsky's 2014 Noah film, see Justin Reed, "'How—How Is This Just?!': How Aronofsky and Handel Handle Noah's Curse," in *Noah as Antihero: Darren Aronofsky's Cinematic Deluge*, ed. Rhonda Burnette-Bletsch and Jon Morgan (New York: Routledge, 2017), 145–60.

3. Phyllis Trible spoke of texts that caused harm to women as "texts of terror" in *Texts of Terror: Literary Feminist Readings in Biblical Narratives* (Philadelphia: Fortress, 1984).

4. A. Leon Higginbotham Jr., *Shades of Freedom: Racial Politics and Presumptions of the American Legal Process* (New York: Oxford University Press, 1996), 9.

5. Stephen Steinberg, *The Ethnic Myth: Race, Ethnicity, and Class in America* (Boston: Beacon, 2001), 31.

6. John Crowley, "The Politics of Belonging: Some Theoretical Considerations," in *The Politics of Belonging: Migrants and Minorities in Contemporary Europe*, ed. Andrew Geddess and Adrian Favell (Brookfield, VT: Ashgate, 1999), 22.

7. Erika Harris, *Nationalism: Theories and Cases* (Edinburgh: Edinburgh University Press, 2009), 22–23.

8. Nira Yuval-Davis, *The Politics of Belonging: Intersectional Contestations* (London: Sage, 2011), 48.

52   *Chapter 2*

9. Natalie Masuoka and Jane Junn, *The Politics of Belonging: Race, Public Opinion, and Immigration* (Chicago: University of Chicago Press, 2013), 42.

10. Winthrop Jordan, *The White Man's Burden: Historical Origins of Racism in the United States* (Oxford: Oxford University Press), 1974, 6.

11. John Stanfield, "Theoretical and Ideological Barriers to the Study of Race-Making," *Research in Race and Ethnic Relations* 4 (1985): 161.

12. Thomas Peterson, *Ham and Japheth: The Myth World of White in the Antebellum South* (Metuchen, NJ: Scarecrow, 1978), 5.

13. Bereshit Rabbah 23:3 resolves the anonymity of Noah's wife by identifying her as the "sister of Tuval Kain" of Genesis 4:22 fame, whose name was Na'amah, or "pleasant one." Although the wife of Noah is included among unnamed mothers in the primordial period, the text is ambiguous regarding whether she is the mother of Noah's sons. This is due to the absence of the phrase, "knew his wife" and the *toledoth begot* formula. Thus, Alice Laffey refers to Noah's "wives" in *An Introduction to the Old Testament: A Feminist Perspective* (Philadelphia: Fortress, 1988), 9.

14. Ilona N. Rashkow, "Daddy-Dearest and the 'Invisible Spirit of Wine'" in *A Feminist Companion to Genesis*, ed. Athalya Brenner (Sheffield: Sheffield Academic, 1998), 82–107.

15. Tikva Frymer-Kensky, *Reading the Women of the Bible* (New York: Schocken, 2002).

16. Wilda Gafney, *Womanist Midrash: A Reintroduction to the Women of the Torah and the Throne* (Louisville: Westminster John Knox, 2017).

17. Julie Ringold, "Noach (6:9–11:32): Mrs. Noah" in *The Women's Torah Commentary: New Insights from Women Rabbis on the 54 Weekly Torah Portions*, ed. Elyse Goldstein (Woodstock, VT: Jewish Lights, 2000), 53–56. See also, Carol L. Meyers, Toni Craven, and Ross Shepard Kraemer, eds., *Women in Scripture: A Dictionary of Named and Unnamed Women in the Hebrew Bible, the Apocryphal and Deuterocanonical Books, and the New Testament* (Boston: Houghton Mifflin, 2000). It mentions the women in Genesis 9 among lists of unnamed women in the Hebrew Bible.

18. Susan Niditch, "Genesis" in *Women's Bible Commentary*, rev. and updated, ed. Carol A. Newsom, Sharon H. Ringe, and Jacqueline E. Lapsley (Louisville: Westminster John Knox, 2012), 27–45.

19. Kåre Berge, "Categorical Identities: 'Ethnified Otherness and Sameness'—A Tool for Understanding Boundary Negotiation in the Pentateuch?" in *Imagining the Other and Constructing Israelite Identity in the Early Second Temple Period,* ed. Ehud Ben Zvi and Diana V. Edelman (London: Bloomsbury, 2014).

20. Nira Yuval-Davis "Nationalist Projects and Gender Relations," *Nar. Umjet* 40, no. 1 (2003): 12.

21. The Hebrew is literally "man and his woman/wife" and is attributed to the J source. The phrase "male and female" is attributed to the Priestly circle.

22. There is an interruption in the pattern in Genesis 5:32 with the birth of Noah. The genealogical list does not report that Noah became the father of named firstborn son but rather lists all three of his sons at once. Moreover, the report is followed by a

lengthy narrative about Noah and the flood, only to return to the genealogical pattern in Genesis 9:28–29 with the notice of his death.

23. Elizabeth Goldstein, *Impurity and Gender in the Hebrew Bible* (Lanham, MD: Rowman & Littlefield 2015), 17; see also Julie Kelso, *O Mother, Where Art Thou? An Irigarayan Reading of the Book of Chronicles* (London: Equinox, 2007), 144, who points to the use of "3ms, mono-productive verbs" in the birth narratives in the genealogies in 1 Chronicles 1–9, which suppresses the maternal body in the religio-political construction of Israel's past in Chronicles. Procreation also occurs without women in the genealogical lists in 1 Chronicles, which include Noah and his sons (1 Chron. 1:4) but with a significant difference. In the NRSV the Hebrew verb *yalad* is translated "became the father of" in both Genesis 5 and 1 Chronicles 1–9, obscuring the distinction between the forms of the verb in each instance. The *hiphil* form of *yalad* translated "beget" in Genesis 5 means "to cause the birth of." The participation of women is at least inferred here. However, in 1 Chronicles the *qal* perfect form translated "to bear or give birth to" indicates that the males give birth. "It is this decorporealized, symbolic understanding of 'origin' that makes possible an appropriation of this verb of giving birth, ילד, by the men of this story." Kelso, 212.

24. Elleke Boehme, *Stories of Women: Gender and Narrative in the Postcolonial Nation* (New York: Manchester University Press, 2005).

25. Martin Kessler and Karel Deurloo, *A Commentary on Genesis: The Book of Beginnings* (New York: Paulist, 2004).

26. Hermann Gunkel, *Genesis,* trans. Mark E. Biddle (Macon, GA: Mercer University Press, 1997); see also, Claus Westermann, *Genesis 1–11: A Commentary*, trans. John J. Scullion (Minneapolis: Augsburg, 1984).

27. John Skinner, *A Critical and Exegetical Commentary on Genesis* (New York: Charles Scribner's Sons, 1910), 182.

28. Gerhard von Rad, *Genesis: A Commentary*, Old Testament Library, trans. John H. Marks (Philadelphia: Westminster, 1972), 135–36.

29. The general consensus is that Genesis 19:18–28 is a conflation of J and P, as evidenced by the use of both divine names in verses 26–27. Moreover, aside from the introduction of Noah's three sons in verses 18–19, all other references to the names Shem, Ham, and Japheth belong to the Priestly tradition.

30. Thomas Brodie, *Genesis as Dialogue: A Literary, Historical, and Theological Commentary* (Oxford: Oxford University Press, 2001), 191.

31. Devora Steinmetz, "Vineyard, Farm, and Garden: The Drunkenness of Noah in the Context of Primeval History," *Journal of Biblical Literature* 113, no. 2 (Summer 1994): 194.

32. Walter Brueggemann, *Genesis*, Interpretation: A Bible Commentary for Teaching and Preaching (Atlanta: John Knox, 1982), 89.

33. Ronald Gowan, *Genesis 1–11: From Eden to Babel* (Grand Rapids: Eerdmans, 1989), 107.

34. Brodie, *Genesis as Dialogue*, 192.

35. Skinner, *A Critical and Exegetical Commentary on Genesis*, 182.

36. The Book of the Covenant consists of Exodus 20:23–23:19 and is largely regarded by scholars as reflecting the premonarchic period (1200–1000 BCE).

54   *Chapter 2*

37. *Pudenda* is a Latin term meaning "the shameful (parts)," from the verb *pundēre*, "to be ashamed."

38. The Holiness Code is largely regarded as post-exilic supplemental material to the priestly strata of the Priestly redaction.

39. See, for example, Frederick Bassett, "Noah's Nakedness and the Curse of Canaan: A Case of Incest?" *Vetus Testamentum* 21, no. 2 (1971).

40. Genesis 19:30–38 is the other narrative about drunkenness leading to parent-child incest when Lot engaged in an incestuous relationship with his daughters while under the influence.

41. G. Johannes Botterweck, trans. David E. Green, *Theological Dictionary of the Old Testament,* Vol. XI 'zz–pānîm (Grand Rapids, MI: Eerdmans, 2001), 346.

42. Steinmetz, "Vineyard, Farm, and Garden," 198.

43. Anthony Phillips, "Uncovering the Father's Skirt," *Vetus Testamentum* 30, no. 1 (1980): 41.

44. Randall Bailey, "'They're Nothing But Incestuous Bastards': The Polemical Use of Sex and Sexuality in Hebrew Canon Narratives," in *Reading from This Place*, vol. 1, ed. Fernando F. Segovia and Mary Ann Tolbert (Minneapolis: Fortress, 1993), 133.

45. David Gilmore, "Introduction: The Shame of Dishonor," in *Honor and Shame and the Unity of the Mediterranean*, ed. David Gilmore (Washington, DC: American Anthropological Association, 1987), 2–21.

46. Bailey, "They're Nothing But Incestuous Bastards," 134.

47. Until Genesis 9:25 the deity did the blessing and cursing (see Gen. 9:1).

48. Bassett, "Noah's Nakedness and the Curse of Canaan," 232.

49. According to *The Book of the Cave of Treasures*, Noah's wife told him that Ham had seen his nakedness and laughed at his father and made a mockery of him. *The Book of the Cave of Treasures*, trans. E. A.Wallis Budge, ed. Christopher M. Weimer (London: The Religious Tract Society, 1927), Sacred Texts, https://sacred-texts.com /chr/bct/bct06.htm.

50. Hermann Gunkel, *Genesis*, trans. Mark E. Biddle (Macon, GA: Mercer University Press, 1997), 80; see also Nahum Sarna, *Genesis: The JPS Torah Commentary* (Philadelphia: The Jewish Publication Society, 1989).

51. As an example, F. W. Bassett, who argues that the offense was sexual in nature based on the idiom "to uncover the nakedness of someone," contends that Ham had sexual relations with Noah's wife. He concludes that Canaan is the offspring of this union in "Noah's Nakedness and the Curse of Canaan," 235.

52. b. Sanh 70a opines that Ham sodomized then castrated Noah, as an explanation for why Noah did not have any progeny after the flood. Some modern scholars maintain that an ancient castration myth lies behind Genesis 9:24. However, Albert Baumgarten, "Myth and Midrash: Genesis 9:20–29," in *Christianity, Judaism, and other Greco-Roman Cults, Studies for Morton Smith at Sixty*, vol. 3, ed. Jacob Neusner (Leiden: Brill, 1975), 67, argues that the motif of castration of the father is not a suppressed pre-existing biblical tradition but is a third century CE rabbinic creation. Stephen Gero, "The Legend of the Fourth Son of Noah," *Harvard Theological Review* 73, nos. 1–2 (Jan–Apr 1980): 329, agrees that the castration story was not a

Outsider Within 55

rabbinic invention to explain an obscure biblical text, but rather argues that underneath the castration story is an attempt to suppress the Jewish legend Yonton, Noah's postdiluvian fourth son, by accusing him of emasculating his father.

53. Thomas W. Mann, *The Book of the Torah: The Narrative Integrity of the Pentateuch* (Atlanta: John Knox, 1988), 25.

54. Bailey, "They're Nothing But Incestuous Bastards," 134.

55. Cheryl Anderson, *Women, Ideology and Violence: Critical Theory and the Construction of Gender in the Book of the Covenant and the Deuteronomic Law* (London: T&T Clark, 2006), 13.

56. Jennifer Knust, "Who's Afraid of Canaan's Curse? Genesis 9:18–29 and the Challenge of Reparative Reading," *Biblical Interpretation* 22 (2014): 393.

57. Fredrik Barth, *Ethnic Groups and Boundaries* (Boston: Little, Brown and Company), 1969.

58. Kathryn Manzo, *Creating Boundaries: The Politics of Race and Nation* (Boulder, CO: Lynne Rienner, 1996), 49.

59. Eugene F. Roop, *Genesis. Believers Church Bible Commentary* (Scottdale, Ontario: Herald, 1987). For example, Ham's son Kush, the eponymous ancestor of the nation of Kush in sub-Saharan Africa or modern-day Sudan, has many descendants identified as countries located on the southern and southwestern parts of the Arabian Peninsula (Gen. 10:6–7). A separate tradition is inserted following Genesis 10:7, evidenced by the shift in style ("the descendants of"), which links Assyria (Asshur) to Ham through Nimrod and Kush (Gen. 10:8–12; cf. 10:22).

60. For an extensive treatment on the varying geographical locations of Kush and Ethiopia and the ethnic identities of Kushites and Ethiopians see David Goldenberg's section on the biblical land of Kush in *The Curse of Ham: Race and Slavery in Early Judaism, Christianity, and Islam* (Princeton: Princeton University Press, 2003).

61. The phrase "black Africa" or "black African" is used in this chapter to mean the groups of people located on the continent of Africa considered black-skinned and would be deemed "Negro" or "Black" by modern racial constructs. For an extensive treatment of the arguments on whether the ancient Egyptians were Black see, Ann Macy Roth, "Building Bridges to Afrocentricism: A Letter to My Egyptological Colleagues," University of Pennsylvania—African Studies Center, January 26, 1995, http://www.africa.upenn.edu/Articles_Gen/afrocent_roth.html.

Roth includes in her discussion on the color of the ancient Egyptians that modern Egyptians, by contemporary western standards, would consider themselves as White. However, a recent study by Meda Maghbouleh, Ariela Schachter, and René D. Flores, "Middle Eastern and North African Americans May Not Be Perceived, nor Perceive Themselves, to Be White," in *The Proceedings of the National Academy of Sciences* 119, no. 7 (2022), https://doi.org/10.1073/pnas.2117940119, found that a majority of people of Middle Eastern and North African (MENA) origins in the United States see themselves as other than White, while Whites also may not see themselves as White despite the US government classifying MENA as White.

62. See, for example, Gay L. Byron, *Symbolic Blackness and Ethnic Difference in Early Christianity* (New York: Routledge, 2002); also, David Goldenberg, *The Curse of Ham: Race and Slavery in Early Judaism, Christianity, and Islam*

56   *Chapter 2*

(Princeton: Princeton University Press, 2003); also. Rodney Sadler, *Can A Cushite Change His Skin? An Examination of Race, Ethnicity, and Othering in the Hebrew Bible* (New York: T&T Clark, 2005).

63. Prudence Jones, "Africa: Greek and Roman Perspectives from Homer to Apuleius," Center for Hellenic Studies: Harvard University, https://chs.harvard.edu/read/jones-prudence-j-africa-greek-and-roman-perspectives-from-homer-to-apuleius.

64. Goldenberg, *The Curse of Ham*, 17. Goldenberg cites Georges Posener, who contends in an article that the name Kush might have Nubian, not Egyptian origins. See also Goldenberg's cited sources for others who have attempted to locate the origin of the name Kush (215n1, 216n5).

65. Sadler, *Can A Cushite Change His Skin?*, 17.

66. BDB lists חם as both a personal name and geographical location. Ham is described as the second son of Noah, "called father of Canaan and of various peoples; these people were inhabitants of southern lands." חם is also referred to collectively as a name for Egyptians (see, e.g., Ps. 105:23–27, 106:22, 75:51), and an adjective for "warm," "hot." HALOT III lists חם as the son of Noah, father of Canaan, poetic for Egypt, and "all those who dwell in the lands of the south."

67. David Neiman, "The Two Genealogies of Japheth" in *Orient and Occident: Essays Presented to Cyrus H. Gordon on the Ocassion of His Sixty-Fifth Birthday*, ed. H. A. Hoffner (Kevelaer: Butzon & Bercker, 1973).

68. M. G. Kyle, "Entry for 'Mizraim,'" in *International Standard Bible Encyclopedia*, 1915, https://www.biblestudytools.com/encyclopedias/isbe/mizraim.html.

69. Kyle, "Entry for 'Mizraim.'"

70. David Goldenberg, *Black and Slave: The Origins and History of the Curse of Ham. Studies of the Bible and Its Reception* (Berlin: De Gruyter, 2017), 149.

71. Goldenberg, *The Curse of Ham*, 136.

72. See also Thomas Gossett, *Race: The History of an Idea in America* (Dallas: Southern Methodist University Press, 1963) and David Brion Davis, *The Problem of Slavery in Western Culture* (Ithaca, NY: Cornell University Press, 1966), who earlier expressed similar views but were not as well known as Jordan, the former whom Jordan relied on.

73. Jordan, *The White Man's Burden*, 18. The Talmud contains mostly legal writings but also includes fables, folklore, legends, theology, and ethics.

74. Gene Rice, "The Curse that Never Was (Genesis 9:18–27)," in *Biblical Studies Alternatively: An Introductory Reader*, ed. Susanne Scholz (Upper Saddle River, NJ: Prentice Hall, 2003), 223.

75. Bereshit Rabbah 36:7 (The Sefaria Midrash Rabbah, 2022), https://www.sefaria.org/Bereshit_Rabbah?tab=contents. Sanhedrin 108b:15 (The William Davidson Talmud), https://www.sefaria.org/Sanhedrin.108b?lang=bi, an earlier Talmudic interpretation (third-century CE) maintains that Ham was afflicted with black skin for cohabiting in the ark—the very thing that Noah is supposed to have condemned Ham for preventing him from doing—as God had forbidden it.

76. Stacy Davis, *This Strange Story: Jewish and Christian Interpretation of the Curse of Canaan from Antiquity to 1865* (Lanham, MD: Unversity Press of America, 2008), 40.

77. Charles Copher, "The Black Presence in the Old Testament" in *Stony the Road: African American Biblical Interpretation*, ed. Cain Hope Felder (Minneapolis: Fortress, 1991), 147.

78. Cain Hope Felder, "Race, Racism, and the Biblical Narratives" in *Stony the Road We Trod: African American Biblical Interpretation*, ed. Cain Hope Felder (Minneapolis: Fortress, 1991), 132. See also, Joseph Washington, Jr., *Anti-Blackness in English Religion, 1500–1800* (New York: Edwin Mellen, 1984).

79. Edward Wimberly, "Beyond the Curse of Noah: African American Pastoral Theology as Political" in *African American Religious Life and the Story of Nimrod*, ed. Anthony Pinn and Dwight Allen Callahan (New York: Palgrave MacMillan, 2008), 181–82.

80. Charles Copher, "The Black Presence in the Old Testament," 147.

81. Rice, "The Curse that Never Was (Genesis 9:18–27)," 223. By contrast, Gay Byron, in *Symbolic Blackness and Ethnic Difference in Early Christianity* (London; New York: Routledge, 2002) examines attitudes towards Egyptians, Ethiopians, and Blacks in ancient Christian literature and contends that Snowden over-emphasized the positive evaluation of Blacks in antiquity.

82. *Book of the Cave of Treasures*.

83. Goldenberg, *Black and Slave*.

84. See, for example, Davis, *The Problem of Slavery in Western Culture*; also, Bernard Lewis, *Race and Slavery in the Middle East* (New York: Oxford University Press, 1990); also, Goldenberg, *Black and Slave*.

85. Lewis, *Race and Slavery in the Middle East*, 55.

86. Edwin Yamauchi, "The Curse of Ham," *Criswell Theological Review* 6, no 2 (Spring 2009): 45–60.

87. Manzo, *Creating Boundaries*, 61.

88. Manzo, 61.

89. Yamauchi, "The Curse of Ham."

90. Ronald Hendel, *The Book of Genesis: A Biography* (Princeton: Princeton University Press, 2013).

91. Hendel, 197.

92. Stephen R. Haynes, *Noah's Curse: The Biblical Justification of American Slavery* (Oxford: Oxford University Press, 2002), 8.

93. John Patrick Daly, "Holy War: Southern Religion and the Road to War and Defeat," *North & South: The Magazine of the Civil War Conflict* 6, no. 6 (2003): 36.

94. Mitochondrial DNA has since shown that all humans are descended from the same ancestor from Africa. John McClendon III begins with the premise that as a legend, Noah can be imaged as Black in *Philosophy of Religion and the African American Experience* (Leiden: Brill, 2017).

95. Terence D. Keel, "Religion, Polygenism and the Early Science of Human Origins," *History of the Human Sciences* 26, 2 (2013): 26.

96. For example, Josiah Priest was certain that the skin color of the first human was red, to include Shem but that God turned Noah's sons Japheth and Ham's skin white and black, respectively. Josiah Priest, *Slavery, as It Relates to the Negro, or African Race, Examined in the Light of Circumstancs, History and the Holy Scriptures; with*

an *Account of the Origin of the Black Man's Color, Causes of His State of Servitude and Traces of His Character as Well in Ancient as in Modern Times; with Strictures on Abolitionism* (Albany: C. Van Benthuysen, 1843), https://archive.org/details/slaveryasitrela00priegoog/page/n6/mode/2up.

97. Isaac de la Preyére first published the theory of pre-Adamism in 1655. Keel, "Religion, Polygenism," 5.

98. Richard H. Colfax, *Evidence Against the Views of the Abolitionists: Consisting of Physical and Moral Proofs, of the Natural Inferiority of the Negroes* (New York: J. T. M. Bleakley, 1833), 26, https://www.loc.gov/item/11006103/.

99. Keel, "Religion, Polygenism," 4.

100. Keel, 12.

101. W. S. Brown, publisher's preface to *Bible Defence of Slavery: and Origin, Fortunes, and History of the Negro Race,* 5th ed., by Josiah Priest (Glasgow, KY: W. S. Brown, 1852), vi, https://www.loc.gov/item/11011710/.

102. Alexander Crummell, "The Negro Not Under a Curse," *Black Abolitionist Papers,* http://blackfreedom.proquest.com/wp-content/uploads/2020/09/crummell8.pdf.

103. Crummell, "The Negro Not Under a Curse."

104. Priest, *Slavery.* The book was reprinted in 1853 as *Bible Defence of Slavery.*

105. Priest, *Slavery.*

106. Haynes, *Noah's Curse,* 67.

107. Priest, *Slavery.*

108. Priest, *Slavery.*

109. Priest, *Slavery.*

110. Haynes, *Noah's Curse,* 76.

111. Nott was building on the theories of his mentor Morton who used the term "hybrids" to refer to the biracial offspring of Blacks and Whites according to Gabriel Alvarez, "Defining Race: Antebellum Racial Scientists' Influences on Proslavery Writers," *The Concord Review,* 2011, https://www.commschool.org/uploaded/publications/cm/cm-1-spring-2012/Concord-Review-Alvarez.pdf.

112. Colfax, *Evidence Against the Views of the Abolitionists,* 31.

113. David G. Croly, *Miscegenation: The Theory of the Blending of the Races, Applied to the American White Man and Negro,* Alfred Whital Stern Collection of Lincolniana, and Joseph Meredith Toner Collection (New York: H. Dexter, Hamilton & co, 1864). https://www.loc.gov/item/05009520/.

114. Colfax, *Evidence Against the Views of Abolitionists.*

115. Becky Little, "How the Union Pulled Off a Presidential Election During the Civil War," *History.com,* April 3, 2020, https://www.history.com/news/civil-war-presidential-election-abraham-lincoln.

116. Mark Sussman, "The 'Miscegenation Troll,'" *JSTOR Daily,* February 20, 2019, https://daily.jstor.org/the-miscegenation-troll/.

117. Keith Sealing, "Blood Will Tell: Scientific Racism and the Legal Prohibitions Against Miscegenation," *Michigan Journal of Race & Law* 5, no. 2 (2000): 559–609, https://repository.law.umich.edu/mjrl/vol5/iss2/1.

118. Masuoka and Junn, *The Politics of Belonging,* 59.

119. Kelly Brown Douglas, *Sexuality and the Black Church: A Womanist Perspective* (Maryknoll, NY: Orbis, 1999), 23–24.

120. Sylvester A. Johnson, *The Myth of Ham in Nineteenth-Century American Christianity: Race, Heathens, and the People of God* (New York: Palgrave MacMillan, 2004), 37.

121. Martha S. Jones, *Birthright Citizens: A History of Race and Rights in Antebellum America* (Cambridge: Cambridge University Press, 2018), 90.

122. Jones, 90.

Chapter 3

Mammies, Jezebels, Prophetesses, and Royal Women

Symbolic Border Guards in the Deuteronomistic History

It took only two days after the inauguration of Kamala Harris, the first woman, Black, and South Asian, as vice president of the United States on January 21, 2021, to be called "Jezebel." The epithet was hurled at her by Pastor Tom Buck of First Baptist Church in Lindale, Texas, who tweeted, "I can't imagine any truly God-fearing Israelite who would've wanted their daughters to view Jezebel as an inspirational role model because she was a woman in power" in reference to the Phoenician princess Jezebel in 1 and 2 Kings.[1] However, even before Harris's inauguration as vice president, another Texas pastor, Steve Swofford of First Baptist Church of Rockwall, Texas, used the appellation for Harris in a January 3 sermon in reference to then president-elect Joseph Biden's cognitive abilities. Swofford proclaimed, "What if something happens to him? Jezebel has to take over—Jezebel Harris; isn't that her name?"[2]

Such a response by conservative White males to a Black woman occupying the second most powerful position in the US government was not a surprise. White men have been calling Black women jezebels since slavery as a racial trope to justify sexual violence against Black women by portraying them as hypersexual, promiscuous seductresses. However, by labeling Harris a jezebel, Buck and Swofford were also signaling that they held control over her body. They could cause her harm for having the audacity to step outside her place in the racial and gender hierarchy in a White supremacist society where US Black women occupy the lowest position in the American racial hierarchy.

Jezebel is one among several stereotypes of Black women that originated during slavery to dehumanize Black women and maintain their subordination

62   *Chapter 3*

in America's racial caste system. Patricia Hill Collins in *Black Feminist Thought* identified four interrelated controlling images emerging from the dominant ideology that form interlocking systems of race, gender, sexuality, and class oppression of Black women: the mammy, the matriarch, the welfare mother (also known as the welfare queen), and the jezebel. Others have included variations of Collins's images to include the angry Black woman, also known as Sapphire.[3]

Of all the stereotypes of Black women by the dominant culture only the jezebel trope is an appropriation of a biblical figure. The controlling image of the biblical figure Jezebel is of a foreign, dangerous seductress who leads men astray.[4] It is in line with the use of biblical texts such as Genesis 9:20–27 explored in chapter 2 to dehumanize Blacks to justify their enslavement and specifically Black women to justify the control of their reproductive and maternal capacities to perpetuate the institution of slavery. As such, of all the controlling images of Black women, the jezebel is the most dangerous because of the sexual violence it engenders with impunity. Usually characterized as a sexually aggressive woman with excessive fecundity, the jezebel image was intended to justify White male sexual abuse and economic exploitation of Black women:

> The controlling image of jezebel reappears across several systems of oppression. For class oppression, the jezebel image fosters the sexual exploitation of Black women's bodies through prostitution. The jezebel image reinforces racial oppression by justifying sexual assaults against Black women. Gender ideology also draws upon the jezebel image—a devalued jezebel makes pure White womanhood possible.[5]

Kelly Brown Douglas explains that the association of Black women with Jezebel is rooted in European travels to Africa: "Travelers often interpreted African women's sparse dress—dress appropriate to the climate of Africa—as a sign of their lewdness and lack of chastity."[6]

Although the jezebel stereotype in antebellum southern culture was originally intended to control the behavior of White women, as the growing dependence on Black labor by southern Whites necessitated an all-out defense of slavery, the racialization of the trope to control Black women's sexuality by burdening Black women with the jezebel image was juxtaposed with the mammy image. Mammy, the domestic servant who cared for the master's children, was according to Kimberly Wallace-Sanders created to assuage the fears of some White Southerners that they were placing their children in the supervision of immoral caretakers, such as the jezebel. Therefore, mammy's creators portrayed her as a trusted house slave who was loyal to her slave owners, especially her young White charges, to the neglect of her own children.[7]

Tina Pippin noted, "The white masters created these images to control and dominate the female slave. The mammy represents the desire for a positive image for African Americans. The jezebel was an excuse—of masters to justify their own adolescent and later adulterous behavior."[8] Deborah Gray White contends that although White Southerners were not on one accord in their view of Black women, they were still able to embrace both controlling images of Black women, alternating between the two as it was convenient: "On the one hand there was the woman obsessed with matters of the flesh, on the other hand was the asexual woman. One was carnal, the other maternal. One was at heart a slut, the other was deeply religious."[9]

This chapter explores the symbolic use of women and gender in the construction and maintenance of boundaries in the politics of belonging first by examining how the writers of the Deuteronomistic History (DH) or Former Prophets in the Hebrew Bible juxtaposed the images of the two named women prophets Deborah and Huldah in the DH with the two named royal women Jezebel and Athaliah. I agree with the literary observations of Duane Christensen that the only two women prophets in the DH, in contrast with Jezebel and Athaliah, form an inclusion on the literary boundaries of the DH. However, contrary to Christensen's argument that the Deuteronomistic historian held a "high regard for the place of women in roles of leadership, both religious and political"[10] as part of a larger concern for the powerless in Israelite society, I contend that Deborah and Huldah's inclusion is largely symbolic rather than an endorsement of their power and influence in religious and political circles. Instead, I argue that Deborah and Huldah function as symbolic border guards to signify the boundaries between those who are in "good Yahwistic standing (observers of ritual and other religious laws and regulations)"[11] and those who are outside covenantal fidelity.

Second, I show how the stereotypes of Jezebel as a seductress and whore over against the motherless women prophets to symbolize covenantal fidelity function the same as the "mammy" and "jezebel" tropes for Black women in the United States in the construction and maintenance of the boundaries of White supremacy. One consequence is that Black women are made to bear the burden of representation to refute White supremacists' persistent attitudes about the inferiority of Blacks by proving that Blacks are exemplary citizens.[12] In the process, Black women become outsiders within American society. Yet, Tamura Lomax refuses to absolve Black religion and Black popular culture of being purveyors of the jezebel trope. According to Lomax, the Black Church, Black religion, and Black popular culture have constructed a Black feminine piety that insists on modesty in dress, moral, and sexual behavior (the "black lady trope") by Black females. However, this trope is dependent on its opposite, the jezebel or "ho" trope to succeed. The effect is to problematize Black women's and girls' sexual identities and situate Black

64   *Chapter 3*

women and girls as outsiders *within* the Black Church and Black cultural representations.[13]

Stacy Davis reiterates this sentiment when she writes, "It seems as if since the nineteenth century, the fear of black women's sexuality and the insistence upon controlling it has been the goal of white men, black nationalists, and Christians of all colors."[14] Thus, while Black women's and girl's sexuality and obsession with its control have been dominated mostly by Whites and Black males, it is Black people's response to the dehumanizing "false racial narratives"[15] about Blacks that has mostly driven the discourse on Black womanhood.

THE DEUTERONOMISTIC HISTORY

Martin Noth coined the term "Deuteronomistic History" (DH) in the early twentieth century to refer to the books of Joshua, Judges, Samuel, and Kings (also known as the Former Prophets) because he believed that they formed a distinctive literary unity based on their shared linguistic and theological views with those found in the book of Deuteronomy. Noth referred to the anonymous author responsible for their composition as the Deuteronomist (Dtr), also referred to as the "historian."[16] Noth placed the *terminus a quo* for the date of this work, around the middle of the sixth century BCE, during Israel's exilic period.[17]

In describing the scope of the composition, Noth explains that Dtr composed the work to interpret Israel's history from the standpoint of the covenantal relationship between YHWH and Israel. Noth explains that in Dtr's view, "The special relationship between God and people is confirmed through the promulgation of the law, which the Deuteronomic law is, according to Deuteronomy 5:28ff., the authentic divine exposition."[18] Covenantal infidelity, most pronounced in the form of the worship of YHWH at proscribed cultic sites outside Jerusalem and worshipping deities besides YHWH, is blamed for Israel and Judah's demise. Noth contends that in Dtr's interpretation the exile is YHWH's final judgment in Israel's long history of disobedience; the relationship between YHWH and the people had come to an end. In explaining Dtr's perspective Noth states, "Clearly he saw the divine judgement which was acted out in his account of the external collapse of Israel as a nation as something final and definitive and he expressed no hope for the future."[19]

Although Noth's theory of an original unity behind the Former Prophets is widely accepted in biblical scholarship, there have been modifications of Noth's theory of a single exilic author of the DH.[20] An example is the theory offered by Göttingen school adherents Rudolf Smend, Jr. and his students Walter Dietrich and Timo Veijola. As explained by Thomas Römer and Albert de Pury, although they agreed with Noth that the original composition was during the exile, they maintain that in contrast to a single literary unity by a single author, two subsequent Dtr editors—one who detailed the successful conquest and extermination of the inhabitants of Canaan by Joshua (DtrH) and a second (DtrN) who was concerned with adherence to the covenant in light of Joshua's failure to annihilate the inhabitants as commanded.[21] Additionally, Dietrich and Veijola argued that a third author and redactor consisting of prophetic stories and speeches (DtrP) was inserted between DtrH and DtrN.

Frank M. Cross split the difference between dates and authorship. He argued for two editions of the DH with multiple authors or editors: a preexilic edition dating to the era of Josiah in the seventh century that had an original theme of hope, and an exilic sixth century edition by an exilic editor, "who retouched or overwrote the Deuteronomistic work to bring it up to date in the Exile, to record the fall of Jerusalem, and to reshape the history . . . into a document relevant to exiles for whom the bright expectations of the Josianic era were hopelessly past."[22]

Likewise, Thomas Römer not only rejected the existence of the DH as an original unit composed by a single author but also expanded the range of its composition. He proposed a three-stage theory for the development of the DH. According to Römer the DH went through a three-stage editing/redacting process during the Assyrian, Neo-Babylonian, and Persian periods by a group of "Deuteronomists." Römer identifies them as royal scribes, who preserved and copied scrolls from the royal library.[23] He contends that these ancient preservationists eventually carried the scrolls with them during the Babylonian captivity where they underwent revision, followed by a third and final editing during the Persian period.

While these scholars are concerned mostly with issues of authorship and dates, other scholars such as Kenton Spark, Diana Edelman, and E. Theodore Mullen investigate such issues related to this study as ethnicity, religion, and politics as organizing principles by the writers of the historical narratives to define Israel's identity formation and boundaries. Their work examines questions around ethnic sentiments, textual authority and group identity, and kingship and identity.

Kenton Sparks, for example, explores ethnicity as a mode of identity and boundaries as it developed throughout parts of Deuteronomy and the DH. Although he finds ethnic sentiments—feelings of attachment based on shared ancestry, fictive or biological, that form group solidarity—important to the Deuteronomic author, ethnicity is a less significant defining criterion for community membership in early Israel than the worship of YHWH as a factor delimiting the boundaries of belonging. However, by the exilic period,

66 *Chapter 3*

the threatened dissolution of their community by foreigners who refused to assimilate, according to Sparks, required the group that came to identify themselves as Israelites to "establish and preserve ethnic distinctions" and adjust "the criteria used to decide who was 'in' and who was not."[24]

Diana Edelman discusses the possibility of the DH as a "written, authoritative depository of valued social memories that are to be learned and passed on by those considering themselves to belong to the group."[25] Similarly, E. Theodore Mullen argues in his monograph on ethnic construction and maintenance in the DH that the historical narratives function as a collection of "archaic originals" that underwent constant reproduction and updating for the purpose of establishing ethnic boundaries based on shared memories of a common history for the postexilic community that would come to constitute biblical "Israel."[26]

While several scholars who explore ethnicity in the DH posit that the narratives rely on myths of a common past or shared ancestry, religion, culture, language, and geographical location to establish an Israelite identity that distinguished ethnic "insiders" and "outsiders," Nira Yuval-Davis argues that the importance of a common destination among the criteria should be included. She maintains that this element is crucial because it is oriented towards the future rather than the past, which can solidify people around a collective identity despite not having a shared myth of origin. Yuval-Davis adds that a common destination "can also explain the dynamic nature of any national collectivity and the perpetual processes of reconstruction of boundaries."[27]

Although these studies of ethnicity as a methodological approach for exploring how the historical narratives might have functioned to provide an exilic community with an ethnic identity and boundaries based on shared memories and ancestry is helpful, except for Yuval-Davis, few have included an analysis of female sexuality and gender in the collectivity's boundary construction and maintenance. For example, while Mullen addresses Athaliah's usurpation of the Davidic line of the throne in Judah, he does not offer an analysis of Athaliah's gender in Dtr's account of her reign and assassination. Duane Christensen's treatment of the women in the DH does not interrogate issues of ethnicity and group formation. Ken Stone's (1996) important work on sexual rhetoric, male honor and power, and gender differences in sex and culture between men and women in the DH does not explore the link between sex, gender, and prestige and ideologies of ethnicity and nation in the historical narratives. Specifically, these studies and others do not go as far as to explore the relationship between gender, sexuality, ethnicity, and nation. Yet, for feminist theorists of gender and nation, an intersectional analysis is essential: gender, ethnicity, and national processes are inextricable.

Among such scholars is Anne McClintock who contends, "All too often in male nationalisms, gender difference between women and men serves

Mammies, Jezebels, Prophetesses, and Royal Women 67

to symbolically define the limits of national difference and power between men."[28] Similarly, Tamar Mayer observes, "when sexed bodies comprise the nation we can no longer think of the nation as sexless. Rather, by exploring the gender ironies of nationalism we expose the fact that sexuality plays a key role in nation-building and in sustaining national identity."[29] Yet, as mentioned in chapter 1, women are affected by national and ethnic processes but also affect them in several different ways, including cultural reproduction. As Yuval Davis points out, "gendered bodies and sexuality play pivotal roles as territories, markers and reproducers of the narratives of nations and other collectivities."[30] Thus, women are frequently made to bear the burden of both embodied and symbolic representation as the polity's boundaries.

Given all this, although Noth's famous thesis regarding the DH has undergone revisions and even faced some fundamental challenges, it is still useful for examining how the stories of women such as Deborah and Huldah form an inclusion making them symbolic border guards that signify the dividing line between Israelite "us" and "them" in the historical narratives. Yet, borrowing Mayer's sentiment, the gender irony might be that these women in their symbolic representation are depicted as asexual or fruitless (Deut. 18:18), not unlike the controlling image of the mammy, in contrast to their religious rivals who bear children. As such, Deborah and Huldah bear the symbolic weight of the curse on the fecundity of Israel and Judah in the interest of the Deuteronomists at the sacrifice of their own maternal interests.

SYMBOLIC BORDER GUARDS

John Armstrong, in his book *Nations before Nationalisms*, draws upon Fredrik Barth's theory on ethnic boundaries to speak of "symbolic border guards" or "symbolic border mechanisms."[31] Armstrong describes symbolic border guards as a "peculiar" phenomenon of ethnicity that presents, for example, as linguistic features, architecture, dress, and manners that help to maintain national boundaries.[32] Yet, Yuval-Davis contends that "any culturally perceived sign could become a boundary signifier to divide the world into 'us' and 'them.'"[33] Although John Hutchinson and Anthony Armstrong do not dispute this, they add that it is important to recognize that symbolic boundary mechanisms should be understood as "attitudinal." While they are emblematic resources distinguishing one group from another, they "exist in the minds of their subjects rather than as lines on a map or norms in a rule book."[34] Still, Yuval-Davis contends that male theorists have placed more emphasis on symbolic boundary mechanisms as peculiar linguistic features, architecture, dress, and manners than as gender symbols. Instead, she has demonstrated that women have not only embodied the collectivity's symbolic boundaries

68   *Chapter 3*

and honor but also are subject to the same boundaries as a means of legitimizing control and oppression of women.[35]

An example of a gendered symbolic border guard is the *hijab* (head covering) in Iranian nationalist projects to control women and their sexuality.
In the early 1900s Iranian women were required to wear the *hijab* as a sign
of religious piety and sexual modesty. Reza Shah of Iran compelled Iranian
women in the early 1930s to remove the *hijab* because he viewed it as a symbol of backwardness and regression. Yet, Iranian women voluntarily removed
the *hijab* when the Shah's son Muhammad Rezah Shah succeeded him. He
reframed the unveiling in terms of progress and modernization. However,
following the 1979 Iranian Revolution, clerics reimposed the compulsory
wearing of the *hijab*. Hamideh Sedghi maintains that with each era of veiling,
unveiling, and reveiling in Iran "the state used gender as a source of legitimacy in order to consolidate its power."[36] Still, Sedghi asserts that the women
from various socioeconomic and political positions were not passive social
actors in these male struggles for state power in deciding for themselves
whether to wear the *hijab*.

Women's bodies can also be made to signify borders. Women have long
been recognized as border guards symbolizing the nation's honor by their
dress and behavior. Yuval-Davis has noted, "Women, in their 'proper' behaviour, their 'proper' clothing, embody the line which signifies the collectivity's
boundaries."[37] Moreover, women are often expected to uphold and reaffirm
"the demarcation between that which they represent and the 'other.'"[38] Eva
Maltschnig explains that in overstepping the boundaries of socially accepted
female behavior, women challenge gender roles. Still, when they do, they are
often regarded as having "abandoned their post."[39] Such perceived affronts to
the collectivity's honor by women who have stepped outside their prescribed
social roles can result in public retribution or even death, such as women who
are murdered by their male relatives in so-called honor killings for bringing shame to their family. Such is the fate of the royal women Jezebel and
Athaliah, outsider women within ancient Israel's history. Although they are
not killed by male relatives, they are nonetheless murdered for nonconformist
behavior according to the Yahwist loyalists.

DEBORAH AND HULDAH AS LITERARY
BORDER GUARDS AROUND THE
DEUTERONOMISTIC HISTORY

I have maintained that in the DH Deborah and Huldah are symbolic border
guards. They function as emblematic resources drawn from the cultural
reservoir of Israel's collective memory and placed on the literary borders

of the Deuteronomistic narratives. As J. Cheryl Exum observes, biblical women serve the interests of the male writers or narrators. Therefore, one of the questions she asks that is pertinent to analyzing the literary inclusion formed by Deborah and Huldah is, "What androcentric agenda does this text promote"?[40] Women prophets appear in the Hebrew Bible, but they are so few that Martti Nissinen commented that they "can be counted with the fingers of one hand."[41] There are in fact only five individual women in the Hebrew Bible identified as a *nebia*, the feminine derivative of the Hebrew word *nabi* for prophet: Miriam (Exod. 15:21), Deborah (Judg. 4:4), Huldah (2 Kings 22:14; cf. 2 Chron. 34:14), the unnamed woman prophet (Isa. 8:3) and Noadiah (Neh. 6:14).[42] Thus, it is not surprising that their appearance in the text has long intrigued scholars, regardless of gender.

Such interest has led scholars to examine the social and religious roles and function of women prophets in the texts. Their conclusions have included that women prophets were limited in exercising their prophetic vocation due to family responsibilities,[43] that women prophets within ancient Israelite religion functioned only during times of Israel's social instability or decentralization,[44] or that women prophets were anomalies[45] or anachronisms.[46] Of course, this is speculation, and the paucity of textual or extrabiblical information on women prophets in ancient Israel does not allow one to reasonably reconstruct their social world. Instead, we might look to alternative methodological approaches for analyzing women prophets in the Hebrew Bible.

I am not arguing that Huldah and Deborah are solely a literary construct.[47] It is not my intention to deny that Deborah and Huldah existed as historical figures in ancient Israel or to argue for the historical accuracy of their portrayal given that there is too little about either woman in the text. Instead, I am interested in how the literary inclusion they form around the DH establishes them as symbolic border guards in the political project of constructing biblical Israel's national identity. One of the ways women affect national projects is as biological reproducers of the nation. However, Deborah and Huldah do not fit this criterion. The other is to affect national projects. They do so as figures signifying the boundaries between true and false followers of Yahweh and therefore true members of the nation of Israel according to Dtr.

Duane Christensen was among the first to propose that Deborah and Huldah formed an inclusion or inclusio, a literary framing device, around the historical narratives of the period of settled life in the Promised Land to the exile (Judges through 2 Kings).[48] Klara Butting also noticed that the two women were the first and last prophets in the Former Prophets, framing the literature in an inclusion.[49] H. G. M. Williamson also argued that the Deuteronomistic historian deliberately framed Deborah and Huldah around the DH in his analysis of the women prophets in the Hebrew Bible. Renita Weems, likewise, agreed with this conclusion. However, she suggested that

70   *Chapter 3*

the inclusion extended from Moses' recitation of the law and the warnings in
the book of Deuteronomy to Huldah's oracle in 2 Kings 22.[50]

Williamson based his observation on the similarities of Deborah's introduction in Judges 4:4 to Huldah's in 2 Kings 22:14:

(Judg. 4:4 5) וּדְבוֹרָהֿ אִשָּׁה נְבִיאָה אֵשֶׁת לַפִּידֹות . . . . וְהִיא יֹשֶׁבֶת

(2 Kings 22:14) וְהִיא יֹשֶׁבֶת ..חֻלְדָּה הַנְּבִיאָה אֵשֶׁת שַׁלֻּם

Williamson states, "As is readily apparent, both passages follow the
scheme of citing personal name, designation as prophetess, name of a husband (with some elaboration in Kings) and place of residence."[51] According
to Williamson, the writer of the DH was intentionally drawing a connection
between the two women prophets by stylizing Deborah after Huldah—and
both as the successors of Moses.[52] Thus, the conclusion that Deborah and
Huldah form an inclusion around the DH is not new.

Christensen's main argument for the inclusion formed by Deborah and
Huldah is that a major theme in the DH is the inherent conflict between
"prophet" and "king" in ancient Israel. Citing Frank Moore Cross, Christensen
maintains that two of the major themes in the DH are the sin of Jeroboam and
the faithfulness of Josiah. However, Christensen adds a third theme: the role
of the prophet. Whether it's the clash between prophets and kings, such as
between kings Jeroboam and Ahab and the prophets, or prophets in conflict
with each other, such as Micaiah and Zedekiah in 1 Kings 22, the prophets
clearly have a central role in the DH. According to Christensen, the presentation of the prophets Deborah and Huldah and the royal women Jezebel and
Athaliah by Dtr takes up the three central themes. However, he argues that
rather than Deborah and Huldah being depicted in adversarial roles, they are
set over against Jezebel and her daughter Athaliah as female representatives
of the tension between the prophet and king:

> A—Deborah: a "Prophetess" of Yahweh alongside Barak
> B—Jezebel: A Royal Advocate of Baal in Israel
> B'—Athaliah: A Royal Advocate of Baal in Judah
> A'—Huldah: a "Prophetess" of Yahweh alongside Josiah.[53]

Christensen concludes that Dtr placed this structural schema around
these four women because of the influence of a "Moses group," the "men
of Anathoth," who were members of the Levitical establishment outside Jerusalem. According to Christensen, they disapproved of the social
stratification introduced by the monarchy—"including the subordination of
women."[54] Finally, he asserts that the Deuteronomistic historian brought these
same values towards women to the canonical process in the time of Josiah, as

reflected by the prominent place of Deborah, Huldah, Jezebel, and Athaliah in the text.

While readers can decide whether they agree that the attention paid by the author to these four dominant women was to highlight the low regard for women commencing with the period of the monarchy, as I mentioned above, I agree with Christensen that Deborah and Huldah are structurally set in opposition to Jezebel and Athaliah. However, I contend that rather than providing female examples of the inherent tension between "prophet" and "king" in ancient Israel, I believe that Deborah and Huldah are symbolic border guards highlighting the failure of the judges in the premonarchic period and the kings in the monarchic period to model for the people true worship of YHWH. As women, they are set structurally against the female royal figures who are constructed in opposition to true Yahwism. Thus, all four women, like contemporary US Black women, carry the burden of representation as symbolic bearers of their respective group's identity or honor.

HULDAH: A PROPHET LIKE MOSES

H. G. M. Williamson proposed that to understand why the author framed Deborah's introduction with an eye toward Huldah, one should examine Huldah's role in Josiah's reforms first. He contends that when the ideal Deuteronomic king Josiah needed to inquire of the deity concerning the scroll of the Torah found during the temple renovation (2 Kings 22:8), he consulted a prophet in the Mosaic succession, which Williamson concludes is Huldah in Josiah's reign. He continues by saying,

> If this is correct, then it is obvious that a similar conclusion must be drawn for Deborah . . . Had we only Judges 5 in our text, we should no doubt have concluded that Deborah was a prophetess in the line of Miriam. The prose narrative in ch. 4, however, offers a different perspective . . . it would be hard to disagree that in this respect, at least, one aspect of Judges 4 is to cast Deborah in the role of Moses.[55]

Christensen's earlier point regarding the themes of the sin of Jeroboam and the faithfulness of Josiah are relevant to Williamson's speculation about Deborah and Huldah. By framing the beginning and end of the DH around these two female Mosaic prophets of YHWH, arguably Dtr emphasizes that their voices were needed, at least symbolically, to legitimize the author's challenge to the two female royal advocates of Baal and Asherah who are in the line of Jeroboam. Jezebel and Athaliah represent a danger to Dtr's religious agenda that is supported by Josiah. Therefore, following Williamson's

72   *Chapter 3*

suggestion, I begin with Huldah to explore each woman's role in the inclusion that forms the textual boundaries around the Deuteronomistic History.

A central claim in the book of Deuteronomy is that the mediator of the divine law was the prophet, and Moses was the prophet *par excellence.* During his speech in preparation for entering the promise land, Moses proclaimed that YHWH would raise up for the people a prophet "like me" (Deut. 18:15). Moses' words become YHWH's a few verses later: "I will raise up for them a prophet like you" (v. 18a). Therefore, according to Deuteronomic law, the only legitimate spokespersons for YHWH are those intermediaries who spoke "like Moses." As the Torah mediator, the Mosaic prophet was also the "mouthpiece" of YHWH: "I will put my words in the mouth of the prophet, who shall speak to them everything that I command. Anyone who does not heed the words that the prophet shall speak in my name, I myself will hold accountable (v. 18b NRSV)." Robert Polzin insightfully noted that the "prophet like Moses" is actually the narrator of the DH and, through him, the author himself: "The Deuteronomist uses Moses to explain by a hortatory lawcode the wide-ranging implications of the Decalogue; this same author will soon be using the Deuteronomic narrator to explain in an exemplary history the wide-ranging implications of that lawcode."[56] Huldah is the ideal Mosaic prophet whose Deuteronomic speech inspires Josiah to implement national reforms in Judah that establish the "words of this covenant written in this book" (2 Kings 23:3).

The discovery of a Torah scroll by the high priest Hilkiah during temple renovation precipitates Huldah's entrance in the text.[57] Upon being read the words of the scroll, Josiah rends his clothes in recognition that YHWH's wrath was kindled against the people because they had failed to keep all the words in the scroll (2 Kings 22:9–11). As if to seek confirmation, he commands the officials to, "Go, inquire of the LORD for me" (22:13). The verb "to inquire" דרש means "to ask, search, explain" (*HALOT* s.v.). It also refers to seeking divine counsel of YHWH. It was not uncommon for monarchs to consult prophets in important matters (e.g., 1 Kings 22:5). However, it was not the standard practice in Israel. Esther Hamori also found it interesting that the king required oracular inquiry to validate the scroll, stating, "We have in this story many other officials who have come across the scroll . . . but the three men—the high priest, the scribe, and the king—still must turn to a higher authority."[58] So, the men consulted Huldah.

The text describes her as "the woman prophet Huldah, wife of Shallum son of Tikva, son of Harhas keeper of the wardrobe" (2 Kings 22:14). Despite the deliberation by some scholars whether the נביאה title is anachronistic to Miriam and Deborah or an honorific of the unnamed woman in Isaiah 8:3, Huldah is generally accepted as a prophet. For example, Lester Grabbe, who questioned the prophet title assigned to Miriam and Deborah, sees "no distinction in the story between Huldah and the various prophets in the tradition."[59] Speaking as a true Mosaic prophet, Huldah responds using the Deuteronomistic messenger formula, "Thus says YHWH" three times in her oracle (2 Kings 22:15, 16, 18), as if to emphasize this point.[60] Her two-part oracle (vv. 15–17, vv. 18–20) affirms the conclusion reached by Josiah that the words in the scroll are YHWH's and that the people are in violation of YHWH's words. She said to them:

> Thus says YHWH, the God of Israel, "Say to the man who sent you to me, thus says YHWH," 'Behold, I am bringing evil to this place and upon its inhabitants—all the words of the book that the king of Judah has read—because they have forsaken me and burned incense to other gods; so that they have provoked me to anger by all the deeds of their hands. Therefore, my anger is kindled against this place and will not be quenched.' (2 Kings 22:15–17; author's translation)

Huldah fulfills her prophetic role speaking on behalf of YHWH, making her the first person to authenticate a canonical text. Moreover, as Claudia Camp explains, "Huldah was not simply the authorizer of the book but its interpreter for the present day . . . we find that she did not address the validity of the book for all time but rather set it as an announcement of doom impinging on Judah's current condition."[61]

Huldah uses Deuteronomic language of prohibitions in her oracle—YHWH and the covenant are forsaken, YHWH's anger is kindled, YHWH destroys the land, etc. (Deut. 28:20; 29:24; 31:16)—such that her prophecy has led biblical scholars such as Weems and others to refer to Huldah as a "mouthpiece for Deuteronomi(sti)c ideology."[62] She is used to validate the work of the Deuteronomic writer by authenticating the book of Deuteronomy when she is consulted in 2 Kings 22.[63] Similarly, John Gray stated that upon being consulted, "Huldah's response is so thoroughly developed by the Deuteronomic redactor, that the original oracle is no longer distinguishable."[64]

Without getting into the debate regarding the authenticity of Huldah's oracle, most scholars agree that Huldah is used to promote the Deuteronomistic agenda instituted by Josiah's reform.[65] Yet, despite the author's efforts to mold her in the image of a Mosaic prophet, the reader is nonetheless allowed to hear Huldah's own words in the second part of her oracle—"But to the king of Judah, who sent you to inquire of YHWH, thus you shall say to him" (2 Kings 22:18a)—before returning to the standard messenger formula to pronounce Josiah's demise. Scholars have deliberated whether her prophecy came to pass since he was killed in battle rather dying peacefully as she predicted. On one side are scholars such as Baruch Halpern who contends, "Huldah's prophecy of comfort to Josiah in fact goes unfulfilled no

74   *Chapter 3*

matter how one reads it."[66] On the other side are her defenders such as Diana Edelman, who counters that technically her prophecy was not false but rather that the idiom "to be gathered to your grave in peace" referred to the proper means of Josiah's burial.[67]

Given her impeccable credentials as a Mosaic prophet, Dtr uses Huldah's pronouncement as the pretext for and authorization of Josiah's implementation of a series of Deuteronomic religious reforms in 2 Kings 23 that the king and the people promised to obey. The result is that the historian is allowed to frame the covenantal renewal on one side by Josiah, one of the most righteous of all Judean kings to reign, and on the other side by Huldah, the woman who speaks of the futility of the innovations. Still, other prophets have pronounced the judgment and the destruction of Judah (2 Kings 21:10–15). However, they were male. Thus, it is not difficult to imagine why some interpreters have not only asked why Huldah, a woman, was inquired of but also why others have concluded that she was chosen because of her gender. Blaženka Scheuer is among the scholars who contend, "Huldah was chosen by the redactor of the Book of Kings/DtrH *because* she was a woman" (emphasis original).[68] As such, although it has already been established that Huldah is regarded as a legitimate Mosaic prophet supported by the fulfillment of her prediction concerning Judah's destruction and exile, as a married woman who is childless, she is symbolic of a desolate nation under God's curse due to covenantal infidelity.

We do not know whether Huldah is past childbearing age, is barren, or is yet to conceive and bear a child. Nonetheless, God promises to bless the fruit of the wombs of those who diligently observe all God's commandments (Deut. 28:4, 11) and curse the fruit of the wombs of the disloyal (28:18). Thus, we find her as the embodied literary boundary of the fall of Jerusalem.

JEZEBEL: THE ROYAL OUTSIDER

According to Duane Christensen, Jezebel's story is the central point in the structural pattern that forms the inclusion around the Deuteronomistic History. The Phoenician princess is also the royal opposite of the prophet Huldah. She is arguably the most reviled female figure in the historical narratives. Some scholars, such as Robert Carroll, attribute Dtr's disdain to her foreignness. He and others contend, "the opposing of foreign women is a topos, as may be seen in the ideological critique of Jezebel in the Deuteronomistic History."[69] Yet, other foreign women in the DH are praised. For example, Walter Brueggemann noted that the Queen of Sheba's speech in 1 Kings 10:9 praising Solomon "turns her into a good Yahwist."[70] Likewise, the widow of Zarephath is exalted as a good foreign woman when she proclaims

Mammies, Jezebels, Prophetesses, and Royal Women 75

of Elijah, "Now I know that you are a man of God and that the word of the LORD in your mouth is truth" (1 Kings 17:24) for reviving her dead son.

The problem with Jezebel is two-fold. First, her marriage to King Ahab violates the prohibition in Deuteronomy 7:3 against making treaties and intermarrying with the indigenous peoples of the land for fear the bridegroom would be turned from worshiping YHWH only. In this regard, one might say that she is a victim of circumstances. According to Winfried Thiel, such diplomatic marriages were part of the larger foreign policy of Ahab's father Omri. She asserts, "The marriage of the crown prince Ahab to the Phoenician princess Jezebel, which served to guarantee the accord with the Phoenicians, was certainly proposed by Omri and was brought to fruition during his own lifetime."[71] Sarah Melville maintains that diplomatic marriages between kings and their vassals, as well as between kings of equal status, were commonplace during the Late Bronze Age (1500 –1100 BCE).[72] Thus, Jezebel's marriage to Ahab was likely a matter of convenience, but Dtr nonetheless counts it against her in the negative evaluation of Ahab as an evil king.

Yet, her marriage alone is not why Dtr reviles Jezebel. Jezebel is a threat to the Deuteronomistic theology because she retains her Phoenician cultural identity to include the worship of Baal. According to the historical narrative, not only does she persist in observing her religious practices, but she is also openly antagonistic toward the prophets of YHWH including having them killed (1 Kings 18:4, 13) and gives material support to prophets of Baal and Asherah (v. 19). Bradley Crowell states that the author has constructed Jezebel as "a woman who actively works against Yahweh and Yahweh's kingdom of Judah"[73] and thus is eventually eradicated, but not before the damage is done to her reputation.

For one, Jezebel is depicted as the stereotypical foreign woman who is the sensual *femme fatale* who tempts men to their deaths.[74] The author makes the direct correlation between Ahab's marriage to Jezebel and Ahab doing more than any other king in Israel to incur YHWH's wrath because he built a temple and erected an altar to Baal, his wife's deity, and served and worshiped Baal himself (1 Kings 16:30–33). This is in violation of the command to tear down the altars and sacred poles used in the worship of foreign gods (Deut. 7:5).[75] Thus, although their union was not of Jezebel's making, in pronouncing the end of Ahab's house, Dtr concludes that it is Jezebel's corruptive influence that resulted in the king's disreputable end (1 Kings 21:25–26). As Phyllis Trible observes, the author reserves his vituperative attack on Jezebel's support for Baal stating, "Not surprisingly, the hostility focuses on her religious affiliation. Three times in their censure of Ahab the Deuteronomists spit out the name of her god."[76]

While the vilification of Jezebel for her religious zeal would be enough for readers to be turned against her, she is further assailed with invective

76   *Chapter 3*

rhetoric by the author that has led to the mischaracterization of Jezebel as a hypersexualized vixen over the history of interpretation. For one, while Jehu the usurper pursued his violent campaign to eradicate the Omride dynasty to include Ahab's sons and purge Israel of the cult of Baal, he cast aspersions on Jezebel by referring to Jehoram's mother's "whoredoms and sorceries" (2 Kings 9:22).[77] The inference is that Jezebel is responsible for Israel's apostasy. This supposition is supported by the deuteronomistic assessment, "Indeed, there was no one like Ahab, who sold himself to do what was evil in the sight of the Lord, urged on by his wife Jezebel" (1 Kings 21:25, NRSV). The verb translated "urged" in the (Heb. סות) also means to incite, instigate, or mislead (*HALOT* s.v.), implying that she set in motion Ahab's downfall.

The succeeding "jezebel" epithet is a euphemism from the Hebrew root זנה for Israel's abandonment of its covenantal patron combined with the Hebrew root כשף (BDB s.v.) for "sorcery" to mean "to engage in witchcraft." Here it is used figuratively to mean a "seductive" or "corruptive" influence, as in the evaluation that Jezebel's seductive influence on Ahab turned him and the people against YHWH. In the prophetic literature illicit female behavior is used metaphorically for apostasy or "whoredoms" (e.g., Hosea 4:12; Ezek. 16:33).

For another, there is the report in 2 Kings 9:30 that when Jezebel hears that Jehu has come to kill her, she puts on her royal finery, paints her eyes, styles her hair, and stands at the window to await her fate. While her actions should be seen as that of a proud queen and not as sexually suggestive, some interpreters have likened her conduct to a whore preparing to "welcome a john."[78] Bradley Crowell states that she readies for her imminent death by "preparing to use her sexuality in an attempt to seduce the usurper, Jehu, a zealous Yahwist, who seeks to overthrow the Omride Dynasty in Israel. She attempts to seduce him just like a prostitute."[79] In contrast, Janet Howe Gaines contends, "Jezebel dresses royally not in any hope of beguiling her would-be assassin but because she is proud and wishes to die with dignity."[80] Indeed, Jezebel not only faces her death with defiance, but also with caustic wit.

When Jezebel sees Jehu, she ridicules him with the battle taunt, "Is it peace Zimri, murderer of his master?" (2 Kings 9:31), a sly reference to the general whose coup against King Elah of Israel was short-lived (1 Kings 16:8–20), implying that she already knows the answer but wishes the same fate for Jehu. Melissa Jackson adds that in those "few gutsy words" Jezebel "dismisses Jehu as an incompetent usurper, letting him (and the audience) know exactly the disdain with which she views him."[81] Claudia Camp refers to her words as a "masterful bit of political name calling."[82] Undeterred, Jehu asks whose allegiances are with him. When two or three of her eunuchs appear in the window, Jehu orders them to throw her from the window to the ground below. They do as commanded, and her body hits the wall, spattering her blood on

Mammies, Jezebels, Prophetesses, and Royal Women 77

the wall and on the horses below that trample her underfoot, tearing her from limb to limb.

Following her death, Jehu enters her residence and sits down to eat and drink. Upon consideration, in deference to her royal status, he orders that the daughter of a king be properly buried. However, the servants report back that only her skull, feet, and palms of her hands remain. He pronounces that this was in fulfillment of the prophecy by Elijah, "In the territory of Jezreel the dogs shall eat the flesh of Jezebel; the corps of Jezebel shall be like dung on the field in the territory of Jezreel, so that no one can say, this is Jezebel" (2 Kings 9:36–37; cf. 1 Kings 21:23).

The outsider princess who became an insider queen nonetheless remains an outsider within because she would not disavow her cultural and religious identity and become a good Yahwist adherent. For this she paid the ultimate price and, presumably, the scourge in Israel was purged from the land. As Judith McKinlay explains, in the context of the Babylonian exile, the explanation why YHWH allowed Israel to be taken captive reads like a catechism:

> Answer: because Israel had followed other gods and not heeded Yahweh's word as delivered through the prophets, such as Elijah. Why did Israel do this? Answer: in this case, because of the evil influence of the foreign Baal- and Asherah-worshipping Queen Jezebel.[83]

Thus, although the fall of Israel is blamed on the apostasy of the nation's kings, literarily Jezebel carries the full weight of being the influence that led Israel astray. According to Janet Howe Gaines, from the deuteronomistic writer's view, "Jezebel embodies everything that must be eliminated from Israel so that the purity of the cult of Yahweh will not be further contaminated."[84] Yet, the pollutant cannot be contained by borders, and we soon find another foreign woman blamed for the spread of the cult of Baal, this time in Judah.

ATHALIAH: MONARCH IN JUDAH

If Jezebel was the bad wife who seduced her husband into worshiping other gods, Athaliah was the bad mother who led her children astray. According to 2 Chronicles, her son Ahaziah did what was evil in the sight of YHWH on account of being counseled in evildoings by his wicked mother (2 Chron. 22:3). Peter Leithart describes Athaliah as the "antimother who destroys rather than nurtures the royal seed."[85] She is the biblical version of the controlling image of the mammy figure, who was accused of being a bad mother who neglected her own children's care and nurturing. Along with the jezebel,

78   *Chapter 3*

according to Robin Boylorn and Mark Hopson, controlling images of Black women communicate "their assumed inept ability to mother properly."[86]

Athaliah is the only woman to rule independently as a monarch in the Hebrew Bible. She ruled for six years in Judah. Several commentators refer to her as "Queen Athaliah." However, the Hebrew text never refers to her by this title. Lissa Wray Beal contends that Dtr never refers to Athaliah as "queen" because the author regarded her rule as illegitimate.[87] A member of the Omride dynasty, Athaliah ascended to the throne in Judah by unconventional means. The disputed daughter of Ahab and Jezebel, Athaliah is given in marriage to Jehoram, king of Judah, to form an alliance with the kingdom of Israel. According to 2 Chronicles 21:4, upon ascending the throne, Jehoram murdered all his brothers leaving only his heir Ahaziah to succeed him. However, Jehoram died of a mysterious ailment in his eighth year of rule (2 Chron. 21:6, 20), and Ahaziah is murdered by Jehu. When Athaliah hears of her son's death, perhaps motivated by self-preservation, she kills all those left in line to inherit the throne in Judah and assumes power, making her the first ruler outside the Davidic line to rule in the house of David (2 Kings 11:1).

Athaliah's sin has been described by some scholars as following her mother Jezebel in advancing the cult of Baal in Judah. Whether or not Athaliah was the daughter of Jezebel is questionable. In the NRSV, Athaliah is described as the granddaughter of King Omri of Israel (2 Kings 8:26; 2 Chron. 22:2). However, the succession account of Ahaziah in the MT identifies her as the daughter of King Omri of Israel.[88] In contrast, the succession account of King Jehoram reports that his wife was the daughter of Ahab (2 Kings 8:18; 2 Chron. 21:6). Thus, Athaliah is recognized as the wife of Jehoram, mother of Ahaziah, and perhaps the daughter of Ahab and Jezebel.

Despite the ambiguity in her relationship to the royal couple, it is clear that the author wishes to link Athaliah to the Omride dynasty and the spread of Baal worship in Judah. However, as E. Theodore Mullen notes, there is no explicit relation between Athaliah and baalism in the text, suggesting that gender rather than religious orthodoxy led to her vilification. Nonetheless, he contends that the "general association with the Tyrian Jezebel provides the major impetus to connect Athaliah with the fostering of foreign religious practices"[89] and her violent disposal. Likewise, the structural device of the literary inclusion, as Duane Christensen observed, invites a comparison of Jezebel and Athaliah with Deborah and Huldah. In contrast to the two women prophets who promote Yahwism, Christensen contends that Jezebel "certainly is responsible in the biblical story for advancing the cult of Baal in Israel; as her daughter Athaliah is subsequently in Judah."[90] Like her mother's death, Athaliah's assassination led to a covenant renewal ceremony with YHWH, the people, and the king that was expected to result in the removal of the cult of Baal in Judah. Yet, the downward spiral to Judah's eventual demise continued.

DEBORAH: A PROPHET LIKE HULDAH

The prophet Deborah in Judges 4 completes the inclusion around the Deuteronomistic history. Deborah is intentionally inserted to complement Huldah on the opposite end of the settled period in the DH when charismatic deliverers also called judges ruled in Israel. She is framed like Huldah: both women are introduced using the feminine derivation of *nabi* or prophet; both are identified by their marital status; and both represent all Israel—Huldah resides in Judah in the south and Deborah judges Israel in the north. Yet, there are features of Deborah's introduction that suggest that the similarities between the two women are artificial literary constructions. For one, Huldah is identified by her name and prophetic status, followed by her primary relationship—in this case her husband—and his family relation and profession: "the prophetess Huldah the wife of Shallum son of Tikvah, son of Harhas, keeper of the wardrobe" (2 Kings 22:14). In contrast, Deborah is identified by three feminine singular nouns: her name, gender (Heb. *ishshah* for "woman"), and office. What follows next is the same Hebrew feminine noun *ishshah* as before but in construct form with the masculine noun *lappidoth*, "woman of Lappidoth," which is usually translated "wife of Lappidoth" (NRSV, JPS, KJV, RSV): "At that time Deborah, a prophetess, wife of Lappidoth, was judging Israel" (Judg. 4:4 NRSV).

Yet, several scholars have questioned whether Lappidoth should be translated as a male proper name given its feminine abstract ending for the Hebrew word *lappid*, which means "torch" or "lightning." Some scholars believe that it should be an epithet for Deborah. Thus, as Tammi Schneider observes, "one possible interpretation could be that she was, 'Deborah, a woman, a prophet, a fiery one.'"[91] While agreeing that this is a valid interpretation of Judges 4:4 and perhaps even the original meaning, as part of the inclusion with Huldah around the literary borders of the Deuteronomistic narratives, the reader is intentionally led to read the wife of Lappidoth with the same lens as Huldah the wife of Shallum.

Another reason that the reader should suspect that the original account of Deborah's portrayal underwent revision is her prophet designation. While Huldah's *neviah* title is generally accepted, others contend that the epithet is an editorial addition of Dtr for Deborah. Those who are of this opinion contend that the *neviah* epithet for Deborah is anachronistic on the basis that prophecy in ancient Israel did not emerge until the tenth century BCE beginning with Samuel. Instead, they maintain that Deborah should be regarded as

80 Chapter 3

a seer rather than a prophet (1 Sam. 9:9). Yet, there are no attestations to a female derivative of the Hebrew term for seer in the Hebrew Bible. Perhaps her judging Israel in the forensic sense was understood as a prophetic role.

Therefore, as H. G. M. Williamson observes, the prose version of Deborah as a *neviah* in Judges 4 should be considered as "part of the redaction of the book of Judges as it approached its final form within the Deuteronomic History (DtrH) as we now have it."[92] As such, regardless of whether Deborah's title should be regarded as anachronistic, the *neviah* epithet is intended to model Deborah in the style of Huldah and both as Moses' successors in the prophetic tradition. In the end, according to Williamson, Huldah's story in 2 Kings brings the reader up to current events, and Deborah's is more like an analeptic account recalling the evil deeds that brought Israel to the point of judgment, bringing the inclusion to full circle.

CONCLUSION

Duane Christensen concluded that these four dominant women in the Deuteronomistic History provided an appropriate symbol around which to structure some of the central theological concerns of the Dtr, foremost being fidelity to YHWH. As women prophetic figures, Deborah and Huldah are both successors of Moses as keepers of the covenant and symbolic border guards signifying Israel and Judah's waywardness due to the influences of foreign elements—namely foreign women. For example, E. Theodore Mullen argued that in the book of Judges, Israel jeopardized its ethnic and geopolitical identity by allowing the influence of foreign elements, usually introduced through intermarriage, to turn the Israelites from fidelity to YHWH and YHWH's Torah.[93] Similarly, Judith McKinlay points to the corrupting influence of the worship of the goddess Asherah in Israelite religion, which she argues was justifiably removed by another women, the prophet Huldah. According to McKinlay, "It is only *YHWH* (emphasis original) who speaks, but speaks through a woman whose own voice and interests have been silenced, as Huldah announces the words that give the warrant not only for the fall of Judah but for the fall of Asherah, the female figure of the divine for Israel."[94]

Thus, in a culture where women usually regulate other women's behavior, the fact that women prophets, even if symbolically, judge male Israelites for associating with foreign women figuratively or literally is a sign of the degree to which Israel and Judah had strayed from YHWH.

Esther Hamori observes that in the biblical texts, "There is an observable pattern of female diviners not also being depicted as mothers."[95] She contends that when it comes to female divination and traditional maternal roles, the biblical writers' discomfort with the women prophets' nonnormative gender role led them to keep these roles separate. In this womanist interpretation, I liken Deborah and Huldah's literary construct that views them less than fully human and fully woman for being childless women in a patriarchal society to controlling images of US Black women, such as the "Black Lady" stereotype, an evaluation of childless Black women as "bad" because they refuse or are unable to be mothers.[96] Like the mammy image, Deborah and Huldah conjure the pious, older, trusted woman who are not mothers but nonetheless imbue maternal love and protection for children not their own in how they protect the children of Israel.

Yet, it is Jezebel, unlike Deborah and Huldah, who haunts US Black women the most. As Melissa Jackson contends, "She is so much the reviled outsider that her infamy has travelled well beyond the pages of the books of Kings and into the wider religious and cultural usage as a metaphor for any woman deemed dangerous, seductive, and/or evil."[97] She shows up in at least a couple ways in the American anti-Black female stereotype. For one is the association of Jezebel's religious practices with sexual activity. This is partly a result of Dtr's depiction of her as having used seduction to turn Ahab from worshiping only YHWH but also, in part, because her participation in the cult of Baal portrayed metaphorically as sexual infidelity over the history of interpretation has become literal. As such, "This movement from metaphor to literalness has become complete in culture, so that now a 'Jezebel' is a promiscuous and dangerously seductive harlot."[98] Following from this, like Jezebel, US Black women's physical expressions of worship serve as another site of cultural attacks on their sexuality. African American charismatic or ecstatic displays of worship become interpreted as "sexualized and deeply gendered excesses of African American religious experience,"[99] especially when exhibited by Black women.

For another, Jezebel (as well as Athaliah) is masculinized by the author. As Wil Gafney notes, "There is something almost unnatural about her presentation as a woman in the text. There is no description of her in the primary role for a biblical woman, birthing and mothering the next generation."[100] But Jezebel is also depicted as masculine for usurping male power and authority when she takes on the mantle of kingship to procure Naboth's vineyard for her husband (1 Kings 21:9–10).[101] This depiction of Jezebel as unfeminine extends to the controlling image of Black women as jezebels who are the subjects of racialized gender stereotypes that reserve femininity exclusively for White women. According to Cheryl Townsend Gilkes, "Proper femininity and whiteness are so interrelated that Jim Crow restrooms were designated for 'white ladies' and 'colored women.'"[102] From slavery to today, Black women are masculinized in several ways. For example, since purity and femininity are linked to White womanhood, the sexual abuse and economic exploitation

82 Chapter 3

of Black women's bodies, as mentioned above by Patricia Hill Collins, excluded Black women from being seen as feminine. Direct attacks on Black women's bodies were intended to masculinize Black women and deny their femininity. From persistent rumors of former First Lady Michelle Obama as transgender to tennis great Serena Williams being called an "ape," "gorilla," and "unfeminine" by spectators and competitors for her physical build, the dominant culture's attacks on Black women deny their womanhood.[103]

Where another characteristic of femininity was domesticity, Black women were often forced to perform devalued and poverty-level jobs outside the home—work traditionally limited to men. From 1860 to 1960, Black women were employed as farm laborers, domestic servants, and industrial workers. According to Enobong Branch, "The notions of true womanhood that surrounded White women painted them as frail creatures who were incapable of marshalling the strength to tend crops."[104] However, Black women's labor from slavery to postbellum in occupations usually suited for men was because they were not considered women but rather beasts of burden. The disparity between White and Black women's labor has policy implications. For example, a popular feature of the 1930s New Deal is the Social Security/OAI (Old Age Insurance). It originally excluded farm laborers and domestic workers, which effectively disqualified nine out of ten Black women from participating.[105]

Finally, as a woman's place has long been regarded as the domestic sphere, women who dare venture into the male-controlled public sphere of business and politics are still often deemed unfeminine, overbearing, and emasculating. In a study of the dominance of masculine imagery in public service, Leisha DeHart-Davis, Justin Marlowe, and Sanjay Pandey found, "Public virtue is portrayed in decidedly culturally masculine overtones, in terms of paternalistic guardians, autonomous fame seekers, commanding heroes (not heroines), and citizens who have historically been identified as white and male."[106] As for Deborah and Huldah, read through male interests, these public figures are only symbolic border guards over against Jezebel and Athaliah to warn male members of Israel of the dangers awaiting them if they commit covenantal infidelity. They are outsiders within the Israelite social and religious structures.

NOTES

1. Mark Wingfield, "SBC Pastor Calls Vice President Kamala Harris a 'Jezebel' Two Days after Inauguration," January 22, 2021, https://baptistnews.com/article/sbc-pastor-calls-vice-president-kamala-harris-a-jezebel-two-days-after-inauguration/#.YB8F9I9KjDJ.

2. Reginald Lyles, "Pastors Buck and Swofford, Get the Biblical Story of Jezebel Straight.," February 4, 2021, https://baptistnews.com/article/pastors-buck-and-swofford-get-the-biblical-story-of-jezebel-straight/#.YCBQqo9KjDI 2021.

3. See, for example, Melissa Harris-Perry, *Sister Citizen: Shame, Stereotypes, and Black Women in America* (New Haven: Yale University Press, 2011) for an analysis of stereotypical images of Black women, such as the persistent lascivious Jezebel and the angry Sapphire, both which have been transposed onto former First Lady Michelle Obama by her critics.

4. Tina Pippin, *Apocalyptic Bodies: The Biblical End of the World in Text and Image* (London: Routledge, 1999).

5. Patricia Hill Collins, *Black Feminist Thought: Knowledge, Consciousness, and the Politics of Empowerment*, 2nd ed., rev. 10th Anniversary ed. (New York: Routledge, 2000), 132.

6. Kelly Brown Douglas, *Sexuality and the Black Church: A Womanist Perspective* (Maryknoll, NY: Orbis, 1999), 36.

7. Kimberly Wallace-Sanders, *Mammy: A Century of Race, Gender, and Southern Memory* (Ann Arbor, MI: University of Michigan Press, 2008).

8. Pippin, *Apocalyptic Bodies*, 34–35.

9. Deborah Gray White, *Ar'n't I a Woman? Female Slaves in the Plantation South* (New York: W. W. Norton, 1985), 46.

10. Duane Christensen, "Huldah and the Men of Anathoth: Women in Leadership in the Deuteronomic History," in *Society of Biblical Literature 1984 Seminar Papers*, ed. Kent Harold Richards (Chico, CA: Scholars, 1984), 403.

11. Mercedes Garcia Bachmann, *Women at Work in the Deuteronomistic History* (Atlanta: SBL, 2013), 2.

12. Black British art historian Kobena Mercer coined the term "burden of representation" in response to expectations that Black artists should be the spokespersons for all Black culture. Yuval-Davis, *Gender & Nation* (London: Sage, 1997) also contends that women are often required to carry the burden of representation since they tend to be constructed as the symbolic bearers of the collectivity's identity and honor.

13. Tamura Lomax, *Jezebel Unhinged: Loosing the Black Female Body in Religion and Culture* (Durham, NC: Duke University Press, 2018).

14. Stacy Davis, "The Invisible Women: Numbers 30 and the Politics of Singleness in Africana Communities," in *Womanist Interpretations of the Bible: Expanding the Discourse*, ed. Gay L. Byron and Vanessa Lovelace (Atlanta: SBL, 2016), 41.

15. Lomax, *Jezebel Unhinged*, ix.

16. Martin Noth, *The Deuteronomistic History* (Sheffield: JSOT, 1981), 4. Although Noth believed that a single author was responsible for the Deuteronomistic History, I will follow other scholars who use Deuteronomist, author, or historian in the singular to refer to what was likely a group or school of scholars responsible for the body of work.

17. Noth, 4.

18. Noth, 90.

19. Noth, 97.

84 *Chapter 3*

20. Several scholars acknowledge that the recognition of the Dtr texts as a literary work is a theory and that the Hebrew canon does not recognize a division titled Deuteronomistic History. See Albert de Pury, et al., eds., *Israel Constructs its History: Deuteronomistic Historiography in Recent Research* (Sheffield: Sheffield Academic, 2000).

21. Thomas Römer and Albert de Pury, "Deuteronomistic Historiography (DH): History of Research and Debated Issues," in *Israel Constructs its History*, ed. Albert de Pury, et al. (Sheffield: Sheffield Academic Press 2000), 67.

22. Frank Moore Cross, *Canaanite Myth and Hebrew Epic: Essays in the History of the Religion of Israel* (Cambridge, MA: Harvard University Press, 1973), 285.

23. Thomas Römer, *The So-Called Deuteronomistic History* (New York: T&T Clark, 2005), 47.

24. Kenton Sparks, *Ethnicity and Identity in Ancient Israel: Prolegomena to the Study of Ethnic Sentiments and their Expression in the Hebrew Bible* (Winona Lake, IN: Eisenbrauns, 1998), 315.

25. Diana Edelman, "Huldah the Prophet—of Yahweh or Asherah?" in *Feminist Companion to Samuel and Kings*, ed. Athalya Brenner and Karla G. Shargent (Sheffield: Sheffield Academic, 2014), 2–3.

26. E. Theodore Mullen Jr., *Narrative History and Ethnic Boundaries: The Deuteronomistic Historian and the Creation of Israelite National Identity* (Atlanta: Scholars, 1993), 14.

27. Yuval-Davis, *Gender & Nation*, 19.

28. Anne McClintock, "'No Longer in a Future Heaven': Race, Gender and Nationalism," in *Dangerous Liaisons*, ed. Anne McClintock, Aamir Mufti, and Elai Shohat (Minneapolis: University of Minnesota Press, 1997), 89.

29. Tamar Mayer, "Gender Ironies of Nationalism: Setting the Stage," in *Gender Ironies of Nationalism: Sexing the Nation*, ed. Tamar Mayer (New York: Routledge, 2000), 2.

30. Yuval-Davis, *Gender & Nation*, 39.

31. John Armstrong, *Nations before Nationalisms* (Chapel Hill: University of North Carolina Press, 1982).

32. Armstrong, 6.

33. Yuval-Davis, *Gender & Nation*, 47.

34. John Hutchinson and Anthony D. Smith, *Nationalism* (Oxford: Oxford University Press, 1995), 144.

35. Yuval-Davis, *Gender & Nation*, 46.

36. Hamideh Sedghi, *Women and Politics in Iran: Veiling, Unveiling, and Reveiling* (Cambridge: Cambridge University Press 2007), 7.

37. Yuval-Davis *Gender & Nation*, 46.

38. Lynn Abrams and Karen Hunt, "Borders and Frontiers in Women's History," *Women's History Review* 9, no. 2 (2000): 193.

39. Eva Maltschnig, "Austrian War Brides as Symbolic Border Guards," in *Transgressing Boundaries: Humanities in Flux*, ed. Marija Wakounig and Markus Peter Beham (Münster, Germany: LIT, 2013), 240.

40. J. Cheryl Exum, "Feminist Criticism: Whose Interests are Being Served?" in *Judges & Method: New Approaches in Biblical Studies,* 2nd ed., ed. Gale A. Yee (Minneapolis: Fortress, 1995), 69.

41. Martti Nissinen, "The Dubious Image of Prophecy," in *Prophets, Prophecy, and Prophetic Texts in Second Temple Judaism,* ed. Michael Floyd and Robert Haak (New York: T&T Clark, 2006), 33.

42. Phyllis A. Bird, *Missing Persons and Mistaken Identities: Women and Gender in Ancient Israel* (Minneapolis: Fortress, 1997) excludes Miriam and the unnamed woman prophet in Isaiah 8:3 even though the texts identify each woman as a נביאה. Susan Ackerman, "Why Is Miriam also among the Prophets? (And Is Zipporah among the Priests?)," *Journal of Biblical Literature* 121, no. 1 (Spring 2002): 47–80, includes only the named women prophets in her analysis. However, a few scholars expand the list of the five women with the נביאה title to include the daughters whom the prophet Ezekiel accused of prophesying out their imaginations (Ezek 13:17), as well as the daughters in Joel 2:28 (Heb. 3:1), such as Wil Gafney, *Daughters of Miriam: Women Prophets in Ancient Israel* (Minneapolis: Fortress, 2008), who proposed that the number of women who belong to the prophet category should be expanded to include women in the prophetic guild.

43. Bird, *Missing Persons and Mistaken Identities.*

44. Renita J. Weems, "Huldah the Prophet: Reading a (Deuteronomistic) Woman's Identity," in *A God So Near: Essays on Old Testament Theology in Honor of Patrick D. Miller,* ed. Brent A. Strawn and Nancy R. Bowen (Winona Lake, IN: Eisenbrauns, 2003), 321–39.

45. Susan Ackerman, "Why Is Miriam also among the Prophets? (And Is Zipporah among the Priests?)," *Journal of Biblical Literature* 121, no. 1 (Spring 2002): 47–80.

46. Rita J. Burns, *Has the Lord Indeed Spoken Only through Moses? A Study of the Biblical Portrait of Miriam* (Atlanta: Scholars, 1987).

47. Exum, "Feminist Criticism," 69, contends that women in biblical literature are "male constructs," or more specifically, "the creations of androcentric (probably male) narrators." As such, she maintains that women are made to reflect and serve androcentric ideas and interests.

48. Although the term "inclusio" is used interchangeably with "inclusion," I am following Christensen's use of inclusion since he is my primary interlocutor for this analytical framework. For further details about the inclusio structure in the Hebrew Bible, see Jason M. H. Gaines, *The Poetic Priestly Source* (Minneapolis: Augsburg Fortress, 2015).

49. Klara Butting, *Prophetinnen gefragt: Die Bedeutung der Prophetinnen im Kanon aus Tora und Prophetie* (Knesebeck, Germany: Erev-Rav, 2001), 77, 99–100.

50. Weems, "Huldah the Prophet," 327.

51. H.G.M. Williamson, "Prophetesses in the Hebrew Bible" in *Prophecy and the Prophets in Ancient Israel,* ed. John Day (New York: T&T Clark, 2014), 68.

52. Williamson, 72.

53. Christensen, "Huldah and the Men of Anathoth," 400.

54. Christensen, 403.

55. Williamson, "Prophetesses," 71–72.

86   *Chapter 3*

56. Robert Polzin, *Moses and the Deuteronomist: A Literary Study of the Deuter-onomistic History, Pt. 1* (New York: Seabury, 1980), 61.

57. The Talmud (*bMegillah* 14b) raised the question why King Josiah sent his del-egation to inquire of Huldah for a prophecy rather than her contemporary Jeremiah. The Gemara answered that Jeremiah did not mind because Huldah was his relative. When that response did not satisfy her critics, he replied that the king sent his emis-saries to Huldah because as a woman she would show more compassion in delivering the oracle of doom than her male counterparts.

58. Esther Hamori, "The Prophet and the Necromancer: Women's Divination for Kings," *Journal of Biblical Literature* 132, no. 4 (2013b): 838.

59. Lester Grabbe *Priests, Prophets, Diviners, Sages: A Socio-Historical Study of Religious Specialists in Ancient Israel* (Valley Forge, PA: Trinity Press International, 1995), 73.

60. Her speech also includes *nəʾum*-YHWH "oracle of YHWH" (2 Kings 22:19).

61. Claudia Camp, "Female Voice, Written Word: Women and Authority in Hebrew Scripture," in *Embodied Love: Sensuality and Relationship as Feminist Values*, ed. Paula M. Cooey, Sharon A. Farmer, and Mary Ellen Ross (San Francisco: Harper & Row, 1988), 100.

62. Weems, "Huldah the Prophet," 323, 339.

63. Scholars have debated whether the contents of the scroll were the book of Deu-teronomy in its entirety or only portions. See for example Volkmar Fritz, *1 & 2 Kings*, trans. Anselm Hagedorn (Minneapolis: Fortress, 2003); John Gray, *1 & 2 Kings: A Commentary* (Philadelphia: Westminster, 1963); Richard Nelson, *First and Second Kings* (Louisville: Westminster John Knox, 1987). A more intriguing argument is the one proposed by scholars such as Katherine Stott, "Finding the Lost Book of the Law: Re-reading the Story of 'The Book of the Law' (Deuteronomy—2 Kings) in Light of Classical Literature," *Journal for the Study of the Old Testament* 30, no. 2 (December 2005): 153–69, who argued that the scroll never actually existed, but rather its inclusion in 2 Kings 22:8 is a rhetorical device that is part of the lost and found documents motif that functions to lend credibility to the book of Kings.

64. Gray, *1 & 2 Kings*, 660.

65. For arguments regarding whether the phrasing and theology of Huldah's oracle were assembled from the words of the book of Deuteronomy or the prophet Jeremiah, see Diana Edelman, "Huldah the Prophet—of Yahweh or Asherah?" in *Feminist Com-panion to Samuel and Kings* (Sheffield: Sheffield Academic, 1994) and Mordechai Cogan and Hayim Tadmor, *II Kings*, The Anchor Bible (New York: Doubleday, 1988).

66. Baruch Halpern, "Why Manasseh is Blamed for the Babylonian Exile: The Evolution of a Biblical Tradition," *Vetus Testamentum* 48, no. 4 (1998): 499.

67. Edelman, "Huldah the Prophet," 241.

68. Blaženka Scheuer, "Huldah: A Cunning Career Woman?" in *Prophecy and Prophets in Stories: Papers Read at the Fifth Meeting*, ed. Bob E. J. H. Becking and Hans Barstad (Leiden: Brill, 2015), 108.

69. Robert Carroll, "Coopting the Prophets: Nehemiah and Noadiah," in *Priests, Prophets, and Scribes: Essays on the Formation and Heritage of Second Temple*

Judaism in Honour of Joseph Blenkinsopp, JSOT 149, ed. Eugene Charles Ulrich and Joseph Blenkinsopp (Sheffield: Sheffield Academic, 1992), 94.

70. Walter Brueggemann, *1 & 2 Kings,* Smyth & Helwys Bible Commentary (Macon, GA: Smyth & Helwys, 2000), 134.

71. Winfried Thiel, "Omri," in *The Anchor Bible Dictionary*, Vol. 5 (New York: Doubleday, 1992), 18.

72. Sarah C. Melville, "Royal Women and the Exercise of Power in the Ancient Near East," in *Companion to the Ancient Near East*, ed. Daniel C. Snell (Malden, MA: Blackwell, 2007), 219–28.

73. Bradley Crowell, "Good Girl, Bad Girl: Foreign Women of the Deuteronomistic History in Postcolonial Perspective," *Biblical Interpretation* 21, no. 1 (2013): 11.

74. See for example, John Greenfield, "Transforming the Stereotype: Exotic Women in Shelley's Alastor and The Witch of Atlas," in *The Foreign Woman in British Literature: Exotics, Aliens, and Outsiders*, ed. Marilyn Demarest and Toni Reed Button (Westport, CT: Greenwood Press, 1999).

75. Ahab also made a sacred pole (1 Kings 16:33), which would also indicate the worship of Asherah, Baal's consort.

76. Phyllis Trible, "Exegesis for Storytellers and Other Strangers," *Journal of Biblical Literature* 114, no. 1 (1995): 4.

77. The account of Jehu's assassination of Jehoram of Israel and Ahaziah of Israel (2 Kings 9–10) is disputed by an inscription from a fragment of the Tel Dan Stele, which claims that a king of Aram (Syria) killed the two monarchs in battle. See Steven McKenzie, *King David: A Biography* (Oxford: Oxford University Press, 2000).

78. Peter J. Leithart, *1 & 2 Kings* (Grand Rapids, MI: Brazos, 2006), 221. In some churches wearing makeup is prohibited because it is considered "jezebel," based on 2 Kings 9:30. The rationale is that Jezebel applied makeup to try and sexually entice Jehu, despite the text making no such reference. Therefore, modest women should not wear makeup. I have seldom seen any reference to Job's daughter Keren-happuch (42:14), whose name means "horn of antimony" (BDB s.v.), a black mineral powder used for eye makeup.

79. Crowell, "Good Girl, Bad Girl," 12.

80. Janet Howe Gaines, *Music in the Old Bones: Jezebel through the Ages* (Carbondale, IL: Southern Illinois University Press, 1999), 82.

81. Melissa Jackson, *Comedy and Feminist Interpretation of the Hebrew Bible: A Subversive Collaboration* (Oxford: Oxford University Press, 2012), 174.

82. Camp, "Female Voice, Written Word," 109.

83. Judith McKinlay, *Reframing Her: Biblical Women in Post-Colonial Focus* (Sheffield: Sheffield Phoenix, 2014), 71.

84. Janet Howe Gaines, "How Bad was Jezebel?" *Biblical Archaeology Society*, October 1, 2023, http://www.biblicalarchaeology.org/daily/people-cultures-in-the -bible/people-in-the-bible/how-bad-was-jezebel/.

85. Peter Leithart, *1 & 2 Kings* (Grand Rapids, MI: Brazos, 2006), 225.

86. Robin Boylorn and Mark Hopson, "Learning to Conquer Metaphysical Dilemmas: Womanist and Masculinist Perspectives on Tyler Perry's for Colored Girls," in *Black Women and Popular Culture: The Conversation Continues*, ed. Adria

Y. Goldman, Vanatta S. Ford, Alexa A. Harris and Natasha R. Howard (London: Lexington, 2014), 94.

87. Lissa Wray Beal, *1 & 2 Kings* (Downers Grove, IL: IVP Academic, 2014), 386.

88. Several translations have "granddaughter" of Omri (e.g., ESV, NRSV). Although the MT has עמרי-בת or "daughter of Omri," several scholars note that Athaliah should be understood as a female descendant of Omri and not his daughter.

89. Mullen, *Narrative History and Ethnic Boundaries*, 21n7.

90. Christensen, "Huldah and the Men of Anathoth," 401.

91. Tammi Schneider, *Judges* (Collegeville, MN: Liturgical, 2009), 66.

92. Williamson, "Prophetesses in the Hebrew Bible," 69.

93. Mullen, *Narrative History and Ethnic Boundaries*.

94. Judith McKinlay, "Gazing at Huldah," *The Bible and Critical Theory* 1, no. 3 (2005): 4.

95. Esther Hamori, "Childless Female Diviners in the Bible and Beyond," in *Prophets Male and Female: Gender and Prophecy in the Hebrew Bible, the Mediterranean, and the Ancient Near East*, ed. Jonathan Stokl and Corrine L. Carvalh (Atlanta: Society of Biblical Literature, 2013), 169.

96. Boylorn and Hopson, "Learning to Conquer Metaphysical Dilemmas," 95.

97. Melissa Jackson, "Reading Jezebel from the 'Other' Side: Feminist Critique, Postcolonialism, and Comedy," *Review and Expositor* 112, no. 2 (2015): 239–40.

98. Jackson, "Reading Jezebel from the 'Other' Side," 247.

99. Elizabeth L. Jemison, "Gendering the History of Race and Religion," in *The Oxford Handbook of Religion and Race in America*, ed. Kathryn Gin Lum and Paul Harvey (Oxford: Oxford University Press, 2018), 88.

100. Wilda Gafney, *Womanist Midrash: A Reintroduction to the Women of the Torah and the Throne* (Louisville: Westminster John Knox, 2017), 244.

101. Patrick Moynihan, *The Negro Family: The Case for National Action*, Office of Policy Planning and Research, United States Department of Labor, March 1965, commonly referred to as The Moynihan Report, charged Black women with usurping Black male authority in the home.

102. Cheryl Townsend Gilkes, "Outsiders Within the Higher Circles: Two First Ladies as Cultural Icons in a Racialized Politics of Difference," in *Race in the Age of Obama. Research in Race and Ethnic Relations*, vol. 16, ed. Donald Cunnigen and Marino A. Bruce (United Kingdom: Emerald Group, 2010), 56.

103. See, for example, comedian Joan Rivers joked on a cable news show that Michelle Obama was "tranny," a pejorative for transgender in Ryan Gajewski, "Joan Rivers Calls President Obama Gay, Says First Lady is 'Tranny' (Video)," *The Hollywood Reporter*, July 3, 2014, https://www.hollywoodreporter.com/news/general-news/joan-rivers-calls-president-obama-716738/. Comments on social media platforms Facebook and X, formerly Twitter, questioned Serena Williams's gender identity. She was also called "ape" and "monkey" due to her skin color and physicality. See Chelsea Litchfield, Emma Kavanaugh, Jaquelyn Osborne, and Ian Jones, "Social Media and the Politics of Gender, Race and Identity: The Case of Serena Williams," *European Journal for Sport and Society* 15:2 (2018): 15, https://eprints.bournemouth.ac.uk/30146/3/social%20media%20serena%20williams.pdf.

104. Enobong Branch, *Opportunity Denied: Limiting Black Women to Devalued Work* (New Brunswick, NJ: Rutgers University Press 2011), 4.

105. Jamila Michener and Margaret Teresa Brower, "What's Policy Got to Do with It? Race, Gender & Economic Inequality in the United States," *Daedalus* 149, no. 1 (Winter 2020): 101, https://doi.org/10.1162/DAED_a_01776.

106. Leisha DeHart-Davis, Justin Marlowe, and Sanjay Pandey, "Gender Dimensions of Public Service Motivation," *Public Administration Review* 66, no. 6 (November-December 2006): 873.

Chapter 4

Mothers in Israel, Church Mothers, and Mothers of the Nation

They hold a special place in Black Protestant congregations. Seated at a place of honor on the front pews of Black Baptist, Methodist, and "Sanctified" (Pentecostal, Holiness, Apostolic) sanctuaries, they are the *Church Mothers*, mostly elderly women of position and stature within the patriarchal church hierarchy. Anthea Butler describes Church Mothers as wielding spiritual maturity and temporal authority in educating and disciplining those within the church.[1] Cheryl Townsend Gilkes refers to them as "older, venerated, Spirit-filled women who hold considerable power within nearly autonomous and well-organized parallel women's worlds."[2]

According to Butler, while the historical antecedents of the term Church Mother as an honorific in US Black churches are uncertain, "Generally, pastors and women, when discussing the Church Mother, referred to Judges 5:7, which describes the prophetess Deborah as a 'Mother in Israel.'"[3] Nineteenth century African Methodist Episcopal exhorter Jarena Lee attested to the tradition. She recollected calling on "an elderly woman named Jane Hutt, a 'sister in Christ,' who accompanied her on a visit with a terminally ill young man" to pray for his conversion because Hutt was "still among us as a 'Mother in Israel.'"[4]

Gilkes traces this tradition of venerating elderly Black women back to West African practices where the African queen Mother exercised considerable power and influence in church and society. Whatever the origins of the epithet for these church women, Butler asserts that "it is clear that it denotes some type of fictive kinship relationship between members of the church community and a woman of great spiritual and moral stature."[5] The Church Mother was an esteemed mother figure regardless of her biological relationship to the members, but it also accorded the male pastor the authority of a father figure.

92   *Chapter 4*

The biblical antecedent to the Church Mother, Deborah, called by the epithet *mother in Israel*, is not referred to as a prophet in Judges 5:7 despite regularly being identified as one by readers, to include the church members mentioned above. She is assumed to be a prophet in Judges 5 because of the prose narrative in Judges 4 that introduces Deborah as a prophet whom the people went to for judgment (Judg. 4:4). Judges 5 is the poetic version that recounts the battle in Judges 4.

Some scholars contend that Deborah was an older woman because family responsibilities would have prevented women in their childbearing years from performing their prophetic functions. For example, Phyllis Bird contends that women prophets "exercised their charismatic vocation . . . after their child-rearing duties were past."[6] Victor Matthews described Deborah as a "postmenopausal female" who "functions as an elder" and thus serves in an authoritative position because of her maturity.[7] Interpretations of Deborah as an elderly woman coupled with the respect and authority accorded her as a religious figure may have contributed to the association of the honorific Church Mother in the Black church with the mother in Israel.

Although Deborah is described as married in Judges 4, she is not known to have been a biological mother in either the prose or poetic version. Deborah is a mother in Israel, figuratively speaking. Following Nira Yuval-Davis, at the symbolic level, the role of women, usually mothers, in national processes is to symbolically figure the nation as its boundaries, such as Deborah and Huldah in chapter 3, and as symbolic bearers of the collectivity's identity and/ or honor as in Judges 5. As an example, she points to the French figure *la patrie*, depicted symbolically as a woman in labor during the French Revolution. *La patrie* in French is a female noun translated in English as *fatherland*. However, *la patrie* as symbolic of France is not just a woman in labor but also one giving birth to the nation in need of defense.[8]

The French Legislative Assembly in 1792 issued an address "*La Patrie en danger!*" (The Fatherland in Danger) as a call to arms for volunteers to defend France against the Habsburg Empire.[9] When this appeal met with failure, the French government decreed a *levée en masse* to recruit men for military service. Alan Forrest illustrates how the imagery of the *levée en mass* was often highly gendered. In *levée*-inspired paintings and etchings, young men were depicted as volunteering to serve while women were portrayed in the background sacrificing their sons, brothers, husbands, and lovers for the sake of *la patrie*. According to Forrest, "Their [women's] inclusion in Revolutionary imagery underscored the unity of civil society responding to the call to arms . . . Female figures became powerful symbols of sacrifice and self-abasement, of quiet fortitude and personal heroism."[10]

In this chapter, I propose that in the so-called Song of Deborah, Deborah should also be read as a maternal figure constructed symbolically as the spirit of the collectivity's shared memory of its triumph over an enemy that threatened the national identity and unity while supporting a masculine hegemony.

Although women are often encumbered with the burden of representation, "as they are constructed as the symbolic bearers of the collectivity's identity and honour"[11] in both contemporary society and biblical literature, it is not just any woman who can represent the nation. While Deborah was considered a legitimate symbolic cultural bearer in Israel in the Deuteronomistic historical narratives, outsider women within the nation such as Jezebel in 1 and 2 Kings and the Strange Woman in the book of Proverbs do not qualify to represent the nation. In the United States, race, ethnicity, class, and citizenship status affect which women can symbolize the polity, as will be shown below.

MOTHER IN ISRAEL IN JUDGES 5:7

The epithet mother in Israel (Hebrew *em beyisrael*) conferred on Deborah in Judges 5:7 has puzzled many biblical interpreters for centuries. No other person in the Hebrew Bible is referred to as a mother in Israel.[12] The few clues offered for its significance in Judges 5 are that deliverance came when Deborah arose a mother in Israel and sang her song. Although there is no consensus on what the meaning of mother in Israel might be, a common interpretation is the one proffered by Barnabas Lindars, who suggested that Deborah is referred to as a "mother" to reflect her prophetic role, in much the same way that the leader of a band of prophets has been regarded as a "father" (1 Sam. 10:12). Says Lindars, "A prophet discloses divine knowledge and as such has the teaching responsibility of a father, and the same would be true of a prophetess."[13] Scholars who hold this view are relying on her description as a prophet in Judges 4 despite the absence of the appellation for Deborah in Judges 5. Another interpretation that relies on Judges 4 is Tikva Frymer-Kensky's explanation that the epithet is related to her role judging Israel before the war.[14]

James Ackerman argued that the epithet was a function of Deborah's prophetic role within the context of holy war.[15] Dennis Olson suggests that the title may represent the place and office of a wise woman prophet who delivers divine oracles to resolve disputes like the wise woman at Abel beth-maacah in 2 Samuel 20:16–19.[16] Susan Ackerman contends that the epithet should be understood in the context of Canaanite myths concerning the divine warriors Baal and Anat. She argues that the YHWH and Deborah dichotomy in Judges 5:4b–5, 7 is meant to evoke the parallel to the Baal-Anat cycle of male and female warrior, such that "Yahweh is 'the God of Israel' in verse 5, and Deborah is 'a mother in Israel' in verse 7. This phrasing, along with the entire poetic structure of verses 4b–5 and 7, is designed to make us read these

94   *Chapter 4*

two figures as paired."[17] Based on her analysis, she concludes that the epithet mother in Israel should be understood in military terms, with Deborah as the human female counterpart to the divine male warrior YHWH.

By contrast, Cheryl Exum views the epithet symbolically. Deborah as a mother in Israel symbolizes the "good mother" who delivers her sons from danger and makes their lives secure but who also endangers their lives by sending them off to war to die.[18] Yet, in this act of leading her children into warfare, Exum contends that Deborah's song in Judges 5 is one of several stories where a woman's voice is co-opted by male ideology to further male interests. Whether or not others agree with Exum's interpretation of the honorific mother in Israel as symbolic of a maternal protective figure, her insight into the symbolic figuration of the epithet is much more fundamentally accurate.

FEMALE SYMBOLIC FIGURATION IN THE HEBREW BIBLE

Female symbolization is common in the Hebrew Bible. For example, Claudia Camp's treatment of the figures "Woman Wisdom" and "Strange Woman/ Alien Woman" in Proverbs 1–9 explores the personification of Wisdom and Strangeness as women who represent insider and outsider identities of gender, ethnicity, sexuality, and cultic activity in postexilic Judah.[19] Likewise, Gale Yee examines the Other/Strange Woman in Proverbs, along with Eve in Genesis, the unfaithful Gomer in Hosea, and the two adulterous sisters in Ezekiel to show how certain women in the Hebrew Bible signify the incarnation of moral sin, evil, and death.[20] Mayer Gruber explores the maternal imagery of God in Second Isaiah (42:14, 45:10, 49:15, 66:13) as an expectant mother, a nursing mother, and comforting mother to argue for its positive estimation of femaleness.[21]

In the prophetic texts, capital cities and nations are frequently figured symbolically in the Hebrew Bible as wives, mothers, daughters, and whores. For example, Isaiah likens Babylon to a childless widow (Isa. 47:9); the Assyrian capital Nineveh is likened to a sorceress and hypersexual harlot in the book of Nahum (3:4–7); and Jerusalem has been alternatively depicted metaphorically as the virgin daughter Zion (Isa. 37:22) and the adulterous wife of God (Ezek. 16). Israel is also God's adulterous wife who is wooed back to her abusive husband (Hosea 2:14–16). As mentioned above, Samaria and Jerusalem are sister whores in Ezekiel 23.

Brad Kelle analyzed the phenomenon of the personification of cities as female in Hebrew Bible prophetic literature.[22] The Hebrew noun for "city" is gendered feminine; therefore, it was not surprising to find cities personified feminine. However, Kelle found a pattern of cities in the Hebrew Bible used as metaphors for endangered or sexually violated women to describe the destruction of cities in warfare. For example, Israel's deity threatened metaphorically to lift the skirts of the city Nineveh, personified as female, and publicly expose her nakedness to describe the city's imminent downfall (Nah. 3:5).

Unlike the cities personified in the latter prophets, the epithet mother in Israel in Judges 5 does not symbolize the destruction of a capital city. However, it shares with the above examples of metaphorical language the use of women in wartime rhetoric to either rally warriors, shame men, or signify a moral sin.[23] Like the French *la patrie* who represents the spirit of the polity around whom men rally to defend the "womenandchildren"[24] during wartime, Deborah is elevated to iconic status as female symbolization of the nation of Israel in the emergence of Israel's ethnic sentiments. Judges 5 contributes to the Hebrew Bible literature that distinguishes Israel as a group from other ethnic groups in the surrounding area.[25]

THE SONG OF DEBORAH

Scholars commonly refer to Judges 5 as the Song of Deborah. This is due in large part to the opening stanza (Judg. 5:2–8) of a song celebrating Deborah's role in Israel's victory over the Canaanite army: "Then Deborah and Barak, son of Abinoam, sang in that day" (Judg. 5:1 NRSV). Despite the dual subject of the poem's protagonists, many scholars believe that the song originally implored only Deborah to sing based on the feminine singular verb in the MT which suggests that Deborah is the main subject (cf. Num. 12:1) and that Barak was a later addition.

While the consensus is that the song is a victory hymn much like the Song of Moses in Exodus 15, there is less agreement on which category of victory hymn it belongs to.[26] For example, Charles Echols argues that Judges 5 is a heroic victory hymn.[27] Based on a comparative study of other heroic victory hymns over several periods, he contends that Deborah's Song was originally an ode celebrating ancient Israel's victorious heroes and heroines mentioned in the song with YHWH as a secondary hero added later to give it a liturgical function. However, A. J. Hauser challenges Echols and others to contend that although Judges 5 (and Exod. 15) shares characteristics in common with a victory hymn, such as "the use of the divine name," it does not follow a formal structure associated with one. Nonetheless, he concludes that Judges 5 is a victory song.[28]

While Judges 5 mentions Israel's deity by name, many scholars agree that YHWH's involvement in the battle is minimized, referenced just twice in

96   Chapter 4

passing in two verses (Judg. 5:4–5, 11) rather than central to the hymn, in contrast to other victory hymns in the Hebrew Bible. Instead, Judges 5 emphasizes the centrality of Israel as a nation in the song rather than YHWH's actions. More specifically, the centrality of those tribes who came to Israel's defense contrasts to those that remained on the side. I agree with Gregory Wong that the Song of Deborah may have been intended for a purpose other than celebrating a military victory at the time of the battle. Wong contends that the authors took advantage of the occasion to compose a work of political polemic to chastise the tribes that did not take part in the battle.[29] While the authors do take those tribes to task in the song, without getting into the debate whether or not the song was composed near the time of actual events in ancient Israel's history, I would note that theorists of nation and nationalism point out that nationalisms invent traditions or celebrations to create unity where none existed before.[30] In other words, the song could have been composed much later than the events depicted to coalesce a later audience.

Scholars have noted the difficulty with translating the song, pointing to its archaic features, unusual grammar, syntax, and other complexities. An example of translation difficulties is Judges 5:2. There is not a consensus on the meaning of the root pr' that appears twice in the opening phrase *biperoa peraot* of the song in verse 2. The first translation of the root as "hair" (BDB-II) and the second as "to let loose" or "to unbind" (BDB-III) has led to the commonly accepted renderings of pr' including some version of loosely flowing hair such as "When locks are long in Israel" (NRSV) and "When locks go untrimmed" (JPS). J. Alberto Soggin translates the phrase, "Because in Israel the people have regained their liberty."[31] Although he acknowledges that to "have long hair" is preferred by most scholars, he contends that his translation follows more logically from the rest of the text.[32] In contrast, Robert Miller argues that the phrase should be rendered "When the Pharaohs pharaohed" or "When pharaohs ruled."[33] Those who support hair-related translations often cite ancient Israelite religious traditions and thus translate the parallel verse following in tandem with this interpretation. As Tammi Schneider has opined, "These translations reflect more the intent of the translators or their interpretation than the meaning of the text."[34] Ultimately, we are left to concede that we have an obscure, long-lost Hebrew expression.

These technical challenges have led to debates whether certain terms and expressions identified as archaic in the poem are evidence of its place among the oldest literature in the Hebrew Bible[35] or whether the song should be regarded as late pre-exilic, exilic, or early post-exilic.[36] Those in support of an older date place the composition near the time of the events sung about. Scholars who side with the latter challenge the antiquity of the text and cite the appearance of archaisms, Aramaisms, intertextualities, and other features in the song that appear in later Hebrew Bible texts. Still, others argue that the song is not older than the ninth century BCE.[37] Those scholars contend that the poem is meant to convey a sense of Israel's antiquity and thus authority. In all, the reader is still left with the song's complexities.

The deity makes a first appearance in the song in theophanic terms (Judg. 5:4–5). Yahweh, the God of Israel marches out from Seir in the south "to the accompaniment of thunderstorms while the earth quakes and mountains shake."[38] Such storm imagery of Yahweh the divine warrior alludes to the warrior storm-god, Baal, who moves through battle on a chariot of clouds with wind and thunderbolts as his weapons, attestation to the literary parallels between biblical literature and Ugaritic texts.[39] The epithet "the One of Sinai" for Yahweh is recounted elsewhere (e.g., Ps. 68:7–8).

The circumstances precipitating the battle are recounted in Judges 6–8. The setting is in the days of Shamgar, son of Anath and Jael. Jael is familiar to readers in the prose version of the battle with the Canaanites led by the general Sisera. Shamgar is a judge who appears in Judges 3, but he and Jael are contemporaries in Judges 5. Scholars agree that in these days Israel was living under the hand of oppression by the Canaanites. In keeping with the cycle begun in Judges 2:11, the people again did what was evil in the sight of YHWH by choosing other deities besides YHWH and being sold into the hand of the king of Canaan. These actions caused the Israelites' social and economic condition to deteriorate. However, several scholars disagree on the interpretation of the details of the situation. Susan Niditch discusses how word choice "greatly affects the sociological and political portrayal that one finds behind the poem."[40] Thus, while scholars agree that the problem concerned perilous trade and travel, they cannot agree whether the subject of the Hebrew verb *chadal* "to cease" in verse 6 should be roads, travelers, or inhabitants. In any case, there is a consensus that the dangerous conditions made the region desolate.

The songwriter touts Deborah's role in Israel's victory in Judges 5:7. In a phrase that has been variously translated—"Ways of life in the unwalled towns came to a halt. In Israel they came to a halt"[41]; "The leading class was inactive in Israel, it was inactive in Israel"[42]; "The peasantry prospered in Israel, they grew fat on plunder" (NRSV); "The inhabitants of the village ceased, they ceased in Israel" (KJV)—what follows is a declaration that Deborah's appearance reverses the dire circumstances. The preposition *'ad* ("until") linking the two phrases attests to the reversal of Israel's fortune because Deborah arose as a mother in Israel.

Like *la patrie*, either symbolically or literarily, it is Deborah who the authors of Judges 5 use to mobilize the tribes for battle in defense of the nation. She is the mother sending her sons off to sacrifice their lives in battle. The troops are victorious over the kings of Canaan, and she sings praises to YHWH for those who served voluntarily. But the people were not united in

98   *Chapter 4*

responding to the call to arms (Judg. 5:2, 9). Deborah's song reflects the frustration at the lack of participation by all tribes in a national political agenda.

While several commentaries focus on the rebuke against non-participating tribes, the intersection of nation, gender, and sexuality and their censure is often overlooked in these analyses. Feminist theorists of nation and gender have demonstrated that notions of masculinity and femininity frequently contribute to constructions of nationhood. Judges 5 is an example of how Israel's national identity is constructed not only by "amplify[ing] the past and keep[ing] memories of communal sufferings alive"[43] but also around constructions of gender and sexuality. As such, the call to arms and the failure to respond in defense of the nation of Israel is defined in terms of gender and sexuality.

David Clines writes about gender in the Hebrew Bible in his treatment of the David story (1 Samuel 16 to 1 Kings 2) and the construction of masculinity. Clines explains that one of the fundamental characteristics of being a man in the Hebrew Bible is to be a warrior, a mighty man of valor. Clines contends, "It is essential for a man in the David story that he be strong—which means to say, capable of violence against other men and active in killing other men."[44] Harold Washington asserts, "The language of war in the Hebrew Bible . . . is acutely masculinist. Warfare is emblematically male and the discourse of violence is imbricated with that of masculine sexuality."[45] The capacity for violence is equated with manhood. Thus, men who fail to heed the call to arms are feminized. This evaluation of gender and sexuality is on display in at least two scenes.

The first example is the celebration of masculine performativity of violence led by Deborah in the third stanza (Judg. 5:14–18). She calls the roll of tribes beginning with those who responded to her call to arms. First Ephraim, then Benjamin, followed by Machir and Zebulun, who are joined by Issachar (Judg. 5:14–15a). Zebulun, along with Naphtali, is singled out for the tribe's exceptional sacrifice in battle (v. 18). Deborah sings praises of how they marched out into the valley of one mind in the service of the Lord, each more committed than the other.

She turns her attention to those who searched their hearts but could not find it in them to join the other tribes on the battlefield. Deborah identifies them as Reuben (v. 15b) and Gilead in the south and Dan and Asher in the north (vv. 16–17). They prefer to remain secure where they are rather than heed the call. She assumes a sarcastic tone as she describes why they avoided the combat. She is especially critical of the tribe of Reuben, asking, "Why did you tarry among the sheepfolds, to hear the piping for the flocks?" (v. 16). J. Soggin surmises, "Here we have an effective and insulting comparison with beasts of burden who, either through laziness, or because their load is too heavy, lie down under their loads."[46]

The author may have had the Deuteronomic laws on war in mind when Dtr put these lyrics in Deborah's mouth. The author appears to mock any man who is afraid or disheartened to engage in combat by commanding him to remain home lest he cause "the heart of his comrades to melt like his own" (Deut. 20:8 NRSV). This is one of the few laws that exempt men from going to battle, observes Harold Washington, "lest he compromise the military effectiveness of his fellows."[47] The sentiment of disgust by the author at those who refuse to be men and fight is barely disguised. The establishment of national identity takes for granted acts of violence by men against other men as part of their masculinity and patriotism. The tribes who avoid fighting are not real men and thus do not defend the unity of the nation.

If Dtr composed the historical narratives with national unity in mind for an exilic community threatened with assimilation and ethnic dissolution,[48] then the depiction of the absent tribes is a cautionary tale of the threat to Israel's identity formation. Mercedes Bachmann notes the paradox: "While 'Israel' is a structuring device demarcating stanzas, it becomes apparent that Israel is not all Israel."[49] The lack of unity among the tribes is a theme throughout the book of Judges that later fosters resentment among tribes (e.g., 8:1–3; 12:1–6) and culminates in a civil war that results in the annihilation of the tribe of Benjamin (Judges 21).[50]

The second example demonstrating the intersection of gender, sexuality, and national interests in the song is the unmanning of the Canaanite general Sisera by Jael in stanza 5a (Judg. 5:24–27). If manhood in militaristic terms constitutes violence, as Washington asserts, "Conversely, 'woman' signifies one who succumbs to violence; hence men who are defeated in combat are reckoned as women."[51] Sisera suffers this fate at the hand of Jael although the details in Judges 5 and Judges 4 differ in several ways. For one, in the prose version, Sisera abandons his besieged troops and escapes to the tent of Jael wife of Heber the Kenite who invites him in (Judg. 4:17–18). She drives a tent peg into his temple while he slept weary from the battle and perhaps the milk that she gave him to drink instead of the water he requested (vv. 19–21).

In the song, Barak does not hesitate to go to war in Judges 5 (cf. Judg. 4:8). Moreover, without going into the detail that Sisera fled to Jael's tent, she gives him milk and a bowl of curds instead of water (Judg. 5:25). The most noticeable difference between the two versions is that she appears to approach him from behind and drive the tent peg into his temple while he was standing, shattering his skull. He then sank and fell dead between her legs (v. 27).

Although Jael is not racialized as a stereotypical hypersexualized Black female seductress like Jezebel, she is still victim to being racialized and sexualized as the foreign *femme fatale*, a traitorous, dangerous, sensual woman who is masculinized by some readers for her role reversal as the subject of

100   *Chapter 4*

warfare's violence when she kills Sisera with a tent peg, which some view as a phallic symbol in a reversed rape.[52] For example, Harold Washington describes Jael's killing of Sisera as a "lurid rape-murder, climaxing in the lethal penetration of the man's soft temple by Jael's phallic spike."[53] As a result, Sisera is feminized as the object in relation to violence. The irony is not lost on the reader that in Judges 5 women are used to "un-man" or shame men. Deborah sings, "Most blessed of women be Jael, the wife of Heber the Kenite, of tent-dwelling women most blessed" (Judg. 5:24) for her defeat of Sisera. Steed Davidson, in his exploration of the figure Native Woman in imperializing and postcolonial discourses, writes that Jael is a case where "[t]he role of gender in imperializing discourses foregrounds the Native Woman but implies weakness and inadequacies on the part of the Native Man."[54]

The assignment to male warriors subject positions as invaders acquiring territory and possessions through sexual violence against a feminine object is common in national myths of identity and belonging. According to Julie Mostov, "Popular among these tales are those that tell of the abduction of young girls—whisked away, seduced, or violently torn from their homelands. Such stories reveal the vulnerability or porousness of national boundaries."[55] This expectation is driven home in stanza 5b (Judg. 5:28–30) when Sisera's mother watches from the window for her son's triumphant return from the war. She ponders why his chariot is delayed and she allays her fears—indeed her wisest of advisors joins her—by proclaiming that he is dividing the spoils of victory, to include: "a womb, two wombs for every warrior" (5:30a; AT). As Cheryl Exum observes, Sisera's mother "serves as the mouthpiece for male ideology of war, in which pillage and rape go together."[56]

The Deuteronomic war laws, which encompass the law of the woman captured in war (Deut. 21:10–14), enshrines rape in the Deuteronomic statutes on family and combat. As instructed by the law, if a victorious Israelite soldier sees a beautiful woman among the spoils whom he wishes to marry (Deut. 21:11), then he must bring her to his home where she must shave her head, pare her nails (v. 12), and discard her clothes of captivity (v. 13). She must remain in his home for a month, presumably to assure that subsequent children born to her are his legitimate heirs, all the while mourning her mother and father, the former who may have also been taken captive and the latter who may have been killed. At the end of the month she is transformed into an Israelite wife.[57] Only after these rituals are complete may he engage in sexual relations with her as his wife. In the event he is not pleased with her, he may not sell her but must let her go free since she is now an Israelite wife and no longer a captive slave (v. 14).

In keeping with the notion that men are in subject positions and women objectified in warfare, Caryn Reeder concludes that in the law of the captive woman, "the male Israelite warrior, the addressee of the law, is also the actor in the law, going to war, taking captives, seeing and loving and taking a woman."[58] The taking of women captive in warfare and turning them into slaves or wives "transfers the woman's sexuality to enemy possession and erases and replaces the enemy's population with 'alien seed.'"[59] Tales and songs about illicit border crossings into the enemy's territory eroticize wartime violence, as "each side fantasizes about invading the space of the other, stealing the identity of the alien society and installing its own culture."[60] Additionally, Cheryl Exum does not overlook that in Judges 5, the voice of Deborah, a mother in Israel, is appropriated to "advocate the male ideology of war in which rape is taken for granted as a weapon of terror and revenge."[61]

The Deuteronomistic historian possibly retrieved this tale of human heroism from a "storehouse of national mythologies"[62] and updated and transferred it to the religious realm by inserting YHWH the patron deity of Israel to unite an exilic or postexilic community around an Israelite national identity. Such mythologies, passed down through songs, poetry, and literature, effectively appeal to their audience's emotions with imagery of borders to defend, threats of assimilation by outside influence, and acts of bravery. These scenes play out in Judges 5 in battles at the gates and the cosmic realm in defense of physical and symbolic boundaries, to include women's bodies as boundaries threatened with invasion.

The fact Deborah is included among performers of public musical com memoration, a space usually occupied by men in the Hebrew Bible, is celebrated by some scholars for subverting social inequalities that are bound up with power dynamics of gender and memory.[63] Other scholars contend that in this instance Deborah serves to "sustain rather than disrupt gender constructions in which men are properly aggressors, while women are licit objects of male violence."[64]

MOTHERS OF THE NATION

Mothers, whether symbolically or literally, figure prominently in Judges 5. Mercedes García Bachmann points out to readers that these are the first mothers to appear in the book of Judges.[65] As has already been noted, Deborah, the symbolic figure is identified by the epithet mother in Israel but there is no mention of her bearing children in the text. Instead, she is symbolic of Dtr's masculinized memory of events of the mother figure rallying the sons of Israel to fight, praising those who answer the call to unity, and shaming those who failed to fulfil their duty as unmanly.

102   *Chapter 4*

The symbolic mother of the sons of Israel is paired with the biological mother of Sisera of Canaan. Tammi Schneider explains that this is the only mother/son relationship mentioned in Judges until Samson's annunciation in Judges 13.[66] On one level, she is portrayed as a sympathetic character sitting by the window waiting for her son's return when the reader is aware that he has been killed by Jael. On another level, she is despised for imagining that his delay is because he is raping and dividing the spoils of victory that she expects will be shared with her: "two pieces of dyed work embroidered for my neck as spoil?" (Judg. 5:30).

Other commentators have included Jael as a symbolic mother figure, the "deceptive mother who gives birth (between her legs), offers milk, puts the son to sleep, and then kills him" referring to Jael's murder of Sisera in Judges 5:24–28.[67] For Cheryl Exum, Jael is the "sinister mother" who offers Sisera maternal nurture and security only to deceive him. "The picture of Jael covering Sisera and giving him milk to drink suggests a mother putting her son to bed,"[68] but she turns deadly. Each woman is a death-dealing mother by their actions in Judges 5.

Returning to a point made earlier in this chapter, mothers are often evaluated differently along lines of class, race/ethnicity, and sexuality in binary terms of good and bad or fit and unfit. In the United States, good mothers have been regarded at least since the late eighteenth and early nineteenth centuries as married, White middle-class women ensconced in the domestic realm. Cheryl Exum refers to Deborah as the good mother who "delivers her children from danger and makes their lives secure" while also regarding Deborah as a dangerous mother for sending her sons to near certain death on the battlefield.[69] However, nationalist narratives exalt women symbolically figured as the nation being defended by heroic men sacrificing themselves on her behalf. Good mothers support their sons being sent off to war. Exum is right however, that the good mother is not a sexual mother. As argued in chapter 3, Deborah conjures the pious desexualized mammy, an image imposed on Black women, devoid of sexual attraction, interest, or desire in the interest of caring for her master's children. Paradoxically, Mammy is regarded as a bad mother for neglecting the care of her own offspring.

Ideas about women as good or bad mothers feature prominently in discourses about citizenship and race in the United States. In the antebellum period attempts at defining the roles of women according to certain virtues were defined by historian Barbara Welter (1966) as the "Cult of True Womanhood." Its adherents held that a true woman extolled the virtues of piety, purity, submissiveness, and domesticity. True women were good mothers who fulfilled their patriotic duty by inculcating their children with the virtues of American citizenship from her domestic perch. According to women's magazines of the time, a good mother "stays home with 'her Bible

Mothers in Israel, Church Mothers, and Mothers of the Nation   103

and a well-balanced mind' and raises her sons to be good Americans."[70] Of course, these same sources discounted enslaved Black women, immigrant, and poor working women among those capable of embodying these virtues.

Such sentiments about good and bad mothers and citizenship continued through the twentieth century. Ruth Feldstein analyzed representations of White and Black mothers in New Deal liberalism from the 1930s to the 1960s to argue that beliefs about masculinity, citizenship, and democracy turned on ideas of good and bad motherhood.[71] Her examination of film, scholarship, and policies from this period demonstrated that images of White and Black women's behavior as mothers were interrelated in liberal discourse with ideas about race relations, healthy citizens, and a strong democracy. In this regard, racial liberalism and gender conservatism were not far apart in blaming mothers for rearing sons who could not only function as good citizens but also could be a threat to national security.

Relying on psychological frameworks and using different standards for Black and White women, social scientists and public intellectuals linked racial prejudice, demasculinized men, and weak citizenship to "black and white maternal pathology."[72] Despite their similarities, Feldstein observed that Black and White mothers were evaluated as maternal failures differently according to race and gender. She contends, "If 'momism' produced what was in part a racial problem (prejudice) as a result of gender disorders in white women, then 'matriarchy' produced what was in part a gender problem (unmanly black men) as a result of racial disorders in black women."[73]

Constructions of motherhood in America coincide with citizenship. Certain women are conferred the rights of citizenship based on their ability to perform certain maternal functions for national stability. Feldstein's research showed that some liberal feminists of the 1960s accepted the view that governmental policies should protect and support acceptable women's maternal functions. Likewise state regulators saw their responsibility as preserving "the maternal functions of women who were 'good' mothers and protecting against those women who were 'bad' mothers."[74] "Bad" mothers whose behavior needed controlling included Black women, who were still regarded as family matriarchs who threatened national health and security. A 1961 report of the Presidential Commission on the Status of Women (PCSW) convened by John F. Kennedy asserted that "traditionally, Negro families have been more matriarchal than white families."[75] The report added that this structure caused Black children to be confused about their appropriate gender roles. Feldstein reports that the PSCW determined that "All women needed to avoid the kind of behavior most evident in black women if they were to be good citizens."[76]

Among the commission members were elected officials, college presidents, secretaries of governmental agencies, labor union representatives, US Attorney General Robert Kennedy, Eleanor Roosevelt, chair, Esther

Peterson, Assistant Secretary of Labor, Dorothy Height, National Council of Negro Women President, and civil rights activist and attorney Pauli Murray. Recommendations by the commission included job training, affordable childcare, and paid maternity leave for women. However, in the politics of belonging, "It remained difficult to see black women as citizens or as beyond motherhood."[77] Thus, despite the racial, gender, and religious diversity of the commission members, they privileged White women—more specifically, White middle-class women—over non-White women for governmental programs that were supposed to accord equal opportunity to all women. Thus, morality was a gendered and racialized category dividing us and them as mothers of the nation.

Tamar Mayer noted, "The intersection of nation, gender and sexuality is a discourse about a moral code, which mobilizes men (and sometimes women) to become its sole protectors and women its biological and symbolic reproducers."[78] The moral discourse around maternal functions has been not only about the need to protect good mothers and their offspring to ensure the birth of healthy citizens but also about state regulation of pregnant women, especially poor and Black women, deemed less worthy and capable.[79]

In her article "Producing the Mothers of the Nation: Race, Class, and Contemporary US Population Policies" (1999), Patricia Hill Collins traces how ideas of motherhood influence who gets to belong as a US citizen and the government officials who decide using population policies as their guide. For example, Collins examined US population policies targeted towards middle-class White women, working-class White women, African American women, and undocumented immigrant Latinas to demonstrate how such regulations support the increased fertility of so-called desirable mothers and discourage the fertility of "unfit" mothers. She found that middle-class and affluent White women, who are considered emblematic of the nation, enjoy less intrusive, privatized population policies. Black women, who are treated as second-class citizens are deemed unfit to pass on national culture and, therefore, are subjected to coercive population policies. Collins remarks, "Because Black women are 'unfit' mothers they become 'undeserving' of the benefits of belonging to the American national family."[80]

Working-class White women fared only a little better than Black women. While better off socially than Black women, they are still regarded as less fit social mothers than middle-class White women. As genetic and gestational mothers of White children, they are beneficial for providing middle-class White mothers with adoptive children. Collins argues that the decrease in adoptable White children has contributed to recent efforts to limit access to abortion for working-class and poor White women. Undocumented Latinas are a group that replaced Black women as social mothers for middle-class and affluent White women but are regarded by anti-immigrant activists

Mothers in Israel, Church Mothers, and Mothers of the Nation 105

as "economic welfare burdens."[81] Therefore, their entry into the nation is discouraged.

The social value of women in the United States is in bearing children—not just any children but rather healthy White children for the national interests of the nation. Nira Yuval-Davis makes the connection between population policies, abortion access, and citizenship. She maintains, "Population policies and women's reproductive rights are, therefore, closely interrelated, and both of them affect and are affected by the ways various nationalist projects view the size and quality of the 'pool of genes' in the national collectivity and how these should be controlled and reproduced."[82]

CONCLUSION

Deborah, a mother in Israel, is ostensibly the biblical antecedent to the Church Mother in the Black church. With this symbolic figure at their disposal, Black women in Black Baptist, Methodist, and Sanctified sanctuaries were able to lay claim to church leadership roles because the story of the prophet Deborah in the Bible authorized them to wield real power in male dominated churches. Deborah's maternal image provided both the Black church and the Deuteronomistic authors with a symbolic custodial figure to maintain boundaries around cultural moral systems: the former through racial uplift and moral living in response to being "Othered" and the latter through fidelity to Mosaic law. Nira Yuval-Davis explains, "All societies have a pool of cultural traditions, collective memories and 'common sense' in which the image of the 'Others' and the 'rules' about how they should be handled are to be found."[83]

For Church Mothers in the Church of God in Christ, the rules included Purity Classes established to protect Christian adolescents in the church from the moral decay of the 1920s. "Equipped with creed and a song designed expressly for the Purity Class, the Mothers endeavored to instill in their young members, the Puritans, the basics for a sanctified lifestyle—modest dress, abstinence from sex and alcohol, and pure speech."[84] For Dtr, the song of Deborah was selected and updated from among the collective memories recalled in maternal voices to construct the boundaries between insiders and outsiders.

Mothers are purposefully constructed in the song. Mercedes García Bachmann says, "The result is a poetic masterpiece and an ideologically well-accomplished message, which invites the reader to take sides with the right mother. But is there a right mother?[85] Bachmann warns the reader to proceed with caution "because one very successful patriarchal trick is to set one woman against another, so that there is no solidarity between them (or

106   *Chapter 4*

us)."[86] One way this occurs in contemporary life is to deny the differences in treatment between Black and White women, such as different encounters with population policies based on women's race, class, motherhood, and citizenship.

Audre Lorde acknowledges, "Certainly there are very real differences between us of race, age, and sex. But it is not those differences between us that are separating us. It is rather our refusal to recognize those differences, and to examine the distortions which result from our misnaming them and their effects upon human behavior and expectation."[87] Lorde contends that such distortions prevent us from developing tools for "using human difference as a springboard for creative change within our lives."[88] Instead, she contends that we must "recognize differences among women who are our equals, neither inferior nor superior, and devise ways to use each other's difference to enrich our visions and our joint struggles."[89] Still, as long as the politics of belonging persists in making Black women the constituent boundaries of proper womanhood in America, the differences between White and Black women continue to deem Black women as unsuitable mothers of the nation.

NOTES

1. Anthea D. Butler, "A Peculiar Synergy: Matriarchy and the Church of God in Christ," (PhD diss., Vanderbilt University, 2001), https://etd.library.vanderbilt.edu/etd-0328101-224926.

2. Cheryl Townsend Gilkes, *If It Wasn't for the Women: Black Women's Experience and Womanist Culture in Church and Community* (Maryknoll, NY: Orbis, 2001), 68.

3. Butler, "A Peculiar Synergy," 28.

4. Vanessa Lovelace and Mercedes L. García Bachmann, "Deborah in the African American Tradition," in *Judges*, Wisdom Commentary (Collegeville, MN: Liturgical, 2018), 71.

5. Butler, "A Peculiar Synergy," 28.

6. Phyllis Bird, *Missing Persons and Mistaken Identities: Women and Gender in Ancient Israel* (Minneapolis, MN: Fortress, 1997), 98.

7. Victor Matthews, *Judges and Ruth* (Cambridge: Cambridge University Press, 2004), 64.

8. Nira Yuval-Davis, *Gender & Nation* (London: Sage, 1997), 45.

9. Alan Forrest, *"La Patrie en Danger*: The French Revolution and the First *Levee en Mass,"* in *The People in Arms: Military Myth and National Mobilization Since the French Revolution*, ed. Daniel Moran and Arthur Waldron (Cambridge: Cambridge University Press, 2003).

10. Forrest, 19. In contrast, World War I German propaganda depicts France as a seductively dressed female in the act of being fired upon by a German soldier. Harold

Washington, "Violence and the Construction of Gender," *Biblical Interpretation 5*, 1997: 324–63.

11. Nira Yuval-Davis, "Nationalist Projects and Gender Relations," *Nar. Umjet* 40, no. 1 (2003): 17.

12. The term "mother in Israel" also refers to the city Abel in 2 Samuel 20:19.

13. Barnabas Lindars, *Judges 1–5: A New Translation and Commentary*, ed. A.D.H. Mayes (Edinburgh: T&T Clark, 1995), 239.

14. Tikva Frymer-Kensky, *Reading the Women of the Bible* (New York: Schocken, 2002), 50.

15. James Ackerman, "Prophecy and Warfare in Early Israel: A Study of the Deborah-Barak Story," *Bulletin of the American Schools of Oriental Research* 220 (1975): 5–13.

16. Dennis Olson, *Judges* (Nashville: Abingdon, 1998).

17. Susan Ackerman, *Warrior, Dancer, Seductress, Queen: Women in Judges and Biblical Israel* (New York: Doubleday, 1998), 59.

18. J. Cheryl Exum, "Feminist Criticism: Whose Interests are Being Served?" in *Judges & Method: New Approaches in Biblical Studies*, 2nd ed., ed. Gale A. Yee (Minneapolis: Fortress, 2007), 71.

19. Claudia Camp, *Wise, Strange and Holy: The Strange Woman and the Making of the Bible* (Sheffield: Sheffield Academic, 2000).

20. Gale A. Yee, *Poor Banished Children of Eve: Woman as Evil in the Hebrew Bible* (Minneapolis, MN: Fortress, 2003).

21. Mayer Gruber, "The Motherhood of God in Second Isaiah," *Revue Biblique 90* (1983): 351–59.

22. Brad E. Kelle, "Wartime Rhetoric: Prophetic Metaphorization of Cities as Female," in *Writing and Reading War: Rhetoric, Gender, and Ethics in Biblical and Modern Contexts*, ed. Brad E. Kelle and Frank Ritchel Ames (Boston: Brill, 2008), 95–112.

23. Kelle, "Wartime Rhetoric."

24. Cynthia Enloe coined the phrase "for the sake of the womenandchildren" in *Bananas, Beaches, and Bases: Making Feminist Sense of International Politics* (Berkeley: University of California Press, 1989), to describe how women and children are conflated as a single, defenseless entity in need of protecting to mobilize men to defend the nation at wartime.

25. Kenton Sparks, *Ethnicity and Identity in Ancient Israel: Prolegomena to the Study of Ethnic Sentiments and their Expression in the Hebrew Bible* (Winona Lake, IN: Eisenbrauns, 1998).

26. Scholars note that both Exodus 15 and Judges 15 are narrative poems that follow a prose version of the accounts sung about, both are songs celebrating YHWH's victory over Israel's enemy, and both songs allude to YHWH's control over water to bring about the victory. See, for example, Gregory T. K. Wong, "Song of Deborah as Polemic," *Biblica* 88, no. 1 (2007): 1–22, https://www.jstor.org/stable/42614746.

27. Charles Echols, *"Tell Me, O Muse": The Song of Deborah (Judges 5) in the Light of Heroic Poetry* (New York: T&T Clark, 2008).

108   *Chapter 4*

28. Alan J. Hauser, "Two Songs of Victory: A Comparison of Exodus 15 and Judges 5," in Directions in Biblical Hebrew Poetry, ed. Elaine R. Follis, JSOT Supplements 40 (Sheffield, UK: JSOT, 1987): 281.

29. Wong, "Song of Deborah as Polemic," 3.

30. See, for example, Anne McClintock, "'No Longer in a Future Heaven': Race, Gender and Nationalism," in *Dangerous Liaisons*, ed. Anne McClintock, Aamir Mufti, and Elai Shohat (Minneapolis: University of Minnesota Press, 1997), 89–112.

31. J. Albert Soggin, *Judges, A Commentary*, trans. John Bowden (Philadelphia: Westminster, 1981), 84.

32. Soggin, 84. Less accepted translations include "A revelation was made in Israel" (LXX) and "For the avenging of Israel" (KJV).

33. Robert Miller, "When Pharaohs Ruled: On the Translation of Judges 5:2," *Journal of Theological Studies* 59, no. 2 (2008): 654.

34. Tammi J. Schneider, *Judges*, Berit Olam (Collegeville, MN: Liturgical, 2009), 87.

35. Soggin, *Judges*.

36. Serge Frolov, "How Old Is the Song of Deborah?" in *Journal for the Study of the Old Testament* 36, no. 2 (2011): 163–84.

37. Sparks, *Ethnicity and Identity in Ancient Israel*.

38. Ken Stone, "Judges," in *Theological Bible Commentary*, ed. Gail O'Day and David L. Petersen (Louisville: Westminster John Knox, 2009), 90.

39. Washington, "Violence and the Construction of Gender," 329.

40. Susan Niditch, *Judges* (Louisville: Presbyterian Publishing Corp., 2008), 71.

41. Niditch, 68.

42. Soggin, *Judges*, 82.

43. Tamar Mayer, "Gender Ironies of Nationalism: Setting the Stage," in *Gender Ironies of Nationalism: Sexing the Nation*, ed. Tamar Mayer (New York: Routledge, 2000), 2.

44. David J. A. Clines, *Interested Parties: The Ideology of Writers and Readers of the Hebrew Bible* (Sheffield: Sheffield Academic, 1995), 7.

45. Washington, "Violence and the Construction of Gender," 330.

46. Soggin, *Judges*, 90.

47. Washington, "Violence and the Construction of Gender," 347.

48. E. Theodore Mullen Jr., *Narrative History and Ethnic Boundaries: The Deuteronomistic Historian and the Creation of Israelite National Identity* (Atlanta: Scholars, 1993).

49. Mercedes L. García Bachmann, *Women at Work in the Deuteronomistic History. Society of Biblical Literature*, International Voices in Biblical Studies 4 (Atlanta: SBL, 2013), 66.

50. In all, ten tribes are identified in the stanza, which has led many commentators to propose multiple theories for not only the lack of twelve tribes but also the absence of familiar tribes such as Levi, Simeon, and Judah.

51. Washington, "Violence and the Construction of Gender," 330.

52. Mieke Bal, *Murder and Difference: Gender, Genre, and Scholarship on Sisera's Death* (Bloomington, IN: Indiana University Press, 1988); Danna Fewell and David

Gunn, "Controlling Perspectives. Women, Men and the Authority of Violence in Judges 4 and 5," *Journal of the American Academy of Religion* 58, no. 3 (Autumn 1990): 389–411.

53. Washington, "Violence and the Construction of Gender," 361.

54. Steed Vernyl Davidson, "Gazing (At) Native Women: Rahab and Jael in Imperializing and Postcolonial Discourses," in *Postcolonialism and the Hebrew Bible: The Next Step*, ed. Roland Boer (Atlanta: Society of Biblical Literature, 2013), 75.

55. Julie Mostov, "Our Women/Their Women: Symbolic Boundaries, Territorial Markers, and Violence in the Balkans," *Peace & Change* 20, no. 4 (October 1995): 517.

56. Exum, "Feminist Criticism," 73.

57. Deuteronomy 21:12–13 makes provisions for a captive woman's marriage to her Israelite captor in the absence of normal marriage arrangements between her father or other male relative and her suitor.

58. Caryn Reeder, "Deuteronomy 21.10–14 and/as Wartime Rape," *Journal for the Study of the Old Testament* 41, no. 3 (2017): 325.

59. Reeder, 328.

60. Mostov, "Violence in the Balkans," 517.

61. Exum, "Feminist Criticism," 73.

62. Mostov, "Violence in the Balkans," 516.

63. Ovidiu Creangă, "The Silenced Songs of Victory: Power, Gender and Memory in the Conquest Narrative of Joshua (Joshua 1–12)," in *A Question of Sex? Gender and Difference in the Hebrew Bible and Beyond*, ed. Deborah W. Rooke (Sheffield: Sheffield Phoenix, 2007).

64. Washington, "Violence and the Construction of Gender," 361.

65. Bachmann, *Deuteronomistic History*, 79.

66. Schneider, *Judges*.

67. Mercedes L. García Bachmann, *Judges*, Wisdom Commentary 7 (Collegeville, MN: Liturgical, 2018), 80.

68. Exum, "Feminist Criticism," 71.

69. Exum, "Feminist Criticism," 71–72.

70. Barbara Welter, "The Cult of True Womanhood: 1820–1860," *American Quarterly* 18, no. 2 Part 1 (Summer 1966): 7.

71. Ruth Feldstein, *Motherhood in Black and White: Race and Sex in American Liberalism, 1930–1965* (Ithaca, NY: Cornell University Press, 2000).

72. Feldstein, 8.

73. Feldstein, 61.

74. Feldstein, 159.

75. Feldstein, 160; The Presidential Commission on the Status of Women established by President John F. Kennedy in 1962 met to examine employment policies in place for women and make recommendations. Although the commission promoted equal opportunity for women of all incomes, non-White women were often shut out from programs that supported women and children.

76. Feldstein, 160.

77. Feldstein, 160.

110 Chapter 4

78. Mayer, "Gender Ironies of Nationalism," 6.
79. Feldstein, *Black and White*.
80. Collins, "Mothers of the Nation," 125.
81. Collins, "Mothers of the Nation," 12.
82. Yuval-Davis, "Nationalist Projects and Gender Relations," 16.
83. Yuval-Davis, 19.
84. Butler, *A Peculiar Synergy*, 50.
85. Bachmann, *Deuteronomistic History*, 80.
86. Bachmann, 81.
87. Lorde, *Sister Outsider*, 115.
88. Lorde, 115–114.
89. Lorde, 122.

Chapter 5

Final Thoughts of an Academic Outsider Within

The Seneca Falls (New York) Convention of 1848 is a commemorated historical event in the women's rights movement known for the leading figures who convened to present their list of demands for the social, civic, and religious rights of women. Yet, a less celebrated gathering of historical significance took place nearly twenty years earlier in 1830 at Mother Bethel A.M.E. Church in Philadelphia. This was the Colored National Convention, the first of more than 200 Colored Conventions between 1830 and the 1890s, comprised of Black activists who met to deliberate and strategize on ending slavery, ending anti-Black violence, and securing citizenship for Black Americans.

Although Black women were largely excluded from attending the Colored Conventions as delegates, women such as Mary Ann Shadd Cary, Elizabeth Gloucester, and Maria Stewart were publicly active in supporting the convention platforms of both the Colored Conventions and the women's rights conventions. This intersection of Black women's activism for women's suffrage and the abolition of slavery not only was natural to Black women based on their belief in their divinely inspired call and Constitutional right, as recounted in the introduction, but also is the place where womanist biblical interpretation finds its beginnings. For Black women, race and gender were simultaneously interlocking concerns grounded in biblical teachings on freedom and equality.

I do not believe that it is a coincidence that the first Colored convention convened in 1830. While Black Americans advocated for the end of slavery and the right to citizenship, as mentioned in chapter 2, the abolitionist movement was gaining momentum in America in the 1830s. Whether Blacks were inspired by the growing strength of the movement to hold that first convention in 1830 or the reverse, that the organizing and planning by the convention participants motivated those determined to end slavery, the abolitionist

111

112   *Chapter 5*

movement coalesced into an effective organized, vocal, and radicalized crusade to be reckoned with.

This book opened with the ideals proffered by Black activists and clergy that the biblical witness of God's deliverance of the enslaved in Egypt affirmed their right to freedom and that the US Constitution and the Declaration of Independence guaranteed their right to citizenship by birth. They preached such principles from church pulpits and convention podiums. Chapter 2 details how the burgeoning influence of anti-slavery activism in the 1830s fueled the proliferation of racist publications that linked religious ideologies and scripture to the defense of slavery rather than the manumission of slaves. Fear of the success of the abolitionist movement in ending the involuntary labor of enslaved Africans that drove the economic system in the south only deepened the entrenchment of a racial hierarchy that espoused the inferiority of Blacks. The appeal to the authority of scripture to defend slavery and White supremacy was not a new phenomenon in the United States and would not have surprised anti-slavery advocates. But they likely underestimated the degree to which White Christians would use an interpretation of Genesis 9 that linked Noah's curse of Ham's son Canaan with blackness and servitude to deny Blacks their humanity and citizenship.

Historian Martha Jones explains that free Black Americans had been mulling over the idea of citizenship since the eighteenth century. If the Declaration of Independence of 1776 pronounced that "all men are created equal," then what, free Blacks asked themselves, would preclude them from enjoying the same privileges of White citizens? This was not just a philosophical question. For example, free Blacks in Massachusetts were taxed the same and sometimes more than Whites but were not granted the same privileges—such as the right to vote—as White taxpayers. Blacks petitioned states and the federal government for the right to citizenship, but the courts were at odds over the question of whether freeborn Black Americans were entitled to the "unalienable Rights" submitted by the framers of the Declaration of Independence.[1]

Blacks were met with growing resistance to their demands for citizenship by wealthy and powerful White men determined to preserve "the United States as a white man's country."[2] By the 1820s, the colonization movement in America became a real threat to free Blacks.[3] In their efforts to thwart Black citizenship, wealthy White citizens colluded with courts and legislators, who "pressured free Black Americans into self-exile by enacting local statutes, termed Black laws, that restricted their work, movement, and public gatherings . . . In some states, lawmakers proposed new laws that would require free people of color to leave by threat of force."[4] Undeterred, Blacks petitioned to secure privileges equal to Whites as citizens by birthright or naturalization, and slaveholders and White supremacists fought to prevent the same. The doctrine of Black inferiority prevailed. At the heart of this

Final Thoughts of an Academic Outsider Within   113

Black activism for full citizenship was a desire for belonging. As Martha Jones wrote, "Citizenship is an old concept, with roots that stretch back to the ancient world. To be a citizen is to be an insider. It is to belong."[5]

The biblical narratives explored in the previous chapters, beginning with the Sarah and Hagar narrative, reflect exilic and post-exilic writers' efforts at constructing a national identity of a community called "Israel." The writers sought to construct an identity for an ethnic group threatened with complete dissolution after its dispersion by the Assyrians in 722 BCE and defeat and exile by the Babylonians in 587/86 BCE. Jacob Wright explains,

> A nation needs a narrative. With the political order broken down, the monarchies ousted, and the state armies conquered, the Israelite people would be forced to confront the questions, *Who are we?* and *What—if anything—still holds us together?* The biblical authors responded, preemptively, by weaving (selective) fragments of their people's past into a coherent narrative of its origins.[6]

The writers collected and preserved—some say invented—a narrative comprised of a common origin, common solidarity, and common destiny that divided the world between "us" and "them." Those who followed the covenant of Moses were insiders; those who rejected it were outsiders. These stories interest us as readers because they allow us to examine issues of what it means to belong as a member of society: who is an insider and an outsider, and what are some of the processes that construct the boundaries between us and them—the *politics* of belonging. Each narrative analyzed demonstrated numerous ways different political projects of belonging engaged in the drawing and maintenance of boundaries based on gender, class, and racial/ethnic categories that determined who could be included as a member of Israel.

As we read, in both ancient texts and contemporary contexts, people are constructed as "belonging" on multiple levels. One can belong along lines of social location and social groupings, individual and collective identity narratives and emotional attachments, and ethical and political value systems. Nira Yuval Davis frames these levels of belonging along an intersectional analysis, stating that "while people can identify exclusively with one identity category . . . their concrete social location is constructed along multiple axes of difference."[7]

Another way of looking at it is Patricia Hill Collins's example of the family as constituting a primary site of belonging to various groups. One can belong to a family "as an assumed biological entity; to geographically identifiably, racially segregated neighborhoods conceptualized as imagined families; to so-called racial families codified in science and law; and to the US nation-state conceptualized as a national family."[8] The hegemonic political powers that draw these lines of inclusion and exclusion and their contestation

114   *Chapter 5*

and challenge by political agents are what Yuval-Davis distinguishes as the politics of belonging from just belonging.

WHAT A DIFFERENCE A MOTHER MAKES

The first three chapters developed from separate research projects and therefore the link between motherhood and belonging was not readily evident to me when I began to write this book. However, by the time chapter 4 was taking shape it was undeniable that motherhood, whether genetic, gestational, social, or symbolic, was central in the processes that determined who was included and excluded as a member of Israel (and in the United States). While common descent or the myth of the same as a requisite for belonging is a common theme in the Hebrew Bible, as we saw in the story of Ishmael and Isaac, "Who's your mama?" was a decisive factor. Whether or not one's mother—in both the biblical narratives and contemporary society—had the right pedigree and credentials played a role in different political projects.

In chapter 1, the circumstances of one's birth mother defined the parameters of belonging. The political project of motherhood ultimately decided that it would be Isaac and his descendants who were entitled to belonging as members of Israel to the exclusion of Ishmael. Hagar's ethnicity and social status resulted in the abjection of Ishmael from Abraham's household despite a cultural milieu where primogeniture was standard practice. The political process of membership by descent is at first replaced with a political project that is theologically determinative of the rite of male circumcision. However, this is soon displaced by the political project of motherhood. Motherhood initially elevated Hagar's status in Abraham's household as both the genetic and gestational mother of his firstborn son. However, she loses esteem to Sarah as the social mother of Ishmael, who then rejects him for the genetic, gestational, and social motherhood accorded her by giving birth to Isaac. Hagar then assumes the function of symbolic signifier of ethnic and national difference as a foreign mother to a non-Israelite son.

While Ishmael is evaluated positively by the narrator as a "wild ass of a man" (Gen. 16:12 NRSV) "who bends his neck to no yoke,"[9] he would not be the son of the promise due to his maternal lineage though he was still Abraham's offspring. Nonetheless, God blesses Hagar with a multitude of descendants of which Ishmael would be the progenitor (Gen. 21:10) and represent nations apart from Israel. In chapter 3, the sons of Jezebel and Athaliah are judged negatively for departing from the ways of God: they did what was "evil in the sight of YHWH." They are not condemned so much because they had mothers who were outsiders in Israel but rather because the Deuteronomistic historian has accused their mothers of exercising undue influence over their sons by allegedly leading them and the nation to follow gods other than YHWH (Deut. 7:2–4). The historian relies on sexual tropes to cast aspersions on Jezebel and Athaliah as bad mothers who neglect their sons. The Deuteronomistic historian is successful in this portrayal in part due to the women's foreignness and their usurpation of male positions which casts them as unfeminine and thus unfit for motherhood. Outsider women thus are often portrayed as reproducers of enemies who would turn insiders from following YHWH in the biblical texts or in contemporary narratives from being model citizens as in the case of Black mothers.

The theme of good versus bad mothers continues through chapter 4. While women are biological reproducers of members of the polity, it became evident that the politics of belonging held certain expectations for social motherhood. Deborah and Sisera's mother are symbolic and biological mothers, respectively, who produce sons who sacrifice their lives to defend the nation. The two women are on opposite sides of the national boundaries and are thus assessed as good and bad mothers based on who is telling the story. Still, both praise men for fighting battles that imperil women's bodies and security.

Moreover, it is women's patriotic duty not only to bear sons to fight wars but also to instill patriotism in their sons, defined to a large degree in masculinist terms. Mothers explored in this book were often characterized as good mothers if their sons exhibited masculine traits and blameworthy if their sons were regarded as weak or feminine. It became evident that not all mothers are considered acceptable transmitters of national culture to future citizens. Biblical scholars such as Stephanie Buckhanon Crowder have engaged in womanist readings of biblical motherhood and engaged the disparate treatment of biblical mothers and contemporary Black mothers based on ethnic/racial, class, and religious differences.[10] Patricia Hill Collins observes the high personal costs of mothering under oppressive conditions to Black women. She writes, "Black motherhood is fundamentally a contradictory institution. African-American communities value motherhood, but Black mothers' ability to cope with race, class, and gender oppression should not be confused with transcending those conditions."[11]

In chapter 2, following Nira Yuval-Davis, mothers may participate in national processes by giving birth to members of nations, but they are mostly invisible in Genesis 9–10, where we read that it is men who have the procreative powers to beget nations. Genesis 10:1 mentions the children fathered by the sons of Noah without mention of their mothers, but women still figure in the national processes of boundary creation and maintenance in the Noah story. The Priestly writers responsible for the genealogy in Genesis 10 that lists the eponymous ancestors of Ham as the Cushites, Egyptians, Lybians, and Canaanites later turn and portray the Canaanites and Egyptians (and by association the Cushites and Lybians), Ham's descendants, as morally and

116 *Chapter 5*

sexually deviant based on innuendo. But the association works only with the insertion of the gloss of Ham in Genesis 9:21–25 as the antagonist in the narrative that implies the sexual deviance of Ham towards his father.

The list of sexual taboos in Leviticus 18 depicts the men and women of Egypt and Canaan, Ham's progeny in the Table of Nations, as perverted. Implicit in the sexual taboos is that Israelite men should abstain from marrying or having sexual relations with Egyptian or Canaanite women, who might tempt Israelite men to turn and practice the aberrant behavior of their people as depicted by the Priestly writers. However, only marriage to Canaanite women is opposed or prohibited. For example, Abraham makes his slave swear that he will find a wife for Isaac from among his kin rather than allow him to marry a Canaanite woman (Gen. 24:3; cf. 28:1–9; Exod. 34:16). Although mostly addressed to men, such proscriptions maintain Israel's boundaries by policing women's sexuality. We have seen throughout this book that US Black women have been subject to similar boundary mechanisms by slave owners, state regulators, federal policies, and law enforcement.

MYTHS, LIES AND NATIONAL NARRATIVES

Another observation from writing this book is that although myths in biblical literature and contemporary US culture are important for communicating who we are as a collectivity, they can also devolve into untruths that divide the collectivity into us and them in national processes. For some readers (and scholars), the idea that the Bible contains mythological materials is rejected due to popular notions of myths as having no basis in truth when those same readers view the Bible as historically accurate. However, Susan Ackerman explains that in ancient religious texts "myths, through the use of symbolic language, communicate transcendent meaning within a culture, revealing its cosmic dimensions."[12]

As an example, some scholars regard the Passover story in Exodus 1–15 as containing mythological elements. Robert Oden explains that ancient myths function on one level to "bring together disparate people as a group, and then to support these peoples' group identity."[13] On another level, Oden citing Malinowksi offers that a myth performs an "indispensable function in culture: it 'expresses, enhances, and codifies belief; it safeguards and enforces morality.'"[14] The Passover narrative fits the category of a cultic act that functioned to unite the ancient Israelites during the exile but is not based in historical fact. Where myth evolves into lie, for example, is the narrative shared in chapter 1 about Hagar's alleged sexual fecundity due to her Egyptian ancestry.

Final Thoughts of an Academic Outsider Within   117

Similarly, national myths, according to Gérard Bouchard, are "collective representations conveying a large array of meanings, and more precisely, a set of ideals, beliefs, and values expressed in symbols (objects, places, events, individuals). The core attribute of those representations is to be endowed with a kind of sacredness."[15] In America, that sense of sacredness is instilled with biblical "truths." One such story is the exodus in the book of Exodus. Readers may recall in the introduction how nineteenth century Black Americans' faith in the biblical witness of a God who delivered the ancient Israelites from slavery in Egypt fueled their political aspirations for emancipation in America. However, prior to Blacks' adoption of the exodus story, eighteenth century colonists had appropriated the story as their own. King George III was the antitypical Pharaoh, and the colonists were the oppressed Israelites, God's chosen people seeking freedom from the monarchy. Herbert Marbury writes about prominent minister Cotton Mather and his fellow New England Puritans, who viewed themselves as the new Israelites chosen by God in the New World. These colonists not only owned slaves, but Mather, a slave-holder, "believed slavery was morally redemptive and encouraged fellow colonists to make every effort to convert Africans held in chattel slavery from their Traditional African Religions to Christianity."[16]

Yet, as documented in chapter 2, White America's idea of chosenness relies on a racist mythology of Black inferiority based on certain biblical interpretations. Eddie Glaude explains that whiteness functions as a ritual of consensus around a transmitted shared belief or ideology of a racial hierarchy: thus, "the idea of chosenness was racialized such that members of the chosen people were all white men delineated or distinguished from those who were not chosen on the basis of race."[17] As such, Black bodies in America were encoded with servitude and depravity as the imputed progeny of biblical Ham based on literal readings of Genesis 9. As Sylvester Johnson contends, "To participate in the world of American Christian symbols was to 'locate' racial selves in the world of biblical narratives."[18]

Of course, as Glaude described it, such racialized rituals and symbols perpetuate "the lie," the mechanism that allows America to maintain its myth of innocence in the face of its mistreatment of Black people. In his book *Begin Again* on James Baldwin, Glaude declares that Baldwin's brilliance was his commitment to debunking "the lie" that White lives mattered more than Black lives. As cited by Glaude, Baldwin wrote in 1964:

> The people who settled the country had a fatal flaw. They could recognize a man when they saw one. They knew he wasn't . . . anything *else* but a man; but since they were Christian, and since they had already decided that they came here to establish a free country, the only way to justify the role this chattel was playing in one's life was to say that he *was not* a man. For if he wasn't, then no

118 *Chapter 5*

crime had been committed. That lie is the basis of our present trouble (italics in original).[19]

Stephen Steinberg refers to such inventions as the "ideological smoke screen designed to give moral legitimacy"[20] to an unjust racialized caste system. The prophet Jeremiah warned those who claimed to be wise because they were the preservers of the law but had made it into a lie with their interpretations would cause God to put them to shame (Jer. 8:8–9). The best remedy for falsehoods about Black people is to not keep silent. As Audre Lorde spoke on truths left unsaid, our silence will not protect us.[21] Of course, she writes, the transformation of silence into language and action is fraught with danger. "And it is never without fear—of visibility, of the harsh light of scrutiny and perhaps judgment, of pain, of death. But we have lived through all of those already, in silence, except death."[22]

ANTI-MISCEGENATION AND EZRA'S BAN

One Hebrew Bible text that deals with the intersection of race/ethnicity, gender, and class that I chose not to discuss in this monograph is Ezra 9–10 (Neh. 13:23–27), the narrative of the expulsion of the foreign wives and children in post-exilic Judah. I wrestled with whether or not to include an analysis of this passage given its relevance for the book's content. Ezra's ban on intermarriage between the members of the Jewish exilic returnees or *golah* community and foreigners, boundary construction and maintenance of group membership based on the ethnicity or class of mothers, and divine justification for exclusion resemble US anti-miscegenation laws for some US scholars. Cheryl Anderson, for one, compares the intermarriage ban in Ezra to segregationist policies in the United States that prohibited marriage or sexual relations between Whites and Blacks. Anderson contends that the same categories of race/ethnicity, class, and gender used to exclude the foreign wives and children "[w]ere used to consign African Americans to the excluded and marginalized group in the segregationist era."[23]

While such comparisons deserve analysis, apologists for anti-miscegenation laws preferred the myth about the origins of humans. They adhered to the commonly held belief that three distinct racial groups derived from Noah's three sons Shem, Ham, and Jephthah. Following from Noah's curse, White separatists believed that peoples occupying the geographical territory of Africa were deemed to be subservient to Shem and Japheth's descendants, Asians and Europeans, respectively. Therefore, those who pointed to the Bible as justification for their defense of racial separation were more inclined to cite Genesis 9–10 rather than Ezra 9–10. For example, in referring to the legal provision in the United States prohibiting interracial marriage, Anderson cites Judge Leo Bazile of Caroline County Circuit Court in Virginia who upheld the state's intermarriage ban based on his opinion that, "Almighty God created the races white, black, yellow, malay and red, and he placed them on separate continents. And but for the interference with his arrangement there would be no cause for such marriages. The fact that he separated the races shows that he did not intend for the races to mix."[24] While Anderson rightly notes that both the intermarriage ban in Ezra and the US anti-miscegenation laws share features such as justification for the distinctions between groups on racial/ethnic ground as divinely warranted, Bazile and others do not cite Ezra's ban among their arguments.[25] Thus, while elected officials, judges, and Congress relied on biblical justification for enacting laws endorsing segregation and anti-miscegenation, they seldom did so on the grounds of Ezra's ban. Nonetheless, I believe that Ezra 9–10 is helpful for contrasting policies of exclusion based on gender and race/ethnicity in post-exilic Judah and US legal statutes based on the same criteria to discriminate against Blacks.

FUTURE CONSIDERATIONS

This book was limited to examining the controlling images of US-born Black women in White American culture used to exclude Black women from the full benefits of citizenship and belonging based on biblical stereotypes, tropes, and archetypes in the books of Genesis, Judges, and 1 and 2 Kings. A topic for future consideration is the study of the Hebrew Bible, exile and migration, and the experiences of Black immigrant women and motherhood in the United States. A recent Pew Research Center report[26] finds that Black immigrants have contributed significantly to the growth and diversity of the overall US Black population. Pew projects that the Black immigrant population will account for roughly a third of the US Black population's growth through 2060.

Since Patricia Hill Collins's research subjects were US-born Black and White women and undocumented immigrant Latinas, there is little in "Producing the Mothers of the Nation" that might contribute to this conversation. Nonetheless, Collins is right that a woman's race/ethnicity, social class, and citizenship status shape her experiences of motherhood and population policies in the United States and that research on immigrant Black women is a welcome addition to the discourse on motherhood and nation. Additionally, given the intersection of race, gender, and class in the national discourse on White nationalism and reproductive rights post the Dobbs v. Jackson Women's Health Organization decision, motherhood will continue to be a contested category of citizenship and belonging for Black women when mothers are held

120   *Chapter 5*

responsible for the progress of the nation. According to Collins, although African-American communities have traditionally had "strong pro-natalist values," certain Black women find that "[c]oping with unwanted pregnancies and being unable to care for one's children is oppressive."[27]

The authors of the book *Young, Gifted and Diverse* found that the new educated US Black elite are disproportionately female, immigrant, mixed race, and higher income.[28] Historically, Whites have been known to set immigrant Blacks and US-born Blacks in competition against each other. Belinda Deneen Wallace noted in a National Public Radio interview that "Non-Black people are—in the United States are often more comfortable dealing with international Blacks because it doesn't carry the same historical weight."[29] How the growing diversity of Black experiences in the United States might lead to changes in attitudes about Black women and population policies towards them is yet to be determined.

These and related topics might be explored with Black immigrant women biblical scholars living and working in the United States such as Margaret Aymer from Barbados and Althea Spencer Miller from Jamaica, who were influenced by the British Methodist Church in the Caribbean, and Dora Mbuwayesango from South Africa. Perhaps the discourse can be expanded to include their analyses of race, gender, sexuality, postcolonialism and biblical types, tropes, and stereotypes and the politics of belonging.

NOTES

1. Martha Jones, "Citizenship," in *The 1619 Project: A New Origin Story*, ed. Nikole Hannah-Jones, Caitlin Roper, Ilena Silverman, and Jake Silverstein (New York: New York Times, 2021), 225.

2. Jones, 223.

3. The American Colonization Society was founded in 1816 to forcibly remove Black Americans and deport them to African nations.

4. Jones, "Citizenship," 226.

5. Jones, 221.

6. Jacob L. Wright, "A Nation Conceived in Defeat," *Azure* (Autumn 5771 / 2010): 86, https://azure.org.il/download/magazine/Az42%20Wright.pdf.

7. Nira Yuval-Davis, "Belonging and the Politics of Belonging," *Patterns of Prejudice* 40, no. 3 (2006): 20.

8. Patricia Hill Collins, "It's All in the Family: Intersections of Gender, Race, and Nation," *Hypatia* 13, no. 3 (1998): 63.

9. Gerhard von Rad, *Genesis: A Commentary*, trans. John H. Marks (Philadelphia: Westminster, 1972), 194.

10. Stephanie Buckhanon Crowder, *When Momma Speaks: The Bible and Motherhood from a Womanist Perspective* (Louisville: Westminster John Knox, 2016).

11. Patricia Hill Collins, *Black Feminist Thought: Knowledge, Consciousness, and the Politics of Empowerment* (Boston: Unwin Hyman, 1990), 133.

12. Susan Ackerman, "Myth," in *The Oxford Companion to the Bible* (Oxford: Oxford University Press, 1993), https://www.oxfordreference.com/view/10.1093/acref/9780195046458.001.0001/acref-9780195046458-e-0510.

13. Robert A. Oden, Jr., "Myth and Mythology (OT). Vol 3," in *Anchor Bible Dictionary*, ed. David Noel Freedman (New York: Doubleday, 1992), 4:952.

14. Oden, Jr., 4:952.

15. Gerard Bouchard, "National Myths: An Overview," in *National Myths: Constructed Pasts, Contested Presents*, ed. Gerard Bouchard (London: Routledge, 2013), 277.

16. Herbert Robinson Marbury, *Pillars of Cloud and Fire: The Politics of Exodus in African American Biblical Interpretation.* Religion and Social Transformation (New York: New York University Press, 2015), 31.

17. Eddie S. Glaude, Jr., *Exodus! Religion, Race, and Nation in Early Nineteenth Century Black America* (Chicago: University of Chicago Press, 2000), 53.

18. Sylvester A. Johnson, *The Myth of Ham in Nineteenth-Century American Christianity: Race, Heathens, and the People of God* (New York: Palgrave MacMillan, 2004), 45.

19. Eddie S. Glaude, Jr., *Begin Again: James Baldwin's America and Its Urgent Lessons for Our Own* (New York: Crown, 2020), 9.

20. Stephen Steinberg, *The Ethnic Myth: Race, Ethnicity, and Class in America* (Boston: Beacon, 2001), 31.

21. Audre Lorde, *Sister Outsider: Essays & Speeches by Audre Lorde* (Berkeley: Crossing, 2007), 41.

22. Lorde, 43.

23. Cheryl Anderson, "Reflections in an Interethnic/racial Era on Interethnic/racial Marriage in Ezra," in *They Were All Together in One Place? Toward Minority Biblical Criticism*, ed. Randall C. Bailey, Tat-siong Benny Liew, and Fernando F. Segovia (Atlanta: Society of Biblical Literature, 2009), 51.

24. Anderson, 50.

25. David Chappell, "Religious Ideals of the Segregationists," *Journal of American Studies* 32, no. 2 (1998): 237–62, writes that an exception is the Presbyterian clergyman G. T. Gillespie, who included a brief reference to Ezra's condemnation of intermarriage in Ezra 9–10 at the end of his Hebrew Bible arguments for racial separation, that included Genesis 4:11–26 and 9:18–29.

26. Christine Tamir, "Key Findings About Black Immigrants in the U.S," *Pew Research Center*, January 27, 2022, https://www.pewresearch.org/fact-tank/2022/01/27/key-findings-about-black-immigrants-in-the-u-s/.

27. Collins, *Black Feminist Thought*, 133–34.

28. Camille Z. Charles, et al., *Young, Gifted and Diverse: Origins of the New Black Elite* (Princeton: Princeton University Press, 2022).

29. Belinda Deneen Wallace, "A Rise in Black Immigrant Population Changes Understanding of Black America," interviewed by Elissa Nadworny, *All Things Considered*, February 17, 2022, https://www.npr.org/2022/02/17/1081570859/a-rise-in-black-immigrant-population-changes-understanding-of-black-america.

Bibliography

Abrams, Lynn, and Karen Hunt. "Borders and Frontiers in Women's History." *Women's History Review* 9, no. 2 (2000): 191–200.

Ackerman, James. "Prophecy and Warfare in Early Israel: A Study of the Deborah-Barak Story." *BASOR* 220 (1975): 5–13.

Ackerman, Susan. "Myth." In *The Oxford Companion to the Bible*. Oxford: Oxford University Press, 1993. https://www.oxfordreference.com/view/10.1093/acref /9780195046458.001.0001/acref-9780195046458-e-0510.

———. *Warrior, Dancer, Seductress, Queen: Women in Judges and Biblical Israel*. New York: Doubleday, 1988.

———. "Why Is Miriam also among the Prophets? (And Is Zipporah among the Priests?)." *Journal of Biblical Literature* 121, no. 1 (Spring 2002): 47–80.

Ahmed, Sara. *The Cultural Politics of Emotions*. 2nd ed. Edinburgh: Edinburgh University Press, 2014.

———. "Feminist Killjoys (And Other Willful Subjects." *The Scholar & Feminist Online* 8, no. 3 (Summer 2010): 1–8. http://sfonline.barnard.edu/polyphonic/ ahmed_01.htm#text1.

Alvarez, Gabriel. "Defining Race: Antebellum Racial Scientists' Influences on Proslavery Writers." *The Concord Review*, 2011. https://www.commschool.org/ uploaded/publications/cm/cm-1-spring-2012/Concord-Review-Alvarez.

Anderson, Benedict. *Imagined Communities*. London: Verso, 1983.

Anderson, Cheryl. *Women, Ideology and Violence: Critical Theory and the Construction of Gender in the Book of the Covenant and the Deuteronomic Law*. London: T&T Clark, 2006.

———. "Reflections in an Interethnic/racial Era on Interethnic/racial Marriage in Ezra." In *They Were All Together in One Place? Toward Minority Biblical Criticism*, edited by Randall C. Bailey, Tat-siong Benny Liew, and Fernando F. Segovia, 47–64. Atlanta: Society of Biblical Literature, 2009.

Anthias, Floya, and Nira Yuval-Davis. *Racialized Boundaries: Race, Nation, Gender, Colour, and Class and the Anti-Racist Struggle*. London: Routledge, 1992.

Armstrong, John. *Nations before Nationalisms*. Chapel Hill: University of North Carolina Press, 1982.

124   *Bibliography*

Bachmann, Mercedes García. *Women at Work in the Deuteronomistic History. Society of Biblical Literature.* International Voices in Biblical Studies, no. 4. Atlanta: Society of Biblical Literature, 2013.

———. *Judges.* Wisdom Commentary. Vol. 7. Collegeville, MN: Liturgical, 2018.

Bailey, Randall C. "'They're Nothing But Incestuous Bastards': The Polemical Use of Sex and Sexuality in Hebrew Canon Narratives." In *Reading from This Place.* Vol. 1. Social Location and Biblical Interpretation in the United States, edited by Fernando F. Segovia and Marry Ann Tolbert, 121–38. Minneapolis: Fortress, 1993.

———. "The Danger of Ignoring One's Own Cultural Bias in Interpreting the Text." In *The Postcolonial Bible.* Bible and Postcolonialism, 1, edited by R.S. Sugirthirajah, 67–90. Sheffield: Sheffield Academic, 1998.

Bailey, Wilma. "Hagar: A Model for an Anabaptist Feminist." *The Mennonite Quarterly Review* 68, no. 2 (1994): 219–28.

Baker-Fletcher, Karen. "Seeking our Survival, our Quality of Life, and Wisdom: Womanist Approaches to the Hebrew Bible." In *Feminist Interpretations of the Hebrew Bible in Retrospect.* Vol III, edited by Susanne Scholz, 225–42. Sheffield: Sheffield Phoenix, 2017.

Bal, Mieke. *Murder and Difference: Gender, Genre, and Scholarship on Sisera's Death.* Bloomington, IN: Indiana University Press, 1988.

Baldwin, James. *The Fire Next Time.* New York: Dial, 1963.

Barth, Fredrik. *Ethnic Groups and Boundaries.* Boston: Little, Brown and Company, 1969.

Bassett, Frederick W. "Noah's Nakedness and the Curse of Canaan: A Case of Incest?" *Vetus Testamentum* 21, no. 2 (1971): 232–37.

Baumgarten, Albert. "Myth and Midrash: Genesis 9:20–29." In *Christianity, Judaism, and other Greco-Roman Cults. Studies for Morton Smith at Sixty*, vol. 3, edited by Jacob Neusner, 55–71. Leiden: Brill, 1975.

Beal, Lissa Wray. *1 & 2 Kings.* Downers Grove, IL: IVP Academic, 2014.

Bereshit Rabbah 36:7 (The Sefaria Midrash Rabbah, 2022). https://www.sefaria .org/Bereshit_Rabbah?tab=contents. Sanhedrin 108b:15 (The William Davidson Talmud), https://www.sefaria.org/Sanhedrin.108b?lang=bi.

Berge, Kåre. "Categorical Identities: 'Ethnified Otherness and Sameness'—A Tool for Understanding Boundary Negotiation in the Pentateuch?" In *Imagining the Other and Constructing Israelite Identity in the Early Second Temple Period*, edited by Ehud Ben Zvi and Diana V. Edelman, 70–88. London: Bloomsbury, 2014.

Bibb, Eloise. "Poems." American Verse Project, 1895. http://name.umdl.umich.edu/ BAD9461.0001.001.

Bible and Culture Collective. "Feminist and Womanist Criticism." In *The Postmodern Bible*, 225–71. New Haven, CT: Yale University Press, 1995.

Bird, Phyllis A. *Missing Persons and Mistaken Identities: Women and Gender in Ancient Israel.* Minneapolis: Fortress, 1997.

Blenkinsopp, Joseph. "The Family in First Temple Israel." In *Families in Ancient Israel.* The Family, Religion, and Culture, edited by Leo G. Purdue, Joseph Blenkinsopp, John J. Collins, and Carol Meyers, 48–103. Louisville, KY: Westminster John Knox, 1997.

Boehme, Elleke. *Stories of Women: Gender and Narrative in the Postcolonial Nation.* Manchester & New York: Manchester University Press, 2005.

"The Book of the Cave of the Treasures." Translated by W. E. Budge. *Sacred Texts.* https://www.sacred-texts.com/chr/bct/bct06.htm.

Botterweck, G. Johannes. *Theological Dictionary of the Old Testament,* Vol. XI 'zz–pānîm. Translated by David E. Green. Grand Rapids, MI: William B. Eerdmans, 2001.

Bouchard, Gerard. "National Myths: An Overview." In *National Myths: Constructed Pasts, Contested Presents*, edited by Gerard Bouchard, 276–96. London: Routledge, 2013.

Boylorn, Robin, and Mark Hopson. "Learning to Conquer Metaphysical Dilemmas: Womanist and Masculinist Perspectives on Tyler Perry's For Colored Girls." In *Black Women and Popular Culture: The Conversation Continues*, edited by Adria Y. Goldman, Vanatta S. Ford, Alexa A. Harris and Natasha R. Howard, 89–108. London: Lexington, 2014.

Branch, Enobong. *Opportunity Denied: Limiting Black Women to Devalued Work.* New Brunswick, NJ: Rutgers University Press, 2011.

Branch, Robin. "Athaliah, a Treacherous Queen: A Careful Analysis of Her Story in 2 Kings 11 and 2 Chronicles 22:10–23:21." *die Skriflig* 38, no. 4 (2004): 537–59.

Brett, Marc G., ed. *Ethnicity and the Bible.* Boston: Brill, 1988.

"A Brief History of Civil Rights in the United States: The Womanist Movement." Howard University School of Law, Vernon E. Jordan Law Library. https://library.law.howard.edu/civilrightshistory/womanist#:~:text=The%20term%20'womanist'%20was%20coined,Mothers'%20Gardens%3A%20Womanist%20Prose.

Brodie, Thomas L. *Genesis as Dialogue: A Literary, Historical, and Theological Commentary.* Oxford: Oxford University Press, 2001.

Brown, W. S. Preface to *Bible Defence of Slavery: and Origin, Fortunes, and History of the Negro Race,* 5th ed., by Josiah Priest, iii–ix. Glasgow, KY: W. S. Brown, 1852. https://www.loc.gov/item/11011710/.

Brueggemann, Walter. *Genesis. Interpretation: A Bible Commentary for Teaching and Preaching.* Atlanta: John Knox, 1982.

———. *1 & 2 Kings.* Smyth & Helwys Bible Commentary. Macon, GA: Smyth & Helwys, 2000.

Burns, Rita J. *Has the Lord Indeed Spoken Only through Moses? A Study of the Biblical Portrait of Miriam.* Atlanta: Scholars, 1987.

Butler, Anthea D. "A Peculiar Synergy: Matriarchy and the Church of God in Christ." PhD diss. Vanderbilt University, 2001. https://etd.library.vanderbilt.edu/etd-0328101-224926.

Butting, Klara. *Prophetinnen gefragt: Die Bedeutung der Prophetinnen im Kanon aus Tora und Prophetie.* Erev-Rav-Hefte: Biblisch-feministiche Texte, 3. Knesebeck, Germany: Erev-Rav, 2001.

Byron, Gay L. *Symbolic Blackness and Ethnic Difference in Early Christianity.* New York: Routledge, 2002.

Camp, Claudia V. "1 and 2 Kings." In *Women's Bible Commentary*, edited by Carol A. Newsom and Sharon H. Ringe, 102–16. Louisville: Westminster John Knox, 1992, 1998.

———. "Female Voice, Written Word: Women and Authority in Hebrew Scripture." In *Embodied Love: Sensuality and Relationship as Feminist Values*, edited by Paula M. Cooey, Sharon A. Farmer, and Mary Ellen Ross, 97–113. San Francisco: Harper & Row, 1988.

———. *Wise, Strange and Holy: The Strange Woman and the Making of the Bible*. Sheffield: Sheffield Academic, 2000.

Carpenter, Delores. "Theological and Spiritual Empowerment of Black Women in Ministry." In *The Quest for Liberation and Reconciliation: Essays in Honor of J. Deotis Roberts*, edited by Michael Battle and James Deotis Roberts, 153–64. Louisville: Westminster John Knox, 2005.

Carroll, Robert P. "Coopting the Prophets: Nehemiah and Noadiah." In *Priests, Prophets, and Scribes: Essays on the Formation and Heritage of Second Temple Judaism in Honour of Joseph Blenkinsopp*. JSOT 149, edited by Eugene Charles Ulrich and Joseph Blenkinsopp, 87–99. Sheffield: Sheffield Academic, 1992.

Center for Barth Studies at Princeton Theological Seminary. "Frequently Asked Questions." https://barth.ptsem.edu/frequently-asked-questions/

Chapman, Cynthia. *The House of the Mother: The Social Roles of Maternal Kin in Biblical Hebrew Narrative and Poetry*. The Anchor Yale Bible Reference Library. New Haven, CT: Yale University Press, 2016.

Chappell, David. "Religious Ideals of the Segregationists." *Journal of American Studies* 32, no. 2 (1998): 237–62.

Charles, Camille Z., Douglas S. Massey, Kimberly C. Torres, and Rory Kramer. *Young, Gifted and Diverse: Origins of the New Black Elite*. Princeton: Princeton University Press, 2022.

Christensen, Duane. "Huldah and the Men of Anathoth: Women in Leadership in the Deuteronomic History." In *Society of Biblical Literature 1984 Seminar Papers*, edited by Kent Harold Richards, 399–404. Chico, CA: Scholars, 1984.

Claassens, Juliana. "Just Emotions: Reading the Sarah and Hagar Narrative (Genesis 16, 21) through the Lens of Human Dignity." *Verbum et Ecclesia* 32, no. 2 (2013).

Clines, David J. A. *Interested Parties: The Ideology of Writers and Readers of the Hebrew Bible*, JSOTsup 205. Gender, Culture, Theory 1. Sheffield: Sheffield Academic, 1995.

Cogan, Mordechai, and Hayim Tadmor. *II Kings: A New Translation with Introduction and Commentary*. The Anchor Bible. New York: Doubleday, 1988.

Coleman, Monica. "Roundtable Discussion. Must I Be A Womanist?" *Journal of Feminist Studies in Religion* 22, no.1 (2006): 85–134.

Colfax, Richard H. *Evidence Against the Views of the Abolitionists: Consisting of Physical and Moral Proofs, of the Natural Inferiority of the Negroes*. New York: J. T. M. Bleakley, 1833. https://www.loc.gov/item/11006103/.

Collins, Patricia Hill. *Black Feminist Thought: Knowledge, Consciousness, and the Politics of Empowerment*. Boston: Unwin Hyman, 1990.

Bibliography

———. *Black Feminist Thought: Knowledge, Consciousness, and the Politics of Empowerment.* 2nd ed. New York: Routledge, 2000.

———. "It's All in the Family: Intersections of Gender, Race, and Nation." *Hypatia* 13, no. 3 (1998): 62–82.

———. "Producing Mothers of the Nation: Race, Class and Contemporary US Population Policies." In *Women, Citizenship and Difference*, edited by Nira Yuval-Davis and Pnina Werbner, 118–29. London: Zed, 1999.

The Combahee River Collective. "The Combahee River Collective Statement." 1978. https://americanstudies.yale.edu/sites/default/files/files/Keyword%20Coalition_Readings.pdf.

Cone, James H. and Gayraud S. Wilmore. *Black Theology: A Documentary History. Vol. 2 (1980–1992).* Maryknoll, NY: Orbis, 2008.

Copher, Charles B. "The Black Presence in the Old Testament." In *Stony the Road: African American Biblical Interpretation*, edited by Cain Hope Felder, 146–64. Minneapolis: Fortress, 1991.

Creangă, Ovidiu. "The Silenced Songs of Victory: Power, Gender and Memory in the Conquest Narrative of Joshua (Joshua 1–12)." In *A Question of Sex? Gender and Difference in the Hebrew Bible and Beyond*, edited by Deborah W. Rooke, 106–23. Sheffield: Sheffield Phoenix, 2007.

Crenshaw, Kimberle Williams. "Demarginalizing the Intersection of Race and Sex: A Black Feminist Critique of Antidiscrimination Doctrine, Feminist Theory and Antiracist Politics." *University of Chicago Legal Forum* 1989, no. 1 (1989):139–67.

Croly, David G. *Miscegenation; the theory of the blending of the races, applied to the American white man and negro.* Alfred Whital Stern Collection Of Lincolniana, and Joseph Meredith Toner Collection. New York: H. Dexter, Hamilton & co, 1864. https://www.loc.gov/item/05009520/.

Cross, Frank Moore. *Canaanite Myth and Hebrew Epic: Essays in the History of the Religion of Israel.* Cambridge, MA: Harvard University Press, 1973.

Crowder, Stephanie Buckhanon. *Simon of Cyrene: A Case of Roman Conscription.* New York: Peter Lang, 2002.

———. *When Momma Speaks: The Bible and Motherhood from a Womanist Perspective.* Louisville: Westminster John Knox, 2016.

Crowell, Bradley. "Good Girl, Bad Girl: Foreign Women of the Deuteronomistic History in Postcolonial Perspective." *Biblical Interpretation* 21, no. 1 (2013): 1–18.

Crowley, John. "The Politics of Belonging: Some Theoretical Considerations." In *The Politics of Belonging: Migrants and Minorities in Contemporary Europe*, edited by Andrew Geddess and Adrian Favell, 15–41. Brookfield, VT: Ashgate, 1999.

Crummell, Alexander. "The Negro Not Under a Curse." In *Black Abolitionist Papers*, 1853. http://blackfreedom.proquest.com/wp-content/uploads/2020/09/crummell8.pdf.

Daly, John Patrick. "Holy War: Southern Religion and the Road to War and Defeat." *North & South: The Magazine of the Civil War Conflict* 6, no. 6 (2003): 34–46.

Darden, Lynne St. Clair. *Scripturalizing Revelation: An African American Postcolonial Reading of Empire.* Atlanta: SBL, 2015.

Bibliography

Davidson, Steed Vernyl. "Gazing (At) Native Women: Rahab and Jael in Imperializing and Postcolonial Discourses." In *Postcolonialism and the Hebrew Bible: The Next Step*. Semeia Studies 70, edited by Roland Boer, 69–92. Atlanta: Society of Biblical Literature, 2013.

Davis, David Brion. *The Problem of Slavery in Western Culture*. Ithaca, NY: Cornell University Press, 1966.

Davis, Stacy. "The Invisible Women: Numbers 30 and the Politics of Singleness in Africana Communities." In *Womanist Interpretations of the Bible: Expanding the Discourse*, edited by Gay L. Byron and Vanessa Lovelace, 21–47. Atlanta: Society of Biblical Literature, 2016.

———. *This Strange Story: Jewish and Christian Interpretation of the Curse of Canaan from Antiquity to 1865*. Lanham, MD: Unversity Press of America, 2008.

DeHart-Davis, Leisha, Justin Marlowe, and Sanjay Pandey. "Gender Dimensions of Public Service Motivation." *Public Administration Review* 66, no. 6 (November–December 2006): 873–87.

Douglas, Kelly Brown. *Sexuality and the Black Church: A Womanist Perspective*. Maryknoll, NY: Orbis, 1999.

Durant, Elizabeth. "It's Complicated: Power and Complicity in the Stories of Hagar and Sarah." *Conversations with the Biblical World* 35 (2015): 78–93.

Echols, Charles. *"Tell Me, O Muse": The Song of Deborah (Judges 5) in the Light of Heroic Poetry*. New York: T&T Clark, 2008.

Edelman, Diana. *Deuteronomy—Kings as Emerging Authoritative Books: A Conversation*. Ancient Near Eastern Texts 6. Atlanta: Society of Biblical Literature, 2014.

———. "Huldah the Prophet—of Yahweh or Asherah?" In *Feminist Companion to Samuel and Kings*. A Feminist Companion to the Hebrew Bible 5, edited by Athalya Brenner and Karla G. Shargent, 231–51. Sheffield: Sheffield Academic, 1994.

"Editors' Introduction." *Journal of Feminist Studies in Religion* 5, no. 2 (1989): 3–5.

Eichelberger, Kacey, Kemi Doll, Geraldine Ekpo, and Matthew Zerden. "Black Lives Matter: Claiming a Space for Evidence-Based Outrage in Obstetrics and Gynecology." *American Journal of Public Health* 106, no. 10 (2016): 1771–72.

Eilberg-Schwartz, Howard. "People of the Body: The Problem of the Body for the People of the Book." *Journal of the History of Sexuality* 2, no. 1 (1991): 1–24.

Enloe, Cynthia. *Bananas, Beaches, and Bases: Making Feminist Sense of International Politics*. Berkeley: University of California Press, 1989.

Exum, J. Cheryl. "Feminist Criticism: Whose Interests are Being Served?" In *Judges & Method: New Approaches in Biblical Studies*, 2nd ed., edited by Gale A. Yee, 65–89. Minneapolis: Fortress, 2007.

———. "Hagar en Procès: The Abject in Search of Subjectivity." In *From the Margins I: Women of the Hebrew Bible and Their Afterlives*, edited by P. S. Hawkins and L. C. Stahlberg, 1–16. Sheffield: Sheffield Academic, 2009.

Felder, Cain Hope. "Race, Racism, and the Biblical Narratives." In *Stony the Road We Trod: African American Biblical Interpretation*, edited by Cain Hope Felder, 127–45. Minneapolis: Fortress, 1991.

Feldstein, Ruth. *Motherhood in Black and White: Race and Sex in American Liberalism, 1930–1965.* Ithaca: Cornell University Press, 2000.

Fewell, Danna and David Gunn. "Controlling Perspectives. Women, Men and the Authority of Violence in Judges 4 and 5." *Journal of the American Academy of Religion* 58, no. 3 (1990): 389–411.

Forrest, Alan. "*La Patrie en Danger*: The French Revolution and the First *Levee En Mass.*" In *The People in Arms: Military Myth and National Mobilization Since the French Revolution*, edited by Daniel Moran, and Arthur Waldron, 8–32. Cambridge: Cambridge University Press, 2003.

Fredrickson, G. M. *The Black Image in the White Mind: The Debate on Afro-American Character and Destiny, 1817–1914.* Middletown, CT: Wesleyan University Press, 1987 [1971].

Fretheim, Terence E. "The Book of Genesis: Introduction, Commentary, and Reflections." In *The New Interpreter's Bible Vol. 1: General Articles on the Bible, General Article on the Old Testament, the Book of Genesis, the Book of Exodus, the Book of Leviticus*, edited by Walter Brueggemann, 319–674. Nashville: Abingdon, 1994.

Fritz, Volkmar. *1 & 2 Kings.* A Continental Commentary, translated by Anselm Hagedorn. Minneapolis: Fortress, 2003.

Frolov, Serge. "How Old Is the Song of Deborah?" *Journal for the Study of the Old Testament* 36, no. 2 (2011): 163–84.

Frymer-Kensky, Tikva. *In the Wake of the Goddesses: Women, Culture, and the Biblical Transformation of Pagan Myth.* New York: The Free Press, 1992.

———. *Reading the Women of the Bible.* New York: Schocken, 2002.

Fuchs, Esther. "Intermarriage, Gender, and Nation in the Hebrew Bible." In *The Passionate Torah: Sex and Judaism*, edited by Danya Ruttenberg, 73–92. New York: New York University Press, 2009.

Gafney, Wilda. "A Black Feminist Approach to Biblical Studies." *Encounter* 67, no. 4 (August 2006): 391–403.

———. *Daughters of Miriam: Women Prophets in Ancient Israel.* Minneapolis: Fortress, 2008.

———. "Translation Matters: A Fem/Womanist Exploration of Translation Theory and Practice for Proclamation in Worship." https://www.sbl-site.org/assets/pdfs/Gafney.pdf.

———. *Womanist Midrash: A Reintroduction to the Women of the Torah and the Throne.* Louisville: Westminster John Knox, 2017.

Gagnon, Robert A. J. *The Bible and Homosexual Practice: Texts and Hermeneutics.* Nashville: Abingdon, 2001.

Gaines, Janet Howe. "How Bad was Jezebel?" *Biblical Archaeology Society.* October 1, 2023. http://www.biblicalarchaeology.org/daily/people-cultures-in-the-bible/people-in-the-bible/how-bad-was-jezebel/.

———. *Music in the Old Bones: Jezebel through the Ages.* Carbondale, IL: Southern Illinois University Press, 1999.

Gaines, Jason M. H. *The Poetic Priestly Source.* Minneapolis: Augsburg Fortress, 2015.

130   *Bibliography*

Gajewski, Ryan. "Joan Rivers Calls President Obama Gay, Says First Lady is 'Tranny' (Video)." *The Hollywood Reporter*, July 3, 2014. https://www.hollywoodreporter .com/news/general-news/joan-rivers-calls-president-obama-716738/.

Gellner, Ernest. *Nations and Nationalism*. Ithaca, NY: Cornell University Press, 1983.

Gerbrandt, Carl. *Sacred Music Drama: The Guide*. 2nd ed. Bloomington, IL: AuthorHouse, 2006.

Gero, Stephen. "The Legend of the Fourth Son of Noah." *Harvard Theological Review* 73, 1–2 (January–April 1980): 321–30.

Gilkes, Cheryl Townsend. *If It Wasn't for the Women: Black Women's Experience and Womanist Culture in Church and Community*. Maryknoll, NY: Orbis, 2001.

———. "Outsiders Within the Higher Circles: Two First Ladies as Cultural Icons in a Racialized Politics of Difference." In *Race in the Age of Obama*. Research in Race and Ethnic Relations, vol. 16, edited by Donald Cunnigen and Marino A. Bruce, 55–76. United Kingdom: Emerald Group, 2010.

Gilmore, David. "Introduction: The Shame of Dishonor." In *Honor and Shame and the Unity of the Mediterranean*. Special Publication of the American Anthropological Society, no 23, edited by David Gilmore, 2–21. Washington, DC: American Anthropological Society, 1987.

Glaude, Eddie S. Jr. *Begin Again: James Baldwin's America and Its Urgent Lessons for Our Own*. New York: Crown, 2020.

———. *Exodus! Religion, Race, and Nation in Early Nineteenth Century Black America*. Chicago: The University of Chicago Press, 2000.

Goldenberg, David. *Black and Slave: The Origins and History of the Curse of Ham. Studies of the Bible and Its Reception*. Berlin: De Gruyter, 2017.

———. "The Curse of Ham: A Case of Rabbinic Racism?" In *Struggles in the Promised Land*, edited by Jack Salzman and Cornel West, 21–51. New York: Oxford University Press, 1997.

———. *The Curse of Ham: Race and Slavery in Early Judaism, Christianity, and Islam*. Princeton: Princeton University Press, 2003.

Goldingay, John. "The Significance of Circumcision." *Journal for the Study of the Old Testament* 25, no. 88 (June 2000): 3–18.

Goldstein, Elizabeth. *Impurity and Gender in the Hebrew Bible*. Lanham, MD: Rowman & Littlefield, 2015.

Gossett, Thomas. *Race: The History of an Idea in America*. Race and American Culture. Dallas: Southern Methodist University Press, 1963.

Gowan, Ronald E. *Genesis 1–11: From Eden to Babel*. International Theological Commentary. Grand Rapids: Eerdmans, 1989.

Grabbe, Lester. *Priests, Prophets, Diviners, Sages: A Socio-Historical Study of Religious Specialists in Ancient Israel*. Valley Forge, PA: Trinity Press International, 1995.

Graves, Robert, and Raphael Patai. *Hebrew Myths: The Book of Genesis*. Garden City, NY: Doubleday, 1963.

Gray, John. *1 & 2 Kings: A Commentary*. Philadelphia: Westminster, 1963.

Grayson, Deborah. "Mediating Intimacy: Black Surrogate Mothers and the Law." *Critical Inquiry* 24, no. 2 (Winter 1998): 525–46.

Greenfield, John. "Transforming the Stereotype: Exotic Women in Shelley's Alastor and the Witch of Atlas." In *The Foreign Woman in British Literature: Exotics, Aliens, and Outsiders*, edited by Marilyn Demarest and Toni Reed Button, 17–26. Westport, CT: Greenwood, 1999.

Grosby, Steven. *Biblical Ideas of Nationality: Ancient and Modern.* Winona Lake, IN: Eisenbrauns, 2002.

Gruber, Mayer. "The Motherhood of God in Second Isaiah." *Revue Biblique 90* (1983): 351–59.

Guest, Deryn. "Modeling the Transgender Gaze: Performance of Masculinities in 2 Kings 9–10." In *Transgender, Intersex and Biblical Interpretation*, edited by Teresa J. Hornsby and Deryn Guest, 45–80. Atlanta: Society of Biblical Literature, 2016.

Gunkel, Hermann. *Genesis.* Translated by Mark E. Biddle. Macon, GA: Mercer University Press, 1997.

Halpern, Baruch. "Why Manasseh is Blamed for the Babylonian Exile: The Evolution of a Biblical Tradition." *Vetus Testamentum* 48, no. 4 (1998): 473–514.

Halsell, Grace. *Soul Sister.* New York: Fawcett Gold Medal, 1969.

Hamori, Esther. "Childless Female Diviners in the Bible and Beyond." In *Prophets Male and Female: Gender and Prophecy in the Hebrew Bible, the Mediterranean, and the Ancient Near East*, edited by Jonathan Stokl and Corrine L. Carvalho, 169–91. Atlanta: Society of Biblical Literature, 2013.

———. "The Prophet and the Necromancer: Women's Divination for Kings." *Journal of Biblical Literature* 132, no. 4 (2013): 827–43.

Harris, Erika. *Nationalism: Theories and Cases.* Edinburgh: Edinburgh University Press, 2009.

Harris-Perry, Melissa. *Sister Citizen: Shame, Stereotypes, and Black Women in America.* New Haven: Yale University Press, 2011.

Hastings, Adrian. *The Construction of Nationhood: Ethnicity, Religion and Nationalism.* Cambridge: Cambridge University Press, 1997.

Hauser, Alan J. "Two Songs of Victory: A Comparison of Exodus 15 and Judges 5." In *Directions in Biblical Hebrew Poetry,* 265–84. Sheffield: JSOT Press, 1987.

Hayes, Diana. *Hagar's Daughters: Womanist Ways of Being in the World.* New York: Paulist Press, 1995.

Haynes, Stephen R. *Noah's Curse: The Biblical Justification of American Slavery.* Oxford: Oxford University Press, 2002.

Hendel, Ronald. *The Book of Genesis: A Biography.* Princeton: Princeton University Press, 2013.

Hiebert, Paula. "Whence Shall Help Come to Me: The Biblical Widow." In *Gender and Difference in Ancient Israel*, edited by Peggy Lynne Day, 125–41. Minneapolis: Augsburg Fortress, 1989.

Higginbotham, Jr., A. Leon. *Shades of Freedom: Racial Politics and Presumptions of the American Legal Process.* New York: Oxford University Press, 1996.

Hobsbawm, Eric. *Nations and Nationalism Since 1780.* Cambridge: Cambridge University Press, 1992.

Hordes, Amy. "Why Doesn't Noah Have More Children After the Flood?" *Jewish Bible Quarterly* 44, no. 4 (2016): 211–20.

Hutchinson, John, and Anthony D. Smith. *Nationalism.* Oxford: Oxford University Press, 1995.

Jackson, Melissa. *Comedy and Feminist Interpretation of the Hebrew Bible: A Subversive Collaboration.* Oxford: Oxford University Press, 2012.

———. "Reading Jezebel from the 'Other' Side: Feminist Critique, Postcolonialism, and Comedy." *Review and Expositor* 112, no. 2 (2015): 239–55.

Jacob, Sharon, and Jennifer Kaalund. "Flowing from Breast to Breast: An Examination of Dis/placed Motherhood in African American and Indian Wet Nurses." In *Womanist Interpretations of the Bible: Expanding the Discourse,* edited by Gay L. Byron and Vanessa Lovelace, 209–38. Atlanta: Society of Biblical Literature, 2016.

Jacobs, Mignon R. *Gender, Power, and Persuasion: The Genesis Narratives and Contemporary Portraits.* Grand Rapids, MI: Baker Academic, 2007.

Jacobs, Sandra. *The Body as Property: Physical Disfigurement in Biblical Law.* Library of Hebrew Bible/Old Testament Studies 582. New York: Bloomsbury T&T Clark, 2014.

Jeansonne, Sharon Pace. *The Women of Genesis: From Sarah to Potiphar's Wife.* Minneapolis: Fortress, 1990.

Jemison, Elizabeth. "Gendering the History of Race and Religion." In *The Oxford Handbook of Religion and Race in American History,* edited by Kathryn Gin Lum and Paul Harvey, 79–95. New York: Oxford University Press, 2018.

Johnson, James Weldon. "Lift Ev'ry Voice and Sing." *Poetry Foundation,* 1900. Accessed January 1, 2022. https://www.poetryfoundation.org/poems/48104/lift-evry-voice-and-sing.

Johnson, Sylvester A. *The Myth of Ham in Nineteenth-Century American Christianity: Race, Heathens, and the People of God.* New York: Palgrave MacMillan, 2004.

Jones, Martha S. *Birthright Citizens: A History of Race and Rights in Antebellum America.* Cambridge: Cambridge University Press, 2018.

———. "Citizenship." In *The 1619 Project: A New Origin Story,* edited by Nikole Hannah-Jones, Caitlin Roper, Ilena Silverman, and Jake Silverstein, 219–36. New York: New York Times, 2021.

Jones, Prudence J. "Africa: Greek and Roman Perspectives from Homer to Apuleius." *Center for Hellenic Studies: Harvard University,* n.d. Accessed January 2020. https://chs.harvard.edu/read/jones-prudence-j-africa-greek-and-roman-perspectives-from-homer-to-apuleius.

Jones-Warsaw, Koala. "Toward a Womanist Hermeneutic: A Reading of Judges 19–21." In *A Feminist Companion to Judges.* A Feminist Companion to the Hebrew Bible 4, edited by Athalya Brenner, 172–86. Sheffield: Sheffield Academic, 1993.

Jordan, Winthrop. *The White Man's Burden: Historical Origins of Racism in the United States.* Oxford: Oxford University Press, 1974.

———. *White Over Black: American Attitudes towards the Negro, 1550–1812.* Chapel Hill: University of North Carolina Press, 1968.

Junior, Nyasha. *An Introduction to Womanist Biblical Interpretation.* Louisville: Westminster John Knox, 2015.

———. *Reimagining Hagar: Blackness and Bible.* Oxford: Oxford University Press, 2019.

———. "Womanist Biblical Interpretation." In *Engaging the Bible in a Gendered World: An Introduction to Feminist Biblical Interpretation in Honor of Katharine Doob Sakenfeld*, edited by Linda Day and Carolyn Pressler, 37–46. Louisville: Westminster John Knox, 2006.

———. "Womanist Interpretation." In *The Oxford Encyclopedia of Biblical Interpretation.* Oxford University Press, 2013. https://www.oxfordreference.com/view/10.1093/acref:obso/9780199832262.001.0001/acref-9780199832262-e-89.

Kaalund, Jennifer. *Reading Hebrews and 1 Peter with the African American Great Migration.* London: T&T Clark, 2018.

Kartzow, Marianne Bjelland. "Navigating the Womb: Surrogacy, Slavery, Fertility – And Biblical Discourses." *Journal of Early Christian History* 2, no. 4 (2012): 38–54.

———. "Reproductive Capital and Slave Surrogacy: Thinking about/with/beyond Hagar." In *Bodies, Borders, Believers: Ancient Texts and Present Conversations*, edited by Marianne Bjelland Kartzow, Anne Hege Grung, and Anna Rebecca Solevag, 396–409. Cambridge, England: Lutterworth, 2016.

Kedourie, Elie. *Nationalism.* London: Hutchinson University Library, 1960.

Keel, Terence D. "Religion, Polygenism and the Early Science of Human Origins." *History of the Human Sciences* 26, no. 2 (2013): 3–32.

Kelle, Brad E. "Wartime Rhetoric: Prophetic Metaphorization of Cities as Female." In *Writing and Reading War: Rhetoric, Gender, and Ethics in Biblical and Modern Contexts*, edited by Brad E. Kelle and Frank Ritchel Ames, 95–112. Boston: Brill, 2008.

Kelso, Julie. *O Mother, Where Art Thou? An Irigarayan Reading of the Book of Chronicles.* London: Equinox, 2007.

Kessler, Martin, and Karel Adriaan Deurloo. *A Commentary on Genesis: The Book of Beginnings.* New York: Paulist, 2004.

Kirk-Duggan, Cheryl. "Divine Puppeteer: Yahweh of Exodus." In *A Feminist Companion to Exodus to Deuteronomy*, Second Series, A Feminist Companion to the Hebrew Bible 2, edited by Athalya Brenner, 75–102. Sheffield: Sheffield Academic, 2000.

Klein, Julie. "Why Scholars Just Can't Stop Talking About Sarah and Hagar." *U.S. News and World Report*, January 25, 2008. https://www.usnews.com/news/religion/articles/2008/01/25/why-scholars-just-cant-stop-talking-about-sarah-and-hagar.

Klock, Susan C., and Steven R. Lindheim. "Gestational Surrogacy: Medical, Psychosocial, and Legal Considerations." *Fertility and Sterility* 113, no. 5 (2020): 889–91.

Knauf, Ernst Axel. "Does 'Deuteronomistic Historiography' (DH) Exist?" In *Israel Constructs its History: Deuteronomistic Historiography in Recent Research*, edited by Albert De Pury, Thomas Römer, and J-D Macchi, 388–98. JSOT Sup, 306. Sheffield: Sheffield Academic, 2000.

Knust, Jennifer. "Who's Afraid of Canaan's Curse? Genesis 9:18–29 and the Challenge of Reparative Reading." *Biblical Interpretation* 22 (2014): 388–413.

Kroeger, Catherine Clark, and Mary J. Evans, eds. *The IVP Women's Bible Commentary.* Downers Grove, IL: InterVarsity Press, 2002.

Kyle, M. G. "Entry for 'Mizraim.'" *International Standard Bible Encyclopedia,* 1915. https://www.biblestudytools.com/encyclopedias/isbe/mizraim.html.

Laffey, Alice. *An Introduction to the Old Testament: A Feminist Perspective.* Philadelphia: Fortress, 1988.

Leithart, Peter J. *1 & 2 Kings.* Brazos Theological Commentary on the Bible. Grand Rapids, MI: Brazos, 2006.

Lewis, Bernard. *Race and Slavery in the Middle East.* New York: Oxford University Press, 1990.

Litchfield, Chelsea, Emma Kavanaugh, Jaquelyn Osborne, and Ian Jones. "Social Media and the Politics of Gender, Race and Identity: The Case of Serena Williams." *European Journal for Sport and Society* 15:2 (2018):154–70. https://eprints.bournemouth.ac.uk/30146/3/social%20media%20serena%20williams.pdf.

Little, Becky. "How the Union Pulled Off a Presidential Election During the Civil War," *History.com.* April 2, 2020. https://www.history.com/news/civil-war-presidential-election-abraham-lincoln.

Lindars, Barnabas. *Judges 1–5: A New Translation and Commentary.* Edited by A.D.H. Mayes. Edinburgh: T&T Clark, 1995.

Lomax, Tamura. *Jezebel Unhinged: Loosing the Black Female Body in Religion and Culture.* Durham, NC: Duke University Press, 2018.

Lorde, Audre. *Sister Outsider: Essays & Speeches by Audre Lorde.* New foreword by Cheryl Clarke. Berkeley: Crossing, 2007.

Lovelace, Vanessa. "Deborah and Huldah: Symbolic Border Guards in the Deuteronomistic History." Ph.D. diss., Chicago Theological Seminary, 2012.

———. "Intersections of Ethnicity, Gender, Sexuality, and Nation." In *The Hebrew Bible: Feminist and Intersectional Perspectives*, edited by Gale A. Yee, 75–107. Minneapolis: Fortress, 2018.

Lovelace, Vanessa and Mercedes L. García Bachmann. "Deborah in the African American Tradition." *Judges.* Wisdom Commentary Series, 70–71. Collegeville, MN: Liturgical, 2018.

Lyles, Reginald. "Pastors Buck and Swofford, Get the Biblical Story of Jezebel Straight." February 4, 2021. https://baptistnews.com/article/pastors-buck-and-swofford-get-the-biblical-story-of-jezebel-straight/#.YCBQqo9KjDI (accessed February 7, 2021).

MacKnight, James Arthur. *Hagar: A Tale of Mormon Life.* New York: A. L. Burt, 1889.

Maghbouleh, Meda, Ariela Schachter, and René D. Flores. "Middle Eastern and North African Americans May Not Be Perceived, nor Perceive Themselves, to Be White." *The Proceedings of the National Academy of Sciences* 119, no. 7 (2022). https://doi.org/10.1073/pnas.2117940119.

Malone, Elizabeth, Nathan E. Hultman, Kate L. Anderson, and Viviane Romeiro. "Stories about ourselves: How national narratives influence the diffusion of large-scale energy technologies." *Energy Research & Social Science* 31 (2017): 70–76.

Maltschnig, Eva. "Austrian War Brides as Symbolic Border Guards." In *Transgressing Boundaries: Humanities in Flux*, Europa Orientalis, no. 14, edited by Marija Wakounig and Markus Peter Beham, 229–44. Münster, Germany: LIT, 2013.

Mann, Thomas W. *The Book of the Torah: The Narrative Integrity of the Pentateuch.* Atlanta: John Knox, 1988.

Manzo, Kathryn. *Creating Boundaries: The Politics of Race and Nation.* Boulder, CO: Lynne Rienner, 1996.

Marbury, Herbert Robinson. *Pillars of Cloud and Fire: The Politics of Exodus in African American Biblical Interpretation.* Religion and Social Transformation. New York: New York University Press, 2015.

Martin, Clarice J. "Biblical Theodicy and Black Women's Spiritual Autobiography: 'The Miry Bog, The Desolate Pit, a New Song in My Mouth.'" In *A Troubling in My Soul: Womanist Perspectives on Evil and Suffering*, edited by Emilie M. Townes, 13–36. Maryknoll, NY: Orbis, 1993.

———. "Womanist Biblical Interpretation" In *Dictionary of Biblical Interpretation*, edited by John H. Hayes, 655–58. Nashville: Abingdon, 1999.

Martyn, Sarah Towne Smith. *Women of the Bible.* New York: American Tract Society, 1868.

Masuoka, Natalie, and Jane Junn. *The Politics of Belonging: Race, Public Opinion, and Immigration.* Chicago: University of Chicago Press, 2013.

Matthews, Victor. *Judges and Ruth.* The New Cambridge Bible Commentary. Cambridge: Cambridge University Press, 2004.

Mayer, Tamar. "Gender Ironies of Nationalism: Setting the Stage." In *Gender Ironies of Nationalism: Sexing the Nation*, edited by Tamar Mayer, 1–24. New York: Routledge, 2000.

Mbuvi, Amanda Beckenstein. *Belonging in Genesis: Biblical Israel and the Politics of Identity Formation.* Waco, TX: Baylor University Press, 2016.

McClendon, John H., III. *Philosophy of Religion and the African American Experience.* Leiden: Brill, 2017.

McClintock, Anne. "'No Longer in a Future Heaven': Race, Gender and Nationalism." In *Dangerous Liaisons*, edited by Anne McClintock, Aamir Mufti, and Elai Shohat, 89–112. Minneapolis: University of Minnesota Press, 1997.

McKenzie, Steven. *King David: A Biography.* Oxford: Oxford University Press, 2000.

McKinlay, Judith E. "Gazing at Huldah." *The Bible and Critical Theory* 1, no. 3 (2005): 1–11.

———. *Reframing Her: Biblical Women in Post-Colonial Focus.* The Bible in the Modern World, 1. Sheffield: Sheffield Phoenix, 2014.

Melville, Sarah C. "Royal Women and the Exercise of Power in the Ancient Near East." In *Companion to the Ancient Near East*, edited by Daniel C. Snell, 219–28. Malden, MA: Blackwell, 2007.

Bibliography

Mercer, Kobena. "Black Art and the Burden of Representation." *Third Text: Third World Perspectives on Art and Culture* 10 (Spring 1990): 61–78.

Meyers, Carol L., Toni Craven, and Ross Shepard Kraemer, eds. *Women in Scripture: A Dictionary of Named and Unnamed Women in the Hebrew Bible, the Apocryphal and Deutercanonical Books, and the New Testament.* Boston: Houghton Mifflin, 2000.

Michener, Jamila, and Margaret Teresa Brower. "What's Policy Got to Do with It? Race, Gender & Economic Inequality in the United States." *Daedalus.* 149, no. 1 (Winter 2020): 100–18. https://doi.org/10.1162/DAED_a_01776.

Miller, Robert D., II "When Pharaohs Ruled: On the Translation of Judges 5:2." *Journal of Theological Studies* 59, no. 2 (2008): 650–54.

Mitchell, Christine. "1 and 2 Chronicles." In *Women's Bible Commentary*, edited by Carol Newsom, Sharon H. Ringe, and Jacqueline E. Lapsley, 184–90. Louisville: Westminster John Knox, 2012.

Moody, Anne. *Coming of Age in Mississippi: The Classic Autobiography of Growing up Poor and Black in the Rural South.* New York: Dell, 1968.

Mostov, Julie. "Our Women/Their Women: Symbolic Boundaries, Territorial Markers, and Violence in the Balkans." *Peace & Change* 20, no. 4 (October 1995): 515–29.

Moynihan, Daniel Patrick. *The Negro Family: The Case for National Action.* Report, United States Department of Labor, Office of Policy Planning and Research. Washington, DC: United States Government, 1965.

Mullen, E. Theodore, Jr. *Narrative History and Ethnic Boundaries: The Deuteronomistic Historian and the Creation of Israelite National Identity.* Atlanta: Scholars, 1993.

Neiman, David. "The Two Genealogies of Japheth." In *Orient and Occident: Essays Presented to Cyrus H. Gordon on the Occasion of His Sixty-Fifth Birthday.* Alter Orient Und Altes Testament, Bd. 22, edited by H. A. Hoffner, 119–26. Kevelaer: Butzon & Bercker, 1973.

Nelson, Richard D. *First and Second Kings.* Louisville: Westminster John Knox, 1987.

Niditch, Susan. "Eroticism and Death in the Tale of Jael" In *Gender and Difference in Ancient Israel*, edited by Peggy Day, 43–57. Minneapolis: Fortress, 1989.

———. "Genesis." In *Women's Bible Commentary. Revised and Updated*, edited by Carol A. Newsom, Sharon H. Ringe, and Jacqueline E. Lapsley, 27–45. Louisville: Westminster John Knox, 2012.

———. *Judges.* Old Testament Library. Louisville: Presbyterian Publishing, 2008.

Nissinen, Martti. "The Dubious Image of Prophecy." In *Prophets, Prophecy, and Prophetic Texts in Second Temple Judaism*, edited by Michael Floyd and Robert Haak, 26–41. New York: T&T Clark, 2006.

———. *Homoeroticism in the Biblical World.* Minneapolis: Fortress, 1998.

Noth, Martin. *The Deuteronomistic History,* JSOTSup. Sheffield: JSOT, 1981.

Oden, Robert A. Jr. "Myth and Mythology (OT). Vol 3." In *Anchor Bible Dictionary*, edited by David Noel Freedman, 946–60. New York: Doubleday, 1992.

Olson, Dennis T. *Judges.* Nashville: Abingdon, 1998.

O'Neal, Cothburn. *Hagar.* New York: Crown, 1958.

Bibliography

Online Etymology Dictionary. "Womanish (adj.)." https://www.etymonline.com /search?q=womanish&utm_campaign=sd&utm_medium=serp&utm_source=ds _search.

Oxford English Dictionary, 3rd ed. Oxford: Oxford University Press, 2011.

Peterson, Thomas. *Ham and Japheth: The Myth World of White in the Antebellum South,* ATLA Monograph Series 12. Metuchen, NJ: Scarecrow, 1978.

Phillips, Anthony. "Uncovering the Father's Skirt." *Vetus Testamentum* 30 no 1 (1980): 38–43.

Phillips, Layli, ed. *The Womanist Reader.* New York: Routledge, 2006.

Pippin, Tina. *Apocalyptic Bodies: The Biblical End of the World in Text and Image.* London: Routledge, 1999.

———. "Biblical Women as Ideological Constructs toward Justice: Ideological Criticism as a Feminist/Womanist Method." In *Feminist Interpretation of the Hebrew Bible in Retrospect. Vol III*, edited by Susanne Scholz, 261–77. Sheffield: Sheffield Phoenix, 2017.

Polzin, Robert. *Moses and the Deuteronomist: A Literary Study of the Deuteronomistic History, Pt. 1.* New York: Seabury, 1980.

Priest, Josiah. *Slavery, as It Relates to the Negro, or African Race, Examined in the Light of Circumstancs, History and the Holy Scriptures; with an Account of the Origin of the Black Man's Color, Causes of His State of Servitude and Traces of His Character as Well in Ancient as in Modern Times; with Strictures on Abolitionism.* Albany: C. Van Benthuysen and Co, 1843. https://archive.org/details /slaveryasitrela00priegoog/page/n6/mode/2up.

Pury, Albert de, Jean-Daniel Macchi, and Thomas Römer, eds. *Israel Constructs its History: Deuteronomistic Historiography in Recent Research.* Sheffield: Sheffield Academic, 2000.

Rashkow, Ilona N. "Daddy-Dearest and the 'Invisible Spirit of Wine.'" In *A Feminist Companion to Genesis.* A Feminist Companion to the Hebrew Bible 1, edited by Athalya Brenner, 82–107. Sheffield: Sheffield Academic, 1998.

———. *Taboo or Not Taboo: Sexuality and Family in the Hebrew Bible.* Minneapolis: Fortress, 2000.

Reaves, Jayme. "Sarah as Victim and Perpetrator: Whiteness, Power, and Memory in the Matriarchal Narrative." *Review & Expositor* 115, no. 4 (2018).

Reed, Justin Michael. "'How—How Is This Just?!': How Aronofsky and Handel Handle Noah's Curse." In *Noah as Antihero: Darren Aronofsky's Cinematic Deluge*, edited by Rhonda Burnette-Bletsch and Jon Morgan, 145–60. New York: Routledge, 2017.

Reeder, Caryn. "Deuteronomy 21.10–14 and/as Wartime Rape." *Journal for the Study of the Old Testament* 41, no. 3 (2017): 313–36.

Rice, Gene. "The Curse that Never Was (Genesis 9:18–27)." In *Biblical Studies Alternatively: An Introductory Reader*, edited by Susanne Scholz, 217–28. Upper Saddle River, NJ: Prentice Hall, 2003.

Ringold, Julie. "Noach (6:9–11:32): Mrs. Noah." In *The Women's Torah Commentary: New Insights from Women Rabbis on the 54 Weekly Torah Portions*, edited by Elyse Goldstein, 53-56. Woodstock, VT: Jewish Lights, 2000.

138   *Bibliography*

Römer, Thomas. *The So-Called Deuteronomistic History: A Sociological, Historical and Literary Introduction.* New York: T&T Clark, 2005.

Römer, Thomas, and Albert de Pury. "Deuteronomistic Historiography (DH): Hiistory of Research and Debated Issues." In *Israel Constructs its History: Deuteronomistic Historiography in Recent Research,* edited by Albert de Pury, Jean-Daniel Macchi, and Thomas Römer, 24–143. Sheffield: Sheffield Academic, 2000.

Roop, Eugene F. *Genesis.* Believers Church Bible Commentary. Scottdale, Ontario: Herald, 1987.

Rose, Martin. "Deuteronomistic Ideology and the Theology of the Old Testament." In *Israel Constructs its History: Deuteronomistic Historiography in Recent Research,* edited by Albert de Pury, Jean-Daniel Macchi, and Thomas Römer, 424–55. Sheffield: Sheffield Academic, 2000.

Roshwald, Aviel. *The Endurance of Nationalism: Ancient Roots and Modern Dilemmas.* Cambridge: Cambridge University Press, 2007.

Roth, Ann Macy. "Building Bridges to Afrocentricism: A Letter to My Egyptological Colleagues." *University of Pennsylvania - African Studies Center.* January 26, 1995. Accessed June 23, 2018. http://www.africa.upenn.edu/Articles_Gen/afrocent_roth.html.

Russaw, Kimberly. *Daughters in the Hebrew Bible.* Lanham, MD: Lexington Books/Fortress Academic, 2018.

Sadler, Rodney Steven. *Can A Cushite Change His Skin? An Examination of Race, Ethnicity, and Othering in the Hebrew Bible.* New York: T&T Clark, 2005.

Sakenfeld, Katharine Doob. *Just Wives? Stories of Power and Survival in the Old Testament.* Louisville, Westminster John Knox, 2003.

Sanders, Cheryl J. "Christian Ethics and Theology in Womanist Perspectives." Journal of Feminist Studies in Religion 5, no. 2 (Fall 1989): 83–91.

Sarna, Nahum. *Genesis: The JPS Torah Commentary.* Philadelphia: The Jewish Publication Society, 1989.

Sasson, Jack. "Circumcision in the Ancient Near East." *Journal of Biblical Literature* 85, no. 4 (1966): 473–76.

Scheuer, Blaženka. "Huldah: A Cunning Career Woman?" In *Prophecy and Prophets in Stories: Papers Read at the Fifth Meeting,* edited by Bob E.J.H. Becking and Hans Barstad, 104–123. Leiden: Brill, 2015.

Schmid, Konrad. *Genesis and the Moses Story: Israel's Dual Origins in the Hebrew Bible.* Siphrut 3. Translated by James D. Nogalski. Winona Lake, IN: Eisenbrauns, 2010.

Schneider, Tammi J. *Judges.* Berit Olam. Collegeville, MN: Liturgical, 2009.

———. *Sarah: Mother of Nations.* New York: Continuum, 2004.

Sealing, Keith. "Blood Will Tell: Scientific Racism and the Legal Prohibitions Against Miscegenation." *Michigan Journal of Race & Law* 5, no. 2 (2000): 559–609. https://repository.law.umich.edu/mjrl/vol5/iss2/1.

Sedghi, Hamideh. *Women and Politics in Iran: Veiling, Unveiling, and Reveiling.* Cambridge: Cambridge University Press, 2007.

Shaftesbury, Edmund. *The Two Sexes: Their Functions, Purposes and Place in Nature.* Washington, DC: The Ralston Club, 1898.

Sherwood, Yvonne. "Hagar and Ishmael: The Reception of Expulsion." *Interpretation: A Journal of Bible and Theology* 68, no. 3 (2014): 286–304.

Skinner, John. *A Critical and Exegetical Commentary on Genesis. International Critical Commentary.* New York: Charles Scribner's Sons, 1910.

Smedley, Audrey, and Brian Smedley. "Race as Biology is Fiction, Racism as A Social Problem is Real: Anthropological and Historical Perspectives on the Social Construction of Race." *American Psychologist* 60, no 1 (January 2005): 16–26.

Smith, Mitzi J., ed. *I Found God in Me: A Womanist Biblical Hermeneutics Reader.* Eugene, OR: Cascade, 2015.

Smith, Shanell T. *The Woman Babylon and the Marks of Empire: Reading Revelation with a Postcolonial Womanist Hermeneutics of Ambiveilence.* Emerging Scholars. Minneapolis: Fortress, 2014.

Snowden, Frank. *Before Color Prejudice: The Ancient View of Blacks.* Cambridge: Cambridge University Press, 1983.

Soggin, J. Alberto. Translated by John Bowden. *Judges, A Commentary.* Philadelphia: Westminster, 1981.

Sparks, Kenton. *Ethnicity and Identity in Ancient Israel: Prolegomena to the Study of Ethnic Sentiments and their Expression in the Hebrew Bible.* Winona Lake, IN: Eisenbrauns, 1998.

Speiser, E. A. *Genesis: Introduction, Translation and Notes, AB 1.* New York: Doubleday, 1962.

Spitzer, Julie Ringold. "Noach (6:9–11:32): Mrs. Noah." In *The Women's Torah Commentary: New Insights from Women Rabbis on the 54 Weekly Torah Portions*, edited by Rabbi Elyse Goldstein, 53–56. Woodstock, VT: Jewish Lights, 2000.

St. Clair, Raquel. "Womanist Biblical Interpretation." In *True to Our Native Land: An African American New Testament Commentary*, edited by Brian K. Blount and Clarice J. Martin, 54–62. Minneapolis: Fortress, 2007.

Stanfield, John. "Theoretical and Ideological Barriers to the Study of Race-Making." *Research in Race and Ethnic Relations* 4 (1985): 161–81.

Steinberg, Stephen. *The Ethnic Myth: Race, Ethnicity, and Class in America.* Boston: Beacon, 2001.

Steinberg, Naomi. *Kinship and Marriage in Genesis: A Household Economics Perspective.* Minneapolis: Augsburg, 1993.

———. *The World of the Child in the Hebrew Bible.* Sheffield: Sheffield Phoenix, 2013.

Steinmetz, Devora. "Vineyard, Farm, and Garden: The Drunkenness of Noah in the Context of Primeval History." *Journal of Biblical Literature* 113, no. 2 (Summer 1994): 193–207.

Stewart, Maria W. "Meditations from the pen of Mrs. Maria W. Stewart: (Widow of the late James W. Stewart) now matron of the Freedman's hospital, and presented in 1832 to the First African Baptist church and society of Boston, Mass." Washington, DC: Garrison & Knap, 1879. https://babel.hathitrust.org/cgi/pt?id=inu .30000011406927&seq=7.

Stone, Ken. "Judges." In *Theological Bible Commentary*, edited by Gail O'Day and David L. Petersen, 87–96. Louisville: Westminster John Knox, 2009.

Stott, Katherine. "Finding the Lost Book of the Law: Re-reading the Story of 'The Book of the Law' (Deuteronomy—2 Kings) in Light of Classical Literature." *Journal for the Study of the Old Testament* 30, no. 2 (December 2005): 153–69.

Sussman, Mark. "The 'Miscegenation Troll.'" JSTOR Daily, February 2019. https://daily.jstor.org/the-miscegenation-troll/.

Tamir, Christine. "Key Findings About Black Immigrants in the U.S." *Pew Research Center.* January 27, 2022. https://www.pewresearch.org/fact-tank/2022/01/27/key-findings-about-black-immigrants-in-the-u-s/ (accessed May 2022).

Taylor, Marion Ann, and Heather E. Weir, eds. *Let Her Speak for Herself: Nineteenth Century Women Writing on Women in Genesis.* Waco, TX: Baylor University Press, 2006.

Thiel, Winfried. "Omri." *The Anchor Bible Dictionary*, vol. 5. Edited by David Noel Freeman, 17–20. New York: Doubleday, 1992.

Trible, Phyllis. "Exegesis for Storytellers and Other Strangers." *JBL* 114, no. 1 (1995): 3–19.

———. *Texts of Terror: Literary Feminist Readings in Biblical Narratives.* Overtures in Biblical Theology 13. Philadelphia: Fortress, 1984.

Tucker, Susan. *Telling Memories Among Southern Women: Domestic Workers and Their Employers in the Segregated South.* Baton Rouge: LA: Louisiana State University Press, 1988.

Van Seters, John. *Abraham in History.* New Haven: Yale University Press, 1975.

Von Rad, Gerhard. *Genesis: A Commentary.* Translated by John H. Marks. The Old Testament Library. Philadelphia: Westminster, 1972.

Walker, Alice. "Coming Apart." In *Take Back the Night: Women on Pornography*, edited by Laura Lederer, 95–104. New York: Harper Perennial, 1979.

———. *In Search of Our Mothers' Gardens: Womanist Prose.* San Diego: Harcourt Brace Jovanovich, 1983.

———. "Review of Gifts of Power: The Writings of Rebecca Jackson (1795–1871), Black Visionary, Shaker Eldress." *The Black Scholar* 12, no. 5 (September/October 1981): 64–67.

Wallace, Belinda Deneen. "A Rise in Black Immigrant Population Changes Understanding of Black America." Interviewed by Elissa Nadworny. *All Things Considered.* February 17, 2022. https://www.npr.org/2022/02/17/1081570859/a-rise-in-black-immigrant-population-changes-understanding-of-black-america.

Wallace-Sanders, Kimberly. *Mammy: A Century of Race, Gender, and Southern Memory.* Ann Arbor, MI: University of Michigan Press, 2008.

Washington, Harold. "Violence and the Construction of Gender." *Biblical Interpretation* 5 (1997): 324–63.

Washington, Joseph Jr. *Anti-Blackness in English Religion, 1500–1800.* Texts and Studies in Religion 19. New York: Edwin Mellen, 1984.

Washington-Williams, Essie Mae. *Dear Senator: A Memoir by the Daughter of Strom Thurmond.* New York: HarperCollins, 2005.

"'We Are Literally Slaves': An Early Twentieth-Century Black Nanny Sets the Record Straight." *History Matters*, 1912. http://historymatters.gmu.edu/d/80/.

Weems, Renita J. *Battered Love: Marriage, Sex, and Violence in the Hebrew Prophets*. Minneapolis: Fortress, 1995.

———. "Gomer: Victim of Violence or Victim of Metaphor." *Semeia 47* (1989): 87–104.

———. "Huldah the Prophet: Reading a (Deuteronomistic) Woman's Identity." In *A God So Near: Essays on Old Testament Theology in Honor of Patrick D. Miller*, edited by Brent A. Strawn and Nancy R. Bowen, 321–39. Winona Lake, IN: Eisenbrauns, 2003.

———. *Just a Sister Away: A Womanist Vision of Women's Relationships in the Bible*. San Diego: Lura Media, 1988.

———. "Womanist Reflections on Biblical Hermeneutics." In *Black Theology: A Documentary History Volume Two: 1980–1992*, edited by James H. Cone and Gayraud S. Wilmore, 216–24. Maryknoll, NY: Orbis, 1993.

Welter, Barbara. "The Cult of True Womanhood: 1820–1860." *American Quarterly* 18, no. 2 (Part 1, Summer 1966): 151–74.

Wenham, Gordon J. *Genesis 1–15, Vol 1*. Word Biblical Commentary. Waco, TX: Word, 1987.

West, Gerald. *Genesis: The People's Bible Commentary. A Bible Commentary for Every Day*. Elsfield Way, Oxford: The Bible Reading Fellowship, 2006.

Westbrook, Raymond. "The Female Slave." In *Gender and Law in the Hebrew Bible and the Ancient Near East*, edited by Victor H. Matthews, Bernard M. Levinson, and Tikva Frymer-Kensky, 214–38. New York: T&T Clark, 1998.

Westermann, Claus. *Genesis 1–11: A Commentary*. Translated by John J. Scullion. Minneapolis: Augsburg, 1984.

———. *Genesis 12–36. A Continental Commentary*. Translated by John J. Scullion S.J. Minneapolis: Fortress, 1995.

White, Deborah Gray. *Ar'n't I A Woman? Female Slaves in the Plantation South*. New York: W. W. Norton, 1985.

Whitford, David. *The Curse of Ham in the Early Modern Era: The Bible and the Justifications for Slavery*. St. Andrews Studies in Reformation History. Farnham, England: Ashgate, 2009.

Williams, Delores. *Sisters in the Wilderness: The Challenge of Womanist God-talk*. Maryknoll, NY: Orbis, 1993.

Williamson, H.G.M. "Prophetesses in the Hebrew Bible." Library of Hebrew Bible/ OT. In *Prophecy and the Prophets in Ancient Israel*, edited by John Day, 65–80. New York: T&T Clark, 2014.

Wiltshire, Ashley, Lynae Brayboy, Kiwita Phillips, et al. "Infertility Knowledge and Treatment Beliefs among African American Women in an Urban Community." *Contraception and Reproductive Medicine* 4, no. 16 (2019). https://doi.org/10.1186/s40834-019-0097-x.

Wimberly, Edward P. "Beyond the Curse of Noah: African American Pastoral Theology as Political." In *African American Religious Life and the Story of Nimrod*, edited by Anthony Pinn and Dwight Allen Callahan, 179–89. New York: Palgrave MacMillan, 2008.

142 *Bibliography*

Wingfield, Mark. "SBC Pastor Calls Vice President Kamala Harris a 'Jezebel' Two Days after Inauguration." January 22, 2021. https://baptistnews.com/article/sbc -pastor-calls-vice-president-kamala-harris-a-jezebel-two-days-after-inauguration/# .YB8F9I9KjDJ.

Wong, Gregory T. K. "Song of Deborah as Polemic." *Biblica* 88, no. 1 (2007): 1–22. https://www.jstor.org/stable/42614746.

Wright, Jacob L. "A Nation Conceived in Defeat." *Azure Online* (Autumn 5771 / 2010): 83–101. https://azure.org.il/download/magazine/Az42%20Wright.pdf.

Yamauchi, Edwin. *Africa and the Bible.* Foreword by Kenneth A. Kitchen. Grand Rapids, MI: Baker Academic, 2004.

———. "The Curse of Ham." *Criswell Theological Review* 6, no 2 (Spring 2009): 45–60.

Yee, Gale A. *Poor Banished Children of Eve: Woman as Evil in the Hebrew Bible.* Minneapolis: Fortress, 2003.

Yuval-Davis, Nira. "Belonging and the Politics of Belonging." *Patterns of Prejudice* 40, no. 3 (2006): 197–214.

———. "Gender and Nation." *Ethnic and Racial Studies* 16, no. 4 (1993): 621–32.

———. *Gender & Nation.* A Theory, Culture & Society Series. London: Sage, 1997.

———. "Borders, Boundaries, and the Politics of Belonging." In *Ethnicity, Nationalism, and Minority Rights*, edited by Stephen May, Tariq Modood, and Judith Squires, 214–30. Cambridge: Cambridge University Press, 2009.

———. "Nationalist Projects and Gender Relations." *Nar. Umjet* 40, no. 1 (2003): 9–36.

———. *The Politics of Belonging: Intersectional Contestations.* London: Sage, 2011.

Index

abolitionist movement, 45, 50, 111, 112
abolitionists, 47, 49
Ahmed, Sara, 3, 21
Anderson, Cheryl, *xxi*, 38, 118
Anthias, Floya, 4
anti-Black, 42, 43, 45, 81, 111
anti-miscegenation, *xxiv*, 118, 119
anti-slavery, 45, 46, 49, 112
artificial insemination, 20
Athaliah, *xxiv*, 63, 68, 70, 71, 77, 78, 81, 82, 114, 115

Bailey, Randall, 36, 38
Bailey, Wilma Ann, 1
barren, 1, 4, 8, 12, 13, 74
barrenness, 5, 11, 12
belonging, *xii, xiii, xviii*, 2–4, 11, 18, 21, 31, 39, 45, 50, 65, 100, 104, 113, 114, 119; political projects of belonging, 2, 3, 10, 11, 113; political projects of motherhood, *xxiii, xxiv*, 2, 18, 19, 21, 114; politics of belonging, *xii, xiii, xxiii, xxv*, 2, 3, 8, 9, 19, 21, 31, 63, 104, 106, 113–15, 120
Bird, Phyllis, 92
birthright, *xii, xiv*, 30, 50, 51, 112
blackness, *xv*, 29–31, 37, 39–42, 44, 46, 50, 112

border guards, 63, 67, 68: symbolic, *xxiv*, 67–69, 71, 80, 82. *See also* symbolic boundaries
borders, *xiii*, 3, 68, 77, 79, 101
boundaries, *xiii, xxiv*, 2–4, 9, 11, 15, 16, 18, 19, 22, 29, 32, 38, 50, 63, 65–69, 72, 92, 100, 101, 105, 106, 113, 115, 116; maintenance, 3, 38, 63, 113, 115; symbolic, 67, 101
breast milk, 15, 16
breastfeeding, 15
Brueggemann, Walter, 34, 74
Butler, Anthea, *xxi*, 91
Byron, Gay L. *xxi, xxii*

Chapman, Cynthia, 15, 16
Church Mother, *xxiv*, 91, 92, 105
circumcision, 10–12, 14, 18, 42–44, 46, 114, 146
citizenship, *xi, xii, xiii, xxv*, 4, 30, 31, 44, 46, 50, 51, 93, 102, 103, 105, 106, 111–13, 119, 143; birthright, *xiv*, 30, 51; second-class, 30, 104
class, *xiii, xiv, xxiv, xxv*, 5, 7, 8, 10, 17, 20, 21, 62, 93, 97, 102, 104, 106, 113, 115, 118, 119
Collins, Patricia Hill, *xx*, 62, 81, 104, 113, 115, 116, 119
Copher, Charles, 43

144   *Index*

Crenshaw, Kimberlé Williams, *xiii*
Crummel, Alexander, 47
Curse of Canaan, 29, 31, 37, 44
Curse of Ham, 29, 43, 44, 45, 48,
    50. *See also* Myth of Ham
Cush/Cushites, 40

Davis, Stacy, 42, 64
Deborah, *xxiv,* 63, 64, 67–72, 78–82,
    91–102, 105, 115
Declaration of Independence, 51, 112
difference, *xiii, xx,* 4, 7, 11, 19, 21, 38,
    66, 67, 113–15
Douglas, Kelly Brown, 50, 62
Durant, Elizabeth, 7

ethnicity, *xxiii, xxv,* 5, 7–9, 16, 17,
    19, 20, 38, 40, 65–67, 93, 94, 102,
    114, 118
Exum, J. Cheryl, 18, 69, 94, 100–102

Felder, Cain Hope, 43
Feldstein, Ruth, 103
fertility, 8, 11, 104
Fourteenth amendment, *xii,* 30

Gafney, Wil, *xxi,* 6, 11, 31, 81
Gaines, Janet Howe, 76, 77
gender, *xiii, xiv, xvi, xvii, xxiv, xxv,* 2,
    4–6, 8, 17, 20, 31, 32, 49, 61–63,
    66–69, 74, 78, 79–81, 94, 98–101,
    103, 104, 111, 113, 115, 118–20, 143
Gilkes, Cheryl Townsend, *xvii,* 81, 91
Glaude, Eddie, *xi,* 17

Hagar, *xxiii,* 1, 2, 4–8, 11–21, 113,
    114, 116
Hamori, Esther, 72, 80
Harris, Kamala, 61
Harris-Perry, Melissa, *xvii,* 21
Higginbotham, Leon, 30
Huldah, 63, 67–74, 78–82, 92

identity, *xii, xiii, xiv, xvii, xxi,* 2, 5,
    8–10, 15, 30, 32, 37, 38, 65–67, 69,

71, 75, 77, 80, 92, 93, 98, 99, 100,
    101, 113, 116
incest, 31, 35, 38
infertility, 11, 12, 20
insider, *xiv, xxiv,* 9, 16–19, 77, 94, 113
insiders, *xxiii, xxiv,* 2, 3, 19, 29, 32, 38,
    66, 105, 113, 115
intersectionality, *xiii*

Jael, 97, 99, 100, 102
Jezebel, *xxiv,* 61–63, 68, 70, 71, 74–78,
    81, 82, 93, 99, 114, 115
jezebel, *xxiv,* 61–63, 76, 77, 81
Jones, Martha, 51, 112, 113
Jordan, Winthrop, 30, 42

Knust, Jennifer, 38
Kush/Kushites, 39, 40

Lee, Jarena, 91
Lincoln, Abraham, 49
Lorde, Audre, *xiii, xiv,* 21, 106, 118

mammy, *xxiv,* 62, 63, 67, 77, 81, 102
Manzo, Kathryn, 44
Martin, Clarice, *xi, xxi*
masculinized, 81, 99, 101
matriarchs, 103
Mbuvi, Amanda, 7, 10, 15, 16, 17
Melville, Sarah, 75
miscegenation, *xxiv,* 49
monogenesis, 46
Mother in Israel, *xxiv,* 91–95, 97,
    101, 105
motherhood, *xxiii, xxiv, xxv,* 1, 2, 12,
    14–16, 18, 20, 103; biological, 12;
    genetic, 12; gestational, *xxiii,* 12, 20;
    social, 12
Mothers of the Nation, *xxiv, xxv,*
    104, 106
Myth of Ham, 31. *See also* Curse
    of Ham

naturalization, 50, 112

Index

Noah's Curse, *xxiv*, 29, 31, 37–39, 43, 44, 49, 112
Noth, Martin, 64, 65
Nott, Josiah, 48

outsider, 12, 18, 68, 77, 81, 93, 94, 113
outsiders, *xiii, xiv, xxiv*, 2, 3, 17, 19, 29, 30, 32, 38, 63, 64, 66, 82, 105, 113, 114

Pippin, Tina, 63
polygenesis, *xxiv*, 46
population policies, 8, 13, 104–6, 119, 120
prejudice, 6, 30, 42, 43, 103
Priest, Josiah, 47, 48

race, *xiii, xiv, xvii, xxi, xxiv, xxv*, 7, 8, 20, 21, 30, 31, 42, 46, 47, 49, 51, 62, 63, 93, 102, 103, 106, 111, 115, 117–20
racism, 43, 47
Reaves, Jayme, 7
Rousseau, Jean-Jacques, 30
Russaw, Kimberly, *xxi*

Sakenfeld, Katharine, 13
Sapphire, 62
Sarah, *xxiii*, 1, 2, 4–21, 113, 114
Sarai, 4, 5, 7, 8, 13
Schmid, Konrad, 9
segregationists, 49, 50
sexuality, *xxiv, xxvii*, 2, 4, 12, 31, 37, 49, 50, 62, 64, 66–68, 76, 81, 94, 98, 99, 101, 102, 104, 116, 120

slavery, *xi, xii, xvii, xxiv*, 6 7, 13, 15, 29–31, 37, 38, 41, 42, 44–50, 61, 62, 81, 82, 111, 112, 117
Steinberg, Naomi, 2, 5, 17
Stewart, Maria, *xi*, 1, 111
surrogacy, 6, 8, 12, 13, 19, 20
surrogate, 12, 13, 17, 19, 20, 21

Taney, Roger, *xii*, 50, 51
Trible, Phyllis, 5, 75

US Constitution, *xi, xii*, 112

Walker, Alice, *xiv, xv, xvi, xvii*
Weems, Renita, *xxi, xxii, xxvii*, 6, 7, 8, 69, 73
welfare queen, 62
White supremacist(s), *xiii*, 48–50, 61, 63, 112
White supremacy, 63, 112
whiteness, 30, 42, 81, 117
Williams, Delores, 1, 6, 7
woman of color, 8
womanhood, 62, 64, 81, 82, 102, 106
womanist, *xiv, xv, xvi, xvii, xviii, xiv, xx, xxi, xxii, xxiii, xxv*, 6–8, 21, 31, 32, 80, 111, 115
women of color, *xiii, xiv, xx*, 21
Wong, Gregory, 96

Yuval-Davis, Nira, *xii,* 3, 4, 9, 10, 11, 32, 66–68, 92, 105, 106, 113–15

About the Author

The Reverend Dr. Vanessa Lovelace is associate dean and associate professor of Hebrew Bible/Old Testament at Lancaster Theological Seminary in Lancaster, Pennsylvania. She is a member of the Society of Biblical Literature, where she serves as an editorial board member for Bible Odyssey and the Committee on the Status of Women in the Profession. She is also a member of the American Academy of Religion and the Society for the Study of Black Religion, and she is an editorial board member for the *Biblical Theology Bulletin*. Her numerous publications and lectures include *Womanist Interpretations of the Bible: Expanding the Discourse* co-edited with Gay L. Byron (SBL Press, 2016), *The Hebrew Bible: Feminist and Intersectional Perspectives* (Fortress Press, 2018), and *The Oxford Encyclopedia of Bible and Gender Studies* (2014).

She previously served as associate professor of Hebrew Bible/Old Testament at the Interdenominational Theological Center in Atlanta, Georgia. Lovelace received her Ph.D. in Bible (Hebrew), Culture, and Hermeneutics from Chicago Theological Seminary, an M.Div. from McCormick Theological Seminary, Chicago, Illinois, and a B.A. in Radio & Television from San Francisco State University. She is an ordained United Church of Christ minister. Her current research interests include Deuteronomistic History; the intersection of the theory of gender and nation, race, and citizenship and biblical studies; womanist hermeneutical approaches.